E
MEDI   ...EAN

JPMGUIDES

CONTENTS

EASTERN MEDITERRANEAN

The Eastern Mediterranean embraces one of the world's most exotic concentrations of cultural diversity. This is reflected in its cuisines, its architecture, its traditional costumes and landscapes. Along the northern perimeter, it extends from Italy's east coast, via the Balkans from Croatia down to Albania and Greece, across to Turkey's Istanbul and Anatolia before turning south along the coast of Syria, Lebanon and Israel. The southern perimeter begins at Egypt's Sinai Peninsula and continues east to Libya.

And away from the coasts, the myriad islands great and small ensure that there need be no fear of monotony when your ship makes for the open sea. Malta, Crete and Cyprus are the major landmarks, with the Ionian islands and Cyclades, Sporadic islands and Dodecanese forming stepping stones in between.

With this endless diversity comes every imaginable opportunity for unusual experiences. Shop in traditional Turkish and Arabic bazaars or fashionable Italian boutiques. Eat the best imaginable seafood or hearty peasant dishes with pasta, rice or cracked wheat. Admire a whole world of architecture from the pharaohs' pyramids near Cairo to the ancient temples of Athens and Crete, the noble palazzi along the canals of Venice, the mosques and palaces of Istanbul and Damascus, and the Crusaders' castles of Rhodes and Cyprus; but also the white homes and tiny churches of the Greek islands—where they offer plenty of clubbing, too.

The Sea in Figures

The Mediterranean as a whole covers an area of over 2 million sq km (772,000 sq miles). It is 3,900 km (2,423 miles) from the Levantine coast of Syria and Lebanon to the Straits of Gibraltar. At its deepest, off the coast of the Greek Peloponnesus, it plunges 5,267 m (17,280 ft) into the Calypso Deep. The eastern half of the Mediterranean has three distinctive seas between the peninsulas of its northern shores. The elongated Adriatic separates

Italy from the Balkans, the broader Ionian extends from the heel and sole of the Italian boot to the Greek mainland, while the east coast of Greece looks across the Aegean to Turkish Anatolia.

Two Rivers and a Canal

Only two major rivers flow into the Eastern Mediterranean: the Nile, estimated, at 6,650 km (4,132 miles) from its furthest headwaters in southern Rwanda to where it empties into the sea at the Delta, to be the longest in the world; and Italy's Po, rising in the Piedmont Alps to flow 652 km (405 miles) into the northern end of the Adriatic near Venice.

Politically and commercially the most important of all Mediterranean waterways is the Suez Canal, just 192 km (119 miles) long. Cutting from Port Said to the Red Sea, it has permitted ships to pass from Europe to Asia since 1869 without having to sail around Africa.

The Mountains

Home of the ancient Greek gods is Mount Olympus, 2,919 m (9576 ft), west of Thessaloniki. Italy's tallest peak is the Corno Grande, 2,912 m (9,553 ft) in the Abruzzo Apennines. Syria's Mount Hermon, 2,814 m (9,232 ft) has been a frequent bone of contention with Israel, currently occupying its Golan Heights.

Vegetation

Geographers consider the olive to be the defining feature of the Mediterranean. With their clusters of leaves turning silver or green as the wind blows, and their gnarled, often centuries-old trunks, the trees mark the inland boundaries wherever they continue bearing fruit to flavour salads and sauces throughout the world. Among the region's other characteristic trees are the Italian cypress, umbrella pines and groves or oranges and lemons. Not forgetting the vineyards.

In the countryside, the shrubland constituting the typical Mediterranean landscape is known to the French as *maquis* or *garrigue*, to the Italians as *macchia* and to the Greeks as *phrygana*. Its densely growing evergreen shrubs, stunted holm oak, strawberry-tree, myrtle and juniper mingle with the fragrant lavender, thyme, sage and rosemary and colourful broom and cistus rock rose.

Populations

In the varied mixture of peoples you will encounter, there is nowhere more spectacular to start than with the Venetians. Visitors will be charmed by the knowing smile and easy elegance appropriate to these descendants of commercial empire-builders. As a former outpost of the Habsburg

Empire, the people of Trieste combine their present-day Italian patriotism with a certain Austrian style and irony and a Slavonic touch from across the Slovene border. The brash, smart citizens of Bari are proud south Italian rivals to the Neapolitans in a port very conscious of its links to the Balkans, Greece and Turkey.

After the long Cold War, the mainly Catholic Croatians have enthusiastically hitched their hospitable wagon to the Western world. Similarly, the Montenegrins, citizens of the smallest of the old Yugoslav republics, offer a subtle blend of Balkan and Mediterranean charm reflecting the styles of their Orthodox Christian churches and Venetian Renaissance and Austrian baroque palaces.

The Albanians of Durrës put a smiling face on what is both a beach resort and one of Europe's most ancient port cities. Similarly, the islanders and coastal dwellers of Greece and Turkey— and Cyprus, too— vie, more peacefully today than in the past, for a dominant role in showing visitors the eastern Mediterranean's historical heritage and the modern pleasures of their coastal resorts.

Along the Levantine coast, Syrians, Lebanon and Israel have each in their own way been happy to show that life can be enjoyed despite the Middle Eastern conflict, though the current situation in Syria makes it inadvisable to visit. Along the North African coast, the Arabs bring to the Mediterranean thousands of years of hospitality steeped in the culture of the desert surrounding their cities. And the people of Malta are out there in the middle of the sea to mirror a potpourri of the cultures that have created the modern island—Phoenicians, Greeks, Romans, Fatimid Arabs, Sicilians, the Crusading Knights of St John, as well as the French and British.

istockphoto.com/Assalve

In the Middle Ages, Venice was an important maritime power.

S. Georgio da lega

S. Biagio Catoldo

Giudeci

FLASHBACK

When man began to migrate out of Africa, the Levant and Anatolia were his first ports of call. Palestine's Jericho can claim to be the world's oldest continuously inhabited town, founded around 8300 BC. About the same time, hunters dwelled in upland caves north of Turkey's Antalya. By 6500 BC, they made way for farming communities scattered across the Anatolian plateau.

In the 4th millennium BC, the pharaohs united north and south Egypt into one country. With its capital moving from Memphis to Thebes (Luxor), Egypt became the dominant power in the Eastern Mediterranean for 1,500 years. Rich farmland and the treasures of its craftsmen attracted invaders from Palestine, Libya and Persia. The Libyan Berbers launched raids into the Nile Delta around 2200 BC. They were subdued by the pharaohs, but some of them rose to seize control in the so-called Libyan dynasties (950–730 BC).

Crete's Great Moment

From 2000 BC, Crete developed over five centuries a civilization synonymous with hedonism, preferring fine living to conquest. The Minoan palaces were built for pleasure—no defensive ramparts, but plenty of roof gardens, bathing pools, banquet halls and spacious bedrooms. Crete formed one of the largest fleets in the Mediterranean, but used it for a thriving trade in luxury goods to pay for the good life at home rather than military conquest abroad.

Enter the Greeks

Greece remained sparsely populated until waves of migrants arrived from the Balkans and Asia Minor from around 4500 BC. By 1400 BC, the dominant force on the Greek mainland was Mycenae in the Peloponnese. To the cultural influence of Crete, the Mycenaeans added a rougher, more "masculine" touch. They adopted Crete's fertility goddesses, but subordinated them to their male deity Zeus. These were the macho heroes Homer's Iliad sent to conquer Troy on the Anatolian coast around 1230 BC.

Then, tough Dorians swept down from the Balkans, destroying Mycenaean civilization and enslaving its peoples. The harsh, warrior-oriented society entered a cultural Dark Age. The Dorians' austerity, characteristic of Sparta, combined with the more amiable serenity of Ionian Athens to create the strength and grace of Greek civilization. Victory over the Persian invasions (499–487 BC), ushered in the Classical Age under Pericles. The period of the great tragedies and splendid architecture ended with the defeat of Athens by Sparta in the Peloponnesian War (431–404).

From Macedonia on Greece's northern frontiers, Alexander set out to conquer the world in 336 BC. He marched through Asia Minor to India and North Africa before dying in Babylon in 323 of malaria and heavy drinking.

The Phoenicians

Based on the Levantine coast of Syria and Lebanon, the Phoenicians patiently built a commercial empire at sea. From their ports of Byblos, Tyre, Sidon and Beirut, they achieved the zenith of their sea power from 1200 to 800 BC, stretching from Cyprus to Malta, Sardinia, Sicily, Spain and Portugal and along the North African coast to Carthage. This became their capital after the Persian conquest of 539 BC. Their trade in tin, copper and other metals even showed up in Ireland and Cornwall. The Phoenicians left their cultural mark in the more sensual "Oriental" features of Greek and Etruscan art.

Roman Rule and Christianity

The Romans invaded the eastern Mediterranean in 224 BC, defeating the Macedonians. Greece became a Roman province by 146 BC, followed by the conquest of Anatolia, Syria, Palestine and Libya. Augustus captured Egypt from Antony and Cleopatra in 31 BC. Jesus grew up in Nazareth and preached in Galilee around AD 27. Roman governor Pontius Pilate had him executed for the perceived threat that the Christian movement posed to Roman law and order. In 49, the apostle Paul began his Christian missions throughout the region.

Byzantine Empire and Islam

In 324, Emperor Constantine made Byzantium capital of the Eastern Empire. Pagan cults were banned, Greek temples closed and the Olympic Games halted. From the 6th century Goths, Visigoths and Slavs invaded and dominated the Greek mainland.

After Mohammed's death in 632, his Arab followers spread Islam to Anatolia and west along the North African coast to cross into Spain in 711.

Venice and the Crusades

From the 11th to 15th centuries, the Venetians created a fabulous maritime empire with masterful shipbuilding and brazen trading methods, including piracy. Defying Constantinople (former Byzantium) and Rome, they traded with Muslims in lumber, salt and slaves. With Arab gold, they bought oriental silks and spices from Constantinople for resale in western Europe at huge profits. Their greatest boost came with the Crusades. From 1095 to 1291, nine Crusades were launched from Christian Europe to "rescue" the so-called Holy Land from the Turkish and Arab Muslims. The Venetians happily provided high-priced shipping and arms. Christian strongholds were established in Cyprus, Crete, Rhodes and throughout Palestine.

The Turks

Arriving from central Asia and converting to Islam in the 10th century, the Seljuk Turks began in 1042 to drive the Byzantines from Anatolia. They in turn succumbed to a tougher breed of Turks who established in 1299 under Osman I—"Ottoman" to the western world—a dynasty that lasted over six centuries. In 1453, Sultan Mehmet II captured Constantinople. The Byzantine emperor died in battle, the church of St Sophia became a mosque and Constantinople became Istanbul. Ottoman power reached its height under Suleiman the Magnificent (1520–66), but over the next three centuries, while Europe was being reinvigorated by the Renaissance and the Industrial Revolution, Turkey rested on its laurels.

19th Century to the Present

The last 200 years saw the rise to national independence. After subservience to the Austro-Hungarian Empire, Venice and Trieste became part of a united Italy. Malta acquired its independence from the British in 1964. With the end of Communism in the 1990s, Croatia and Montenegro split off from Yugoslavia. Albania became a sovereign state in 1912. Greece won its independence from the Turks in 1832 and Turkey became a republic under Atatürk in 1923. Cyprus in 1960, but Greco-Turkish belligerence kept it a partitioned island with a divided capital in Nicosia. The state of Israel was proclaimed in 1948 and has been ever since in conflict with its Arab neighbours over the status to be granted to occupied Palestine.

Syria, Egypt and Libya all went their independent ways after centuries of colonial rule, but entered a period of turbulence and popular uprisings with the Arab Spring of 2011.

tasty specialities

mighty cities

traditional architecture

ITALY

Italy's Adriatic shores are popular, and with good reason: few are the coastlines that can claim such panache, such animation and such variety. It includes some of Italy's stunningly beautiful cities, as well as some of its best beaches. Venice sparkles like a gem cushioned on a blue lagoon, serene in the knowledge of her special place in the sun. Puglia stretches from the Gargano peninsula, the spur of the Italian boot, to the heel. For many centuries, the region has been a vital link between the Italy of yesterday and that of tomorrow.

Venice

The city is divided into six districts, or *sestiere*: San Marco, San Polo, Santa Croce, Dorsoduro, Cannaregio and Castello, with the Grand Canal winding through the centre. Yellow signs are posted everywhere, pointing the way to San Marco (St Mark's), Rialto or Accademia. As for the *vaporetti* (waterbuses), they are an absolute delight with low fares, frequent service and incomparable vistas.

Grand Canal

This compellingly beautiful waterway serves as the main street of Venice. Some 200 palaces built between the 12th and 18th centuries stand along its banks—Byzantine and Gothic, Lombard and baroque, some carefully restored, others sadly crumbling. Their façades have been imitated the world over. Today, they house municipal offices, hotels and museums.

Spanning the Canal roughly at midpoint is the **Rialto Bridge**. With its double row of shops, it was built in 1588 by Antonio da Ponte, having won a competition in which designs were also submitted by Sansovino, Palladio and Michelangelo. The Rialto district is the busiest shopping area in Venice. The bridge leads directly down into the markets. Flowers, fruit and vegetables are on sale at the **Erberia**; there are a few stalls selling clothing and souvenirs. On Campo della

Pescheria, the covered **fish market** with its live crab and lobster and slippery eels is a sight not to be missed—it has been held there for a thousand years. All kind of wares can be found at the bustling and picturesque market held on **Campo delle Beccarie** on the site of the old abattoirs, surrounded by the typical Venetian bistros, *bacari*.

Within the southern loop of the Grand Canal, you will find most of the historic monuments and churches, as well as many restaurants, shops, big hotels and banks. The waterway opens into the San Marco Canal after the Punta della Dogana, the last building on the right bank, and all the vaporetto passengers disembark at St Mark's Square, where the majority of tourists spend their time.

St Mark's Square

Venetians call **St Mark's Square** simply the Piazza, since it has always been the only one in town deemed worthy of the name. It is lined on three sides by splendid palaces. To the north are the Procuratie Vecchie, dating from the 12th century, originally the headquarters of the "procurator" of Saint Mark's and nowadays used as offices. To the south are the Procuratie Nuove, and on the east side the Ala Napoleonica, its façade crowned with statues of Roman Emperors.

St Mark's Basilica encompasses a mixture of styles and irregular construction—each of its five domes, for example, has different dimensions and few of its columns match. Yet it somehow conveys the impression of harmonious beauty.

The first church was built in 830 to house St Mark's body, stolen from Alexandria by two Venetian merchants, and as a chapel for the doges who lived next door. In 976 the largely wooden church burned down and the basilica we know was constructed in the 11th century. St Mark's body was not the only religious treasure "stolen" from the East—almost everything else in the church was brought back as booty from the Levant.

The famous bronze horses on the balcony over the main portal are actually copies—the originals have been moved to the museum inside the basilica.

The magical interior of San Marco is covered with about an acre of mosaics, the earliest dating back to the 11th century. Among the most beautiful are some on the ceiling of the narthex (vestibule). Dating from the 13th century, they relate Old Testament stories.

The **Pala d'Oro**, the shimmering backdrop to the main altar, is one of Christendom's richest treasures. Dating back 1,000 years and bejewelled in its present form in the 14th century, this masterwork of the goldsmiths of Constantinople contained 2,486 pearls, garnets, sapphires, emeralds, amethysts and rubies—before Napoleon helped himself to a gem or two.

For nearly ten centuries, the magnificent **Doge's Palace** (Palazzo Ducale) was the seat of the Republic and residence of most of Venice's doges. It remains almost exactly as it was in the Republic's heyday. The original 9th-century fortress-like palace took its present form—a unique blend of Byzantine, Gothic and Renaissance elements—in the 15th century. The Great Council Chamber (Sala del Maggior Consiglio), a monument from the early days of Venetian democracy, was the place where the citizens assembled to discuss state policies and elect doges. Later, only nobles convened in the vast hall. Covering the wall behind the doge's throne is the largest oil painting in the world, Tintoretto's *Paradise*. This monumental work, based on Dante's *Paradiso*, was undertaken by the artist at the age of 70. Don't miss the Secret Itineraries tour that takes you through rooms where suspects were interrogated.

The famous **Bridge of Sighs** (Ponte dei Sospiri) leads to prison cells in another building. The

Gondolas have been plying the canals since the 11th century. | St Mark's Square, the heart of Venice.

name supposedly came from the sighs of the inmates as they were led over the bridge to torture or execution.

Towering over San Marco and the entire city, the splendid **Campanile** served its Republic proudly in turn as watchtower, beacon, weather vane, gun turret and belfry. The original stood for almost a thousand years, until about 10 a.m. on July 14, 1902, when it collapsed into the Piazza below. The city council quickly decided to rebuild the tower "as it was, where it was" *(com'era, dov'era)*. On April 25, 1912, exactly one thousand years after the erection of the original Campanile, the replica, almost exact, was inaugurated. The new one, many hundreds of tons lighter, is believed to be sound enough to last another millennium. On a clear day, the view from the top is justly celebrated.

Speaking of towers, consider that marvellously colourful example across the Piazza. For nearly five centuries, the two Moors up on the **Torre dell' Orologio** have been hammering the hours on their great bell. The tower itself features the inevitable winged lion and a splendid zodiac clock which shows the time in Arabic and Roman numerals.

The world-famous opera house **La Fenice** has arisen from the flames that destroyed it in 1996. Even more beautiful than before, it was re-inaugurated in December 2003, and re-opened to the public in November 2004.

For a splendid view of the city, climb the magnificent spiral staircase of the **Contarini del Bovolo**

Barbara Ender

Guy Minder

On the menu

Agnello allo squero – spit-roast lamb
Anguilla alla veneziana – eels in tuna sauce
Antipasti di frutti di mare – seafood appetizers
Baccalà al pomodoro – salt cod with tomatoes
Branzino – seabass
Brodetto di mare – fish soup, with regional variations
Carciofata – artichoke hearts sautéed with vegetables
Chiancarelle – pasta with sweet peppers and colrave
Cutturide – lamb stew
Fegato alla veneziana – veal liver with onions
Fritto misto – mixed fry
Gnemeridde – tripe
Marasciule e sinipi – baked vegetables
Migliaccio – dessert of dried and candied fruit
Minestra – soup
Pedeia – stuffed mutton rolls
Porchetta – sucking pig
Risi e bisi – rice with peas
Scaldatelli – bread flavoured with fennel
Vincigrassi – pasta stuffed with meat, chicken, mushrooms, truffles, etc.
Zucchini ripieni – stuffed courgettes

(Palace of the Snail) whose arcaded round tower is adorned with a multitude of columns like icing on a wedding cake.

The **Palazzo Grassi** has been beautifully renovated by the Japanese architect Tadao Ando to house temporary exhibitions based on the modern art collection of French businessman François Pinaut.

Dorsoduro

Cross over the wood and steel Ponte dell'Accademia to enter Dorsoduro, the intellectual district, with the University, museums, public and private collections and foundations.

The **Gallerie dell'Accademia** house an unsurpassed collection of Venetian art. See Carpaccio's *Miracle of the Holy Cross at the Rialto Bridge* (the earlier bridge); Gentile Bellini's *Procession around the Piazza* and Giovanni Bellini's *Madonna and Child* series; Mantegna's *St George* and Giorgione's lyrical *Tempest*; *Feast at the House of Levi,* a compelling canvas by Veronese that covers a whole wall; *Presentation* by Titian; and Tintoretto's dazzling *Transport of the Body of St Mark*.

The **Collezione Guggenheim** gives you a chance to visit one of those intriguing Venetian palaces along the Grand Canal. The Palazzo Venier dei Leoni was the home of

American expatriate Peggy Guggenheim. She died in 1979, leaving behind one of the best collections of modern art in Europe.

The nearby Renaissance **Palazzo Vittorio Cini**, a beautiful 16th-century building in itself, with original furnishings and paintings, holds temporary art exhibitions.

A short walk from Palazzo Cini is the baroque church of **Santa Maria della Salute**, built by Longhena between 1631 and 1687 and acknowledged to be his supreme achievement. The sacristy is adorned with many paintings including works by Titian, Tintoret and Palma the Younger.

The next-door **Punta della Dogana**, the former Customs building, has been converted to display the second half of François Pinault's collections.

Santa Croce

The eastern part of this *sestiere* has retained many of its old palaces. One of them, the baroque marble Ca' Pesaro, houses the **Galleria Internazionale d'Arte Moderna di Ca' Pesaro**, one of the greatest collections of Italian and foreign paintings, sculptures and drawings from the end of the 19th century until the present day. The palace also houses the **Museum of Oriental Art**, displaying a vast collection of Japanese art from the Edo period (1614–1868), and has in addition sections devoted to China and Indonesia.

There are several interesting churches in this district, including the Renaissance-style **Santa Maria Mater Domini**, behind Ca' Pesaro, on a pretty square lined with magnificent Byzantine and Gothic buildings. **San Giacomo dell'Orio** stands on a tree-shaded square that makes a pleasant summer setting for shows and festivals. This church was built in the 9th and 10th centuries; its brick bell tower was added in 1225.

San Polo

The most important sight in this district is the **Scuola Grande di San Rocco**, a guildhall intended to help plague victims. Four architects contributed to the building, which was begun in 1489 and took over a century to complete. Inside is a breathtaking collection of 56 Tintoretto paintings, displayed in one of the most opulent interiors imaginable. Hire a mirror to study the stunning sacred works on the ceiling. It's said that Tintoretto considered the monumental *Crucifixion* (in the Sala dell' Albergo) to be his masterpiece.

The church of **Santa Maria Gloriosa dei Frari**, on Campo dei Frari, boasts two of Titian's most famous paintings—the exquisite *Assumption* (1518) over the high altar and *Madonna di Ca' Pesaro* (1526) above an altar on the left—as well as the great artist's tomb, erected 300 years after his death by the Emperor of Austria. See, too, the fine Bellini triptych of the *Madonna and Saints* (1488) and Donatello's wooden statue of St John the Baptist.

Over by the Rialto bridge, the Renaissance church of **San Giovanni Elemosinario**, opened in early 2002 after 25 years of restoration, has works by Titian and Pordenone.

Cannaregio

This is the living heart of Venice, a district made up of small businesses and workshops. It takes up all of the northwestern sector of the city between the Grand Canal and the lagoon. In the middle is the Ghetto, an area surrounded by water where for three centuries all the Jews were forced to live.

On the ground floor of a synagogue built in 1528, the **Museo Ebraico di Venezia** is the Jewish Museum, displaying examples of Venetian Jewish art of the 17th–19th centuries, tapestries and manuscripts.

Madonna dell'Orto was Tintoretto's parish church and he is buried here with his family near the high altar. Two of the artist's finest works hang by the altar— *Last Judgement* and the *Worship of the Golden Calf*. Look for his dramatic *Presentation of the Virgin* over the sacristy door.

The 15th-century Gothic **Ca' d'Oro** ("Golden House"), with a lacy façade of marble tracery, takes its name from its once-gilded exterior. It houses the **Franchetti Gallery**, which spreads over into the neighbouring Palazzo Giusti. Its displays include collections of Italian and foreign paintings, sculpture in marble and bronze, and ceramics. In addition to Mantegna's famous *St Sebastian*, there are important works by Titian, Tintoretto, Van Eyck, Guardi and Bellini.

Castello

Probably named after a Roman castle, this is the most extensive of the Venetian districts and owes much of its charm to its working-class atmosphere.

The highlight is the **Scuola di San Giorgio degli Schiavoni**. Probably nowhere is there so much spectacular painting on view in such a tiny space. Vittore Carpaccio decorated the chapel of the guildhall of the Dalmatian merchants in Venice between 1502 and 1508 with scenes from the lives of St George and St Jerome.

The **Arsenal**, created in the 12th century, was crucial to the development of this part of town. It is surrounded by a rampart of high walls and a moat of natural and artificial canals and is to be reconverted for cultural and artistic purposes.

On Campo San Bagio, the **Naval Museum** (Museo Storico Navale) displays old trophies and scale models of ships, including the *Bucintoro,* the State galley of the doges, and other fascinating 18th-century Venetian vessels.

The **Giardini Pubblici**, the only park worth mention in the city, was created by Napoleon on marshland, but the original neo-classical design was modified in 1895 when the Biennial International Art Exhibition was introduced. Among the greenery stand 18th-century statues. The *Monument to a Partisan*, in the lagoon, is without doubt the most poignant. Every odd-numbered year, the Biennale Internazionale d'Arte exhibits contemporary painting, sculpture, graphic and decorative art from all over the world. From 1907 to 1964, every participating country built their own pavilion. The result is a fascinating museum of modern architecture.

The Islands

The Venetian lagoon holds many delights for visitors. You can reach the main attractions either by vaporetto or on an organized tour.

La Giudecca is just a stone's throw from Dorsoduro. At the western end there are several small 15th-century palaces and the neo-Gothic Molino Stucky, a flour mill built in 1896 by a Swiss industrialist. After years of neglect and a fire, it has been renovated into shops, convention centre, apartments and a Hilton hotel. The terracotta-coloured Church of the Redeemer was built at the end of the 16th century, in response to a vow made when the plague was ravaging the city. During the Redentore festival in July, it is linked to the Santa Maria della Salute basilica by a bridge of boats. The church contains a *Baptism of Christ* by Veronese, as well as canvases by Tintoretto and Palma the Younger.

Off the eastern tip of La Giudecca, **San Giorgio Maggiore** is taken up almost entirely by a Benedictine monastery. It is now the headquarters of the Cini Foundation, with a permanent collection of paintings, furniture and antiques. There's an open-air theatre in the gardens, the Teatro Verde.

Murano is known the world over for its glass blowing. Take a look into one of the factories to see the craftsmen at work, but be prepared for a hard sell. Some of the finest pieces made over the last five centuries can be seen in the glass museum.

Further east is picturesque **Burano**, the pearl of the Venetian lagoon. The people here still live from fishing and lace-making.

You'll find that the campanile of San Martino has a decided tilt to it, and the trim little red, blue, yellow and gold houses a great deal of charm.

Torcello, on the other side of Burano, was once a thriving community of 20,000, the seat of a bishop. But as Venice grew, Torcello declined and in time it was abandoned, looted and almost forgotten. Today, all that remains is its cathedral, glowing with superb Byzantine mosaics of blue and gold.

The lagoon is enclosed by long strips of beach known as *litorale*. Closest to Venice is the **Lido**, a sandy beach lined with a string of luxury hotels. In summer, the municipal casino offers gambling, puts on film festivals and art shows. This resort was the setting for Thomas Mann's *Death in Venice*, but you'll only experience the funereal atmosphere of the novel if you visit off season, when the crowds have disappeared and the mists and fog banks seep in from the sea.

Gulf of Venice

Grado, Caorle and Jesolo, the three big resorts on the Gulf of Venice, count among the most popular holiday spots on the Adriatic coast.

Set on a peninsula west of the Bay of Trieste, **Grado** was already in Roman times the nearest beach to the ancient city of Aquileia. Nowadays visitors come for the variety of thermal and well-being treatments, such as hot sand baths on the long beaches. In the middle of this fishing town, you will still see some houses in Venetian style. The church of Sant-Eufemia (6th century) has mosaic paving and a 15th-century bell-tower. The octagonal baptistery next to the church has been standing since the 5th century.

The Roman sites of **Aquileia**, only 10 km (6 miles) away, are worth a visit, especially for the fascinating Archaeological Museum. It is also worth having a look at the town's beautiful 11th-century basilica while you are there.

Caorle, a modern touristic town and fishing port at the mouth of the Livenza, was once an island until the lagoon was silted up with debris swept down by the river. The town knew a first Golden Age in the 5th century, when it welcomed inside its walls thousands of refugees fleeing Attila and his mighty hordes. Caorle later came under the protection of Venice. The old historic town is dominated by the cathedral (1038) and its circular belltower. The highlight of the richly decorated interior is the Pala d'Oro, a masterpiece of Byzantine craftsmanship of the 12th–13th centuries.

Holidaymakers looking for a good time will find plenty to do in Caorle: 10 km (6 miles) of beach, a marina, a water park (Aqua-follie) and discothèques to dance the night away.

At the eastern end of the Venetian lagoon, **Jesolo**, with its beach stretching for 15 km (9 miles), has long been a favourite with northern sun-seekers. All the pleasures of a stay by the Adriatic are concentrated in this 1930s beach resort: thalasso-therapy, parks and gardens, well-maintained pedestrian streets with boutiques and restaurants, theme parks, including Aqualan-dia, sporting facilities and discothèques.

The best buys

Antiques (especially in Trieste)

Burano lace

Cartapesta, papier-mâché objects

Gold and silver jewellery (Venetian crafts)

Gondolier's straw hats

Illy coffee in Trieste

Maiolica, pottery

Mosaics from Ravenna

Murano glass

Olive oil from Gargano

Silk scarves and ties

Theatre and carnival masks from Venice

Venetian leather goods

Venetian marbled paper

istockphoto.com/Savoia

The Palazzo Gopcevich in Trieste is home to a museum of theatre and music.

Trieste

Built directly over the landfilled site of the ancient Roman harbour of Tergeste, the vast sea-front **Piazza dell'Unità d'Italia** (or just Piazza d'Italia) is the perfect expression of the city's opening to the Mediterranean. Its eclectic neo-Renaissance and neoclassical palazzi were commissioned by the town's former Habsburg masters. On the north side, a statue of Emperor Karl VI stands in front of the Palazzo del Governo (now the Prefettura), opposite the grand Palazzo del Lloyd Triestino built for the town's great shipbuilding company (now a seat of regional government), with the Palazzo Comunale town hall at the rear.

At Piazza d'Italia 7, Caffè degli Specchi (established in 1839) is just one of many **coffeehouses** that count among the town's most revered monuments. Founded in 1914, Caffè San

Marco (Via Cesare Battisti 18) is the intellectuals' favourite. James Joyce and his fellow writer Italo Svevo met at the venerable Caffè Tommaseo, built in 1830 on the piazza of the same name.

The two literary pals now have their own museums. The *James Joyce Museum* was opened in 2004 to celebrate the centenary of his arrival in the city, with documents and photographs at the Public Library in new premises at Piazza Hortis 4. The museum organizes walks around the great Dubliner's old Trieste haunts. The adjoining **Italo Svevo Museum** (Museo Sveviano) has been restored to be organized on the same lines.

The **harbour** is always lively. Watch the movement of tankers, freighters and cruise-liners while yachts jockey for position in the Porto Sacchetta. For their sacrosanct late-afternoon *passeggiata*, the Triestini like to stroll along the **Molo Audace** pier.

Among the remarkable buildings, the **Teatro Verdi** opera house has been splendidly restored. The **Cattedrale di San Giusto** has combined two Romanesque churches. In the apse are some 13th-century Venetian mosaics, while its campanile incorporates parts of the Roman temple it replaced. Above the cathedral at the top of a park, the Austrian-built **Castello** of 1470 replaced earlier fortresses of the

Venetians, Romans and prehistoric Istrians. A small museum tells their story.

Among the town's many museums, the **Museo Revoltella** (in financier Pasquale Revoltella's palazzo at Via Armando Diaz 27) provides a glimpse of patrician life in Trieste's 19th-century heyday. It combines the baron's personal furnishings and art collections with the **Galleria d'Arte Moderna** by Carlo Scarpa.

The **Museo del Mare** (via Campo Marzio 5) is among the best of the Mediterranean's maritime museums, dedicated to shipping past and present with a special section on Adriatic fisheries.

Ravenna

Though it now lies some 10 km (6 miles) inland, Ravenna was a flourishing seaport under the Romans—250 ships could anchor there at any one time. It rose to prominence when Honorius chose it as the capital of the Western Empire in 402. His sister, Galla Placidia, succeeded him to the throne and enriched the city with monuments. The Goths also established their court here, first Odoacre (in 476) then Theodoric (493–526). In 540, the Byzantine general Belisarius captured Ravenna for Justinian; the city enjoyed a brilliant period of artistic creation, strongly influenced by Eastern tradition.

The **Mausoleo di Galla Placidia** was built in the second quarter of the 5th century in the form of a Greek cross; the small chapel contains superb mosaics, probably the city's oldest. The colours are striking, especially the deep blue. The mosaics depict the Good Shepherd, St Lawrence, the Apostles and Evangelists, while overhead the dome is studded with a constellation of golden stars.

Next to the mausoleum is the **Basilica di San Vitale**, an octagonal structure founded by the Bishop Ecclesius (526). The plain red-brick exterior gives little indication of the ravishing treasures inside—the magnificent green and gold mosaics in the choir and apse are unrivalled. Scenes from the Old Testament are represented, and there are two famous panels of the Emperor Justinian and Empress Theodora surrounded by members of their court. The dome of the apse depicts Christ between two angels, with Bishop Ecclesius and St Vitale holding a model of the church. Eight marble pillars support the Byzantine dome of the basilica with its *matroneum*, or women's gallery.

The adjoining **Museo Nazionale** occupies the cloisters of the San Vitale convent. Also call in at the nearby **Domus dei Tappeti di Pietra**, a house with beautiful mosaic

Part of the Procession of 22 Virgins in Ravenna's Basilica di Sant'Apollinare Nuovo.

floors, accessible from the next-door Saint'Eufemia church.

Another mosaic-filled gem is the **Battistera Neoniano** near the cathedral. The domed octagonal building, originally a Roman bathhouse, is crowned by mosaics dating from 450 and illustrating the baptism of Christ with a procession of the twelve Apostles.

In the centre of the old town, you'll see the **Tomba di Dante**. The poet, exiled from his native Florence, finished writing the *Divine Comedy* in Ravenna, where he died in 1321. His monument, erected in 1780, covers an older structure housing his sarcophagus.

You will be struck by the Venetian influence in the city's principal square, Piazza del Popolo. The main building looks like a small version of the Doges' Palace in Venice, and two Venetian columns bear Ravenna's patron saints, Apollinare and Vitale.

The **Battistero degli Ariani**, on the Piazza Ariani, originally belonged to the Arian Goths (those Germanic tribes that denied the divinity of Jesus). Its mosaics show the baptism of Christ and the Twelve Apostles.

The **Basilica di Sant'Apollinare Nuovo** dates from the time of Theodoric. The mosaics on the walls of the nave, executed in classical Byzantine style, depict the life of Christ. On the left you'll see a procession of virgins, on the right the martyrs, all with jewelled crowns in hand.

The circular **Mausoleo di Teodorico** (526) on the outskirts of town is a curious edifice composed of huge blocks of limestone that were floated across the Adriatic from Istria. The dome, 11 m (37 ft) in diameter, was carved from a single stone weighing about 300 tons.

Some 5 km (3 miles) southeast of Ravenna is the finest example of a Romanesque basilica in Italy, **Sant'Apollinare in Classe** (549). The round campanile, with windows on each storey, was added in the 11th century. Inside the basilica, the lovely mosaics are touching in their naivety and serenity. In the apse is the Transfiguration, with St Apollinare, the first martyr and bishop of Ravenna, surrounded by sheep (representing the chosen ones) in a meadow. Above him are various biblical figures, with a large cross representing Christ at the summit.

Extending down towards the sea from Sant'Apollinare in Classe is the very old and celebrated **Pineta di Classe**. From Dante to Byron, poets have sung the praises of this majestic wood.

Faenza, 31 km (19 miles) inland, is the city that gave its name to the bright and attractive pottery known as faience. The town's magnificent Museo Internationale delle Ceramiche has some fine examples.

Rimini

Rimini is known for its wide and sandy beach stretching almost to infinity, crowded with rows and rows of parasols and beach beds in high season. For many generations, this has been the most popular resort on the coast, with a friendly atmosphere and all the advantages of a modern lifestyle. Pizzerias, gelaterias, restaurants, discothèques and anything else you can think of in the way of entertainment are scattered all over the town.

In fact, Rimini has two distinct and very different faces. On one side is the bathing resort, with its big hotels, holiday apartments and beach clubs, on the other the busy fishing port, where you can go down to the harbour and watch the boats bringing in the daily catch.

Cars have been banned from the town's historic centre, which makes it a charming place for strolling. Founded in the 3rd century BC, Rimini (at the time called Ariminium) was in a strategic position between the Via Aemilia going to Lombardy, and the Via Flaminia which led to Rome. Traces of Roman times can be seen in the huge **Arco di Augusto**, a triumphal arch in white Istrian stone, built to honour Augustus in 27 BC, and a bridge, the **Ponte di Tiberio**, completed in the year 21. The Corso d'Augusto, which connects the arch with the bridge, passes through the site of the old Roman forum, now the busy Piazza Tre Martiri. It was here supposedly that Julius Caesar delivered a stirring speech after crossing the Rubicon.

For a short period in the 13th century, Rimini was an independent republic; the Palazzo dell'Arengo and Palazzo del Podestà date from that time. During the Renaissance, the Malatesta dynasty brought wealth and glory to the town. Among the artists who came to the Malatesta court in the 15th century were Antonio Pisanello, Leon Battista Alberti, Piero della Francesca, Giovanni Bellini and Domenico Ghirlandaio. They had studied in

Venice and Florence, caught the new spirit of the times and introduced the Renaissance to Rimini. In 1509 the city was annexed to the Papal States. In the 19th century, Rimini played an important role in the Risorgimento, the movement for Italian independence, and in 1860 it joined the Kingdom of Italy. It was bombed heavily in World War II before being taken by the Allies in 1944.

The main attraction in the old city is the **Tempio Malatestiano.** Originally a Franciscan church, it was magnificently redesigned during the Renaissance by Sigismondo Malatesta. Its stately façade by the great Florentine architect Battista Alberti was inspired by the Arch of Augustus. Inside, on the right-hand side, you will find the tomb of Sigismondo, the most illustrious of the Malatestas. The Chapel of Relics (between the first and second chapels) contains a fresco by Piero della Francesca; the tomb of Sigismondo's third wife Isotta lies in the second chapel, with a crucifix attributed to Giotto.

At Piazza Cavour, the historical centre of Rimini, you'll find two notable buildings: the 13th-century **Palazzo del'Arengo**, with a façade of pointed arches and crenellated biscuit-coloured brick; and the Gothic **Palazzo del Podestà** where the people's council used to meet.

Adjoining Piazza Cavour in the southwest, Piazza Malatesta is guarded by the **Castel Sismondo**. This 15th-century castle has been restored several times; it used to house the Dinz Rialto ethnographic collections of the Museum of Extra-European Cultures but these have now been moved to new premises at the **Villa Alvarado** in Covignano di Rimini.

Northeast of Piazza Cavour, take Via Gambalunga to reach the **Museo della Città**, with departments of archaeology, medieval and modern art, with many fine paintings including a *Pietà* by Giovanni Bellini.

The **Museo Fellini** honours the great film director who came from Rimini, and illustrates the history of the cinema.

The **Riviera del Sole** is an uninterrupted stretch of beach covering more than 40 km (25 miles) from Cesenàtico north of Rimini to Cattòlica to the south at the border of the Marche. Not far from Cattòlica is the fairytale castle of **Rocca de Gradara**.

Ancona

Beautifully set on a promontory above the sea, the capital of the Marches is the only port of international significance on the Adriatic between Venice and Bari. The history of Ancona has always been linked to the sea.

Founded by Greek colonists in the 4th century BC, it was called Ankon (elbow) because of its position jutting out from the Adriatic coast.

Ancona prospered as a Roman port before coming under the hegemony of the Ravenna Exarchate (the Exarch was the viceroy of the Byzantine emperors). A free city under papal protection from the 12th century, it was annexed to the Papal States in 1532. Bombarded by the Austrian fleet in World War I, Ancona was occupied by the Germans in World War II and bombed by the Allies before being taken by the Poles in 1944. Since then, the town, which lies on a fault line, has suffered much damage from earthquakes. In spite of its battered history, the city has managed to maintain a certain elegance.

The Duomo, or cathedral **San Ciriaco**, crowns Colle Guasco and is dedicated to St Cyriacus, one of the early Christian bishops of Ancona. Built in the form of a Greek cross, on the site of a temple of Venus, the cathedral harmoniously incorporates Byzantine and Romanesque styles; its 12-sided cupola is one of the oldest in Italy. The interior is quite sober and dignified.

The terrace outside overlooks the port and the **Arco di Traiano** erected in AD 115 in honour of the Roman emperor who "modernized" the harbour with a breakwater.

Also noteworthy in Ancona are the elaborate and intriguing sculptures of animals and personages on the façade of the early 13th-century **Santa Maria della Piazza**. Some beautiful examples of Venetian Gothic, to which the Dalmatian sculptor Giorgio Orsini (Juraj Dalmatinac) contributed, are the church of San Francesco, the Portale di Sant'Agostin and the Loggia dei Mercanti with it statues of the Virtues. The **Museo Nazionale delle Marche** is housed in the Palazzo Ferretti. It is mostly devoted to archaeology and traces the old civilizations of the region. The Pinacoteca Comunale has works by old masters such as Titian, Lotto and Vricelli, as well as modern artists.

Gargano Peninsula

The region known to the Italians as Puglia (Apulia in English) stretches from the "spur" of the Gargano peninsula to the heel of Italy's boot. The sun-bleached region has an untamed beauty, with its undulating rocky hills where sheep and goats feed on the sparse greenery.

The peninsula juts into the limpid Adriatic like a spectacular spur. Amidst rugged beauty that inspired the description of "a kingdom of drought and stone", it has something for everyone—beach and forest, history and legend, faith and folklore. It has been inhabited since the early Stone Age.

The Gargano peninsula's easternmost port, **Vieste**, exudes that southern allure of whitewashed houses and a palm-tree-lined waterfront. The town has a long, distinguished history, as witness the castle, begun nearly a thousand years ago, and the medieval Basilica-Cathedral. Among 13th-century dignitaries who made a mark here, if only in transit, were Pope (later Saint) Celestine V and his successor, Pope Boniface VIII. If you are interested in even older history, visit the **Museo Archeologico**. Also of interest is the **Museo Malacologico** (Mollusc Museum) with a fascinating collection of molluscs of all sizes, shapes and colours.

Just south of Vieste, **Pizzomunno** beach is sandy and charming, surveyed by a white pillar of limestone 26 m (85 ft) tall, looking like an austere lighthouse with a fringe of greenery on top. "Pizzomunno" means "tip of the world".

Beyond the beaches south of Vieste (Pugnochusio may be the most frequented), the coastline retreats into a wall of grotto-infested cliffs interspersed with enticing inlets. The view from the corniche road is dazzling.

The coast road descends to sea level at **Mattinata**, a sizable farming centre between the mountains and the Adriatic. Just inland gnarled olive trees mingle with pines. In Mattinata a local chemist's is the site of an off-beat archaeological museum in which more than 3,000 exhibits go back to the 7th century BC when people called Daunians inhabited this part of the Adriatic coast.

The beachy coast continues to the industrial town of **Manfredonia**, founded in 1256 by Manfred, the son of the great Frederick II. Manfred's muscular castle, a classic medieval fortress with circular towers on the corners, has been well preserved. It houses an important archaeological museum, featuring unusual Daunian steles of the 7th and 6th centuries BC. The 11th-century Romanesque basilica of Santa Maria Maggiore stands alongside the site of the ancient city of Siponto, 3 km to the south. Beyond that is the church of San Leonardo, with a notable portal, sculpted in the 13th century.

A road with twists and bends climbs inland to **Monte Sant' Angelo**, a town surrounding the ruins of a castle built by Frederick II. This limestone hill more than 800 m high is riddled with caves and ravines—and legends. The Archangel Michael is supposed to have made three appearances here at times of trouble, even leaving his red cloak as tangible proof of his existence. The phenomenon so impressed the Bishop of Siponto that an abbey was founded and a stream of pilgrims began the descent to the underground sanctuary. Near the Gothic choir of the underground church is a miraculous spring, which, according to legend, started gushing water at the archangel's command.

At **San Giovanni Rotondo,** another cult is pursued. Padre Pio, a 20th-century monk, sanctified in 2002, is buried in a modern church here. The hospital was built with contributions from patients from five continents, grateful for what were deemed miracle cures.

The **Foresta Umbra**, in the centre of the Gargano promontory between Monte Sant'Angelo and Peschici, is an enchanted forest covering some 10,000 ha (25,000 acres). Great oak, maple, beech and ash trees shade a wild population of deer, foxes and badgers. As unspoiled as it may look, the forest is carefully preserved and geared to tourism.

The provincial capital, the 11th-century city of **Foggia**, was one of the favourite bases of Frederick II, but his palace is gone. What was left after the 1731 earthquake was destroyed by World War II bombing raids. The king was originally buried here, but the remains were later moved to his native Sicily. The Duomo (cathedral), which dates from 1179, is the most imposing of a number of historic buildings; its Byzantine-style bell tower, toppled in the earthquake, has been rebuilt. The **Museo Civico**, founded in 1931, covers archaeology and folk traditions. Now an industrial and commercial city with a population of 150,000, Foggia is at the centre of the Tavoliere, the vast golden granary of the Gargano, the biggest plain in the south of Italy.

West of Foggia, **Lucera** had its heyday under the Roman empire. Augustus Caesar built the amphitheatre, now in use again for public spectacles. The castle, its walls still standing, was another of the many projects of the busy Frederick II. The local museum is the owner of a beautiful statue of Venus from the Roman era.

From the road between Lucera and **Troia**, you get wonderful views over the Tavoliera plain. Troia's Romanesque cathedral has a splendid façade.

Bari

This bustling, bumptious commercial Adriatic port was once a magnet for an endless array of foreign "uninvited guests"; in these more peaceful times it welcomes the tourists taking the car ferries for Greece.

The **historic centre** of Bari, set on a peninsula, is a picturesque district of low white houses set along narrow winding streets, with something of the atmosphere of a north African medina.

The Città Vecchia (Old Town) has two imposing Romanesque churches which inspired other religious buildings in Apulia. The **Cathedral of San Sabino** was built in the 12th century on the site of a Byzantine church that had been razed after the death of the Norman king Roger II; a good part of the town disappearing along with it. The cathedral's façade is adorned with a fine rose window, cornices and a sculpted portal that dates from the baroque period. Walk round the elegant bell tower (the second tower was destroyed in the 17th century by an earthquake) and you will see the amazing rear façade, writhing with statues of fantastic animals. The cathedral's interior has been scrupulously restored in Romanesque style. The bishop's throne, the pulpit and the canopy over the main altar were painstakingly pieced together from ancient fragments. The remains of the patron saint of Bari, St Sabino, are kept in the crypt, and greatly revered.

A little further on, the superb **Basilica San Nicola** is the city's most famous building and a popular place of pilgrimage. On the site of the former seat of the Byzantine government, it was begun in 1087, with the prime purpose of housing the relics of St Nicholas, which had been stolen from his tomb in Myra (Turkey) by sailors from Bari. The lofty façade of white limestone, particularly well crafted, is Apulia's most outstanding example of Romanesque style. Inside, you can see a 12th-century tabernacle and a superbly carved bishop's throne. Note also the richly decorated 17th-century ceiling of gilded and painted wood. The remains of the beloved St Nicholas are kept in the crypt.

The former Monastery of Santa Scolastica at the tip of the old town is being converted to house the collections of the **Museo Archeologico Provinciale**. These are composed of ancient artefacts retrieved from excavations all over the region and cover the periods from the Stone Age to the Middle Ages.

West of the old town, the mighty **Castello** looms over the new port. Emperor Frederick II had it built in the 13th century on the ruins of a Byzantine-Norman citadel. In the 16th century, Isabelle of Aragon resided there, then it was converted into a prison. Today the castle makes a striking setting for the **Gipsoteca**, a collection of plaster replicas of the most beautiful Romanesque and Gothic statues to be seen in Apulia's churches and palaces.

Follow Corso Vittorio Emanuele II, a lively thoroughfare linking the old and new districts of the town, to reach the old port and the pretty seafront promenade, **Lungomare Nazario Sauro**, to the east.

The Palazzo della Provinci, further south along the promenade, houses the **Pinacoteca Provinciale**, where you can admire the most important collection of paintings of Apulia, including works by Vivarini, Tintoretto and Veronese. Medieval engravings depicting Bari are also displayed.

In total contrast to the tangle of streets in the old own, the **new town** of Bari was built in the 19th century on a strict grid pattern. Stroll along the elegant traffic-free shopping street of Via Sparano to reach the modern centre on Piazza Umberto I.

Alberobello

In the interior, between Bari and Brindisi, this town is the *trulli* capital, which earned it a place on the UNESCO World Heritage list. As you wander along its streets you'll get the impression you have been transported into a fairytale. Inside the whitewashed *trulli*, all neatly lined up beneath their pointed roofs, are souvenir shops, hotels and holiday apartments. Traditional furniture is

displayed in the well-documented **Trulli Museum**, opposite the cathedral.

A road links Alberobello to **Monopoli**, on the coast, a former Venetian trading port. In the attractive historic centre, the central piazza is surrounded by cafés and bars, perfect for watching the world pass by.

Brindisi

The ancient Roman port of Brindisi is now a thoroughly modern industrial city, familiar to holidaymakers taking the ferry to Greece but with enough interesting sights to merit a visit in its own right.

The **Duomo** (cathedral) was originally built in Romanesque style, but it was remodelled in the 18th-century baroque after a violent earthquake wrecked the town. The church is flanked by an imposing belltower. Inside you can see some fine mosaic paving.

Opposite the cathedral, the **Archaeological Museum** displays antique vases, clay statuettes and a vast collection of Greek, Roman and Byzantine coins.

Behind the bell tower you'll see the remains of two **Roman columns**, long thought to have marked the eastern terminus of the ancient Appian Way (Via Appia), covering nearly 600 km from Rome. The more recent theory is that they were landmarks

Trulli. Apulia is an arid, stony region. Since prehistoric times, farmers built rudimentary huts by piling up coarsely hewn stones, criss-crossed at the top to form a cone-shaped roof. The *trulli* were built without mortar, like dry-stone walls. This simple type of architecture also suited the feudal lords, as the small houses could be easily inspected and controlled. To make more living space, several *trulli* could be joined together.

Historians suggest that there is a connection between this type of dwelling and the "sugarloaf" houses typical of the Alep region in Syria.

Today many of the old *trulli* have been restored, some of them converted into hotels or restaurants, and some incorporating modern materials rather than the old grey stones.

for sailors. Erected at the tip of the promontory that separates the two arms of the city's inner harbour, one column is 19 m high, with a finely carved capital, while only a base and the stump of the other remain, the rest having been taken to Lecce when it collapsed in the 16th century; it now supports the statue of St Orontius.

Less spectacular than the cathedral, the round church of **San Giovanni al Sepolcro** dates from the 12th century. Further southwest, the Romanesque convent of **San Benedetto** is known for its Way of the Cross, one of the oldest in Apulia.

Take a boat trip to the **Monumento al Marinaio**, a high tower shaped like a rudder, erected in memory of sailors lost at sea in 1933. From the top you get a fine view over the town and the Adriatic. The Hohenstaufen citadel perched above the port is not open to the public.

Lecce

This airy, sophisticated town has a place apart in the life of Puglia. It is famous not only for its highly decorative baroque architecture, but also for the good humour and wittiness of the population. The University is renowned for its faculties of history, law and economics. Baroque ornament found its ideal medium in the local fine-grained golden sandstone known

Huber/Simeone

as *pietra di Lecce*. As you stroll around town, notice even on the houses along Via Palmieri and Via Libertini the plethora of ornate doorways, colonnades, balconies and window-arches, alive with nymphs, gods, goddesses, and fanciful monsters among the carved fruit and vines. But a more orderly visit begins at the historic centre, on the bustling **Piazza Sant'Oronzo**. It's named after the city's first bishop and patron saint Orontius, martyred by Nero. His statue, dating from the 18th century, stands near the entrance to the Roman amphitheatre, on the Roman column brought from Brindisi. In an area seating 25,000 spectators, a few bas-reliefs of gladiators and wild animals are still visible, but the best preserved are in the local museum.

Follow **Via Umberto I** to the grand 16th- and 17th-century **Santa Croce** basilica, a true masterpiece of baroque decoration, with richly fashioned figures, grotesques and vegetables. The façade is dominated by the extravagant rose window of Giuseppe Zimbalo, known as Zingarello, the "little gypsy". The 13 creatures supporting the entablature below the window are characteristic of the town's wry humour—men grimly struggling to bear the weight while various monsters watch on, chuckling.

Many of the town's most fashionable boutiques are on or around **Via Vittorio Emanuele** which curves around to the baroque theatre-set of **Piazza del Duomo**. To your right is the Palazzo del Seminario with its splendid windows designed by Giuseppe Cino Zingarello's pupil. Zingarello himself gave the cathedral its grandiose baroque transformation, adding a remarkable five-storey campanile with a balustrade at each level. It's difficult to believe that the exuberant ornament of the baroque altars inside is not stucco, but carved in Lecce sandstone. Zingarello's most elaborately decorated façade can be seen on the **Chiesa del Rosario** at the end of Via Libertini, a profusion of birds and chubby cherubim and interlacing spiral columns.

South of Lecce, the little port of **Otranto** is set at the easternmost point of Italy. Its 15th-century Castello Aragonese is the setting of Horace Walpole's gothic novel, *The Castle of Otranto*. The Norman cathedral was consecrated in 1088.

Gallipoli

In Greek, *Kallipolis* means "beautiful city" and this is certainly still true for the ancient fishing port of Gallipoli's medieval island, now joined by bridge to a more modern city on the mainland. Guarded by an Angevin fortress, the maze of narrow streets winding around the white houses and baroque churches of the old town make a cool and shady haven of tranquillity.

At the centre, the richly decorated baroque façade of the 17th-century **cathedral** offers a distinct echo of Lecce, whose patron saint Orontius is portrayed inside on paintings by Giovanni Andrea Coppola. At sundown, go for a stroll along the sea front.

Taranto

Founded by the Spartans in 706 BC, Taranto became one of the richest of Italy's ancient Greek colonies. Practically all vestiges of the great seaport's proud civilization were subsequently laid low by 19th-century industrial and urban development. Today Taranto (with the accent on the first syllable) is a military naval base and centre of heavy industry (steel, oil and cement). However, masterpieces of the region's Greek and Roman art are preserved in the great **Museo Archeologico** (Corso Umberto).

As at Gallipoli, Taranto's medieval quarter is set on an island now joined to the mainland by a bridge. Here the 15th-century castle is Spanish. The old **Duomo** has a baroque façade. Inside notice the fine Roman and Byzantine capitals on the recycled Greek temple columns.

Tremiti Islands

For escapism, there's nothing to match an island. A mysterious archipelago rises off the Gargano shore, the only such sprinkling of isles along Italy's Adriatic coast. The Isole Tremiti are appreciated for their cliffs, grottoes and sea sports. Legend says that Diomedes of Trojan War fame was buried here and that his companions, transformed into birds *(aves diomedae)*, mourn him on moonless nights with their cries.

San Domino, the largest, highest and most westerly of the islands, used to house a colony of Lateran monks, who called it paradise on earth. The sea caves are intriguing, and so are the birds—albatross and falcons—nesting here.

San Nicola, the traditional administrative and religious centre of the archipelago, is crowned by the abbey of Santa Maria al Mare, founded in the 8th century. The Benedictine monks held forth there as an independent domain; from the cloisters you'll get a fetching view of San Domino. The fortifications recall the pirate attacks of the middle ages.

The third sizable island, **Capraia**, is named for the capers that grow in abundance along the coasts. Another uninhabited isle is the rocky **Pianosa**, with little vegetation and some small reptiles, toads and wild rabbits.

PRACTICAL INFORMATION

Banks. Generally open Monday to Friday 8.30 a.m.–1.30 p.m. and 3–4 or 5 p.m. ATMs are plentiful.

Climate. The weather is mild in winter, pleasantly warm in spring and autumn. Summer is hot and dry, with the sea comfortable for bathing.

Clothing. Pack light clothing, preferably cotton or other natural fibres. Make sure you don't wear revealing clothes when you visit churches: miniskirts, shorts and sleeveless clothes are frowned upon.

Credit cards. The major international cards are accepted practically everywhere.

Currency. The Euro divided into 100 *centesimi*.

Electricity. The current is 220 V, 50 Hz; plugs are the European type with two round pins.

Emergencies. Ambulance/first aid 118; *carabinieri* (police) 112; *pompieri* (fire brigade) 115.

Gondolas and vaporetti. The fare charged by Venetian gondoliers depends on the number of passengers and length of the ride, and it is more expensive after 7 p.m. There are official prices but the gondoliers tend to do as they please. Agree on the price before you climb aboard. The vaporetti are very useful for quick trips; for longer distances take a *motonave* or a watertaxi, *taxi acquei*.

Museums and historic sites. Most close on Mondays.

Post office. Monday to Friday 8.30–2 p.m., Saturday to noon.

Shops. Most open Monday to Saturday 8.30 a.m.–1 p.m. and 4–8 p.m. Some close on Monday mornings or afternoons.

Tipping. In most restaurants and hotels, the service charge and VAT are included. It is the custom to add a tip of 5 to 10 per cent. Taxi drivers also expect a 10 per cent tip.

Tourist information. The APT offices provide free brochures. See the website of the city of Venice: www.comune.venezia.it (in Italian and English), as well as www.turismofvg.it (for Trieste) and www.viaggiareinpuglia.it (for Puglia).

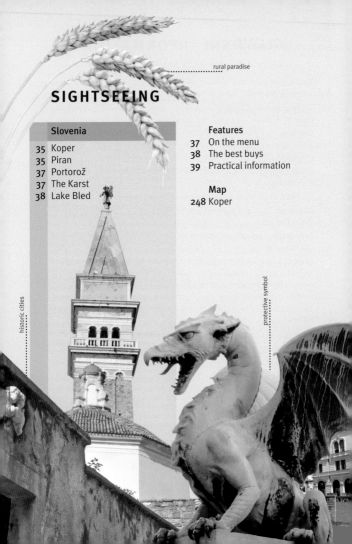

rural paradise

SIGHTSEEING

historic cities

protective symbol

SLOVENIA

Slovenia's 40 km (25 miles) of Adriatic coastline was ruled by Venice for five centuries until Napoleon destroyed the Venetian Republic in 1797. But the picturesque little coastal towns retain the rich flavour of Italy, with their Venetian Gothic architecture, narrow medieval streets and close-packed red-roofed houses.

Slovenia packs a remarkably diverse range of scenery into a very small space. What's more, this tiny nation of only 2 million people has a delightful and vibrant capital city in Ljubljana, while historic provincial towns, medieval castles and impressive Roman ruins abound.

Koper

Koper was the capital city of the Istrian peninsula under the Venetians (its Italian name is Capodistria). After World War II it was developed as a major industrial town and is today Slovenia's premier port. However, the Old Town has kept its medieval character largely intact. Here you'll find the 36-m high **City Tower**, dating from 1480 and with fantastic views from the top. The tower was once the belfry of the **Cathedral of St Nazarius** situated next to it. The cathedral's façade is largely an 18th-century renovation of the Gothic original. On the north side of the square, the arcaded **Loggia** (1463) now serves as a café, while on the south can be found the former Mayor's residence, the **Praetorian Palace** of 1452, both of which are stunning examples of Venetian Gothic.

A historical perspective on the town can be gained at the **Koper Regional Museum** on Kidričeva ulica, where paintings, maps and photos show how the town has developed over the years.

Piran

Another 17 km (10 miles) along the coast, Piran sits at the end of a tiny peninsula jutting out into the Adriatic. It's a delightful, photogenic little town, whose stone streets, lively squares and medieval Venetian beauty make it extremely popular with visitors from around the region.

The main focus of the town is **Tartinijev trg**, which was once the

istockphoto.com/Mokotar

hemis.fr/ Rabouan-Fiori

hemis.fr/ Rabouan-Fiori

inner harbour and only filled in during the 1860s. The square is named in honour of Piran's most famous son, the virtuoso violinist and composer Giuseppe Tartini (1692–1770). His statue stands in the centre of the square. Tartini was born at No. 7, next to the early 19th-century **Church of St Peter**. The house now contains the **Tartini Memorial Room**.

Piran has always been dependent on the sea, and a couple of small museums pursue this theme. Behind the square, next to the marina, there's an interesting old **aquarium**, while located in a sumptuous 17th-century palace opposite, the **Maritime Museum** is packed with antique model ships and figureheads, and displays on the seafaring and salt trades that were essential components of Piran's wealth from the medieval era onwards.

Dominating the whole town is the **Church of St George**, built on a ridge overlooking the sea. Begun in the 1340s and revamped in 1637, it's a splendid mix of Renaissance and baroque styles. The tall campanile, based on the

With its medieval architecture and narrow streets, Piran seems like an open-air museum. | At the Lipica stud farm, they have been raising horses since 1580. | The church of the Assumption on the little island of Bled.

one in St Mark's Square in Venice, is closed, but there are good views of both Piran and the Adriatic from the church's terrace, and even better ones from the medieval town walls, which can be reached a couple of hundred metres to the east.

Portorož

It may be only 5 km (3 miles) from Piran, but Portorož is a world apart in terms of atmosphere, for this is Slovenia's own version of a glitzy seaside tourist resort. **Obala**, the main waterfront boulevard, is a place of high-rise hotels, discos and bars, and the sandy beaches are packed with sunbathers.

The "Port of Roses" nonetheless exudes a real charm and is a fun spot for discovering how to let your hair down Slovenian style. And if it proves too much, you can always head off on a hydrofoil for a day-trip to Venice.

The Karst

The Karst region, a limestone plateau of more than 6,000 caves, chasms and potholes, is located in the southwest of the country. The caves were formed 2 million years ago by underground rivers eating away at the soft limestone, leaving a vast geological Swiss cheese that's a speleologist's paradise.

Postojna Cave is Slovenia's single most visited tourist spot. Guided tours take you through a fifth of its 27 km (17 miles), more than enough to appreciate this natural phenomenon to the full, with its amazing stone columns,

---

On the menu
Dunajski zrezek – breaded scallop
Golaž – goulash
Govedina – beef
Goveja juha z rezanci – clear soup with egg noodles
Postrv – trout
Pršut – raw ham
Riba – fish
Rižota – risotto
Srna – venison
Štruklji – sweet or savoury ravioli
Svinjska pečenka – roast pork
Teletina – veal
Vipavska jota – sauerkraut soup with potatoes and beans

Huber/Pavan

istockphoto.com/Michelizza

The best buys

Apple, plum or pear brandies
Basketware from Ribnica
Black pottery from Prekmurje
Crystal glass from Rogaška
  Slatina
Honey, beeswax, royal jelly
Lace from Železniki and Idrija
Silver jewellery
Woodcarvings from Lake Bohinj

colourful stalactites, gorges and rivers. Bear in mind, the temperature is 8°C year-round, so you'll need a jacket even in summer.

The **Škocjan Caves**, 30 km (18 miles) to the southwest, provide another spectacular foray into the Karst's subterranean wonderland. They are more difficult to reach and on a smaller scale than Postojna, but many cave cognoscenti prefer them for their less developed, more natural state.

Not far from Škocjan is the village of **Lipica**, where the famous white Lipizzaner horses used by the Spanish riding-school in Vienna were bred. The **Lipica Stud Farm** still flourishes, and you can watch the horses going through their paces in special exhibitions given on Tuesday, Friday and Sunday during the summer.

Lake Bled

Idyllic Lake Bled has a picture-postcard beauty that's hard to match, an island graced by a church, a medieval clifftop castle and views that reach to Slovenia's highest snow-capped alps. The lake can be comfortably circumnavigated in a less than two-hour walk, but an even better way to admire the scenery is to take a boat out onto the water. If you do, stop off at Bled Island. The baroque church here is 17th-century, built on the foundations of a much older church, and contains part of a pre-Romanesque chapel in the nave. Perched on a hill overlooking the lake, the castle, **Blejski Grad**, is a marvellous mixture of towers and turrets. It dates from the 11th century, but has been much altered over the years. The views from the ramparts are, of course, breathtaking. The castle also houses a museum, with an interesting collection of armour, weapons, period furniture and artworks.

PRACTICAL INFORMATION

Banks. Open Monday to Friday 9 a.m.–5 p.m. (some close between noon and 1 p.m.)

Climate. The northeast of the country is Alpine, and the mountains are covered in snow from December to March or later, while the summers are warm. The Adriatic coast is hot and sunny in summer, mild in winter. Eastern continental Slovenia has hot summers and cold winters.

Currency. The Euro, divided into 100 centimes.

Electricity. 230 Volts, 50 Hz; plugs are the European type with two round pins.

Emergencies. The European emergency number is 112, or 113 for the police.

Language. The Slovenian language is Slavic but uses the Latin alphabet. Young people generally speak some English. In the Adriatic towns practically everyone speaks Italian.

Museums. Generally closed on Mondays, opening the other days 9 or 10 a.m.–5 or 6 p.m.

Post office. Open Monday to Friday 8 a.m.–6 p.m., and Saturdays 8 a.m.–noon.

Shops. Generally open Monday to Friday between 7 and 9 a.m. to 7 or 9 p.m., Saturday to 1 or 3 p.m. Some also open Sundays.

Time. UTC/GMT +1 from November to March, UTC/GMT +2 from April to October.

Tipping. Service is included in hotel and restaurant bills, but it is customary to leave a tip of 10 per cent for the waiter. Porters and chambermaids also appreciate a tip, and taxi drivers expect 10 per cent of the fare.

Tourist information. See the website of the Slovenian tourist office: www.slovenia.info.

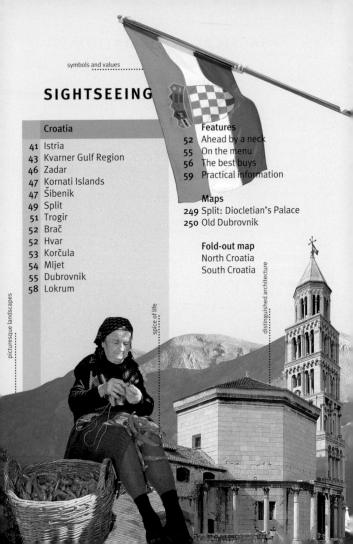

symbols and values

SIGHTSEEING

picturesque landscapes

spice of life

distinguished architecture

CROATIA

Croatia is poised at the edge of Europe's cultural frontier with the East. Its strategic location and rich Mediterranean beauty have attracted a potent mixture of visitors over the centuries. The Greeks came to trade, the Romans to build, the Barbarians to loot. Later, the Venetians colonized, the Turks raided and the Habsburgs ruled. They have all left their traces, be it in the Ottoman-influenced love of strong coffee or the Venetian-style piazzas and red-roofed houses that colour the coastal towns.

Istria

Named after the Illyrian Histri tribe, who were defeated by the Romans in 177 BC, this triangular peninsula is known for its lush farmland, superb Roman ruins, lively seaside towns and marvellous summer sunshine.

Poreč, the major tourist resort, has a combination of fascinating ancient buildings in the old town and hotel complexes stretching 6 km (4 miles) along the popular beaches of the Adriatic coast. The town itself, founded by the Romans as a military camp, juts out on a peninsula. One of the original Roman roads, the Dekumanus, is still the main street. On *Trg Marafor* (Forum of Mars) at its west end, are the ruins of two Roman temples dedicated to Mars and Neptune. Further along,

past a Romanesque mansion on the right, there's the regional museum, housed in an 18th-century baroque palace and containing the altar from the temple of Neptune. But the jewel in Poreč's crown is the 6th-century Basilica of Euphrasis *(Eufrazijeva bazilika)*, north off Dekumanus. Here you can see stunning Byzantine gold mosaics and fine sculptures in one of the most splendid early Christian churches in Europe.

To enjoy the late afternoon sun, head down to Poreč's bustling harbour, a pleasant place to stroll around or to sit outside a waterfront café. From here you can take a 5-minute boat ride across to the small island of **Sveti Nikola** (St Nicholas). For a longer trip, catch a hydrofoil to Venice, an hour away.

The town of Rovinj will no doubt remind you of Venice.

Picturesque **Rovinj**, 38 km (23 miles) to the south, was once part of a chain of 14 small islands just off the coast, until the channel separating it from the mainland was filled in a couple of centuries ago. The old stone houses of this delightful medieval fishing port are dominated by the great Church of St Euphemia *(Sveta Eufemija)*. The tomb of the eponymous 4th-century saint is near the altar inside the church. Built in the 1730s on the site of two earlier churches, its 60-m-high bell tower is topped by a statue of St Euphemia, and gives a fantastic overview of the colourful town and the nearby islands.

Rovinj has a relaxed atmosphere and thriving café scene that has made it extremely popular with Croatian and Italian artists. The working harbour is especially scenic, with fishing boats unloading their morning catch and ferries taking people to the islands. The biggest, **Crveni Otok** (Red Island), is really two islands joined by a narrow strip of land, one of which is used by naturists.

At the tip of the Istrian Peninsula, **Pula** has long been a vital port for whoever has wished to rule the northern Adriatic. The Romans established it as a naval base 2,000 years ago, followed by the Byzantines, the Franks and the Venetians. In the 19th century it became the Austro-Hungarian empire's main harbour, and during the 1920s the Italians took possession.

The most outstanding monument on the entire Istrian peninsula is Pula's spectacular Roman amphitheatre, completed around AD 80 and with a seating capacity of 23,000. Countless gladiators and Christian martyrs would have lost their lives in the arena for the entertainment of Roman soldiers and sailors. The amphitheatre is in remarkably good condition and still used as a venue—each summer the Croatian International Film Festival is held here.

Head towards the centre of the old town to the Archaeological Museum, which is entered through double gates dating from the 2nd century. Inside there's a fine collection of Roman artefacts, while at the back are the ruins of a Roman theatre. Further along, on ulica Prvog Maja, the triumphal arch was erected in 29–27 BC to honour the military successes of the Sergi family. Look for the plaque on the nearby yellow-painted house marking the place where James Joyce taught English to Austrian naval officers.

Follow Prvog Maja towards the waterfront. At the old Roman forum the Temple of Augustus (*Augustov hram*), with its distinctive Corinthian columns, was a focal point of the Roman town. Built 12 centuries later, the Gothic old town hall (*Vijecnica*) was the political centre of medieval Pula. Go round the back to see ancient vestiges incorporated into the later construction.

Just back from the forum, the Franciscan monastery (*Sveti Franjo*) dates from the early 14th century and has an attractive cloister with a Roman mosaic. Notice the church's external pulpit, from which sermons were given when the congregation was too large to fit inside.

Kvarner Gulf Region

At the meeting point of the Istrian peninsula, the Adriatic coast and the Croatian interior, the Kvarner Gulf region encompasses a fascinating variety of landscapes. Glamorous resorts built during the heyday of the Austro-Hungarian empire, ancient castle towns and rugged island idylls all rub shoulders here. The major boost to the tourist trade came in the 19th century when direct train links were established with Vienna and Budapest.

Arriving at **Opatija** after visiting the towns of the Istrian peninsula is like crossing from medieval Italy to fin-de-siècle Austria. A host of grand hotels and luxurious villas were built in the 19th century to receive the wealthy bourgeoisie of Vienna and Budapest, and the town became a Central European alternative to the French Riviera. Famous figures such as Gustav Mahler, Chekhov, Isadora Duncan and the German Kaiser came to take in the health-giving properties of the sea air. The superb seafront promenade, extending several kilometres along the gulf, is named after the Austrian Emperor Franz Josef I, who had trysts with his mistress here. Numerous restaurants and cafés, where you can sample strudel and coffee, complete the Vienna-by-the-sea experience.

Rijeka, Croatia's largest port, has plenty of character. Nowhere better encapsulates this than the Korzo, a wide precinct of shops, banks and cinemas running parallel to the harbour and the perfect place for the city's large population of young people to parade up and down. The best-known landmark, the old City Tower, with figures of the Austrian emperors

Charles VI and Leopold I over the portal, is halfway along the precinct. This was once the sea entrance to the city, before the present-day harbour was built. It gives access to what's left of the old town, Stari Grad. Pass through the arched Roman Gate, and turn right to reach the circular St Vitus's Cathedral, an impressive structure built in 1638. Inside, be sure to see the renowned Gothic crucifixion, carved in wood in the 13th century. The city also has a municipal museum, north of the old town, as well as the History and Maritime Museum next door in an 1890s' palace.

In the Middle Ages, the area around this part of Croatia belonged to the Frankopans, Croatian nobles from the island of Krk who managed to retain independence from Venice and Hungary and who built great fortresses along the coast to prove it. **Crikvenica** came to prominence much later, however, when it found favour at the end of the 19th century as a health resort and playground for the well-to-do of the Austro-Hungarian empire. The legacy of those opulent Habsburg days can be seen in the splendid Austrian hotels and pleasant promenades. And it's still a health resort: Crikvenica specializes in thalassotherapy, a seawater-based health treatment.

Modern visitors are also attracted to the long sandy beaches and the same fine climate that invigorated the pallid Viennese of the fin-de-siècle. This popular resort town comes alive at night, when you can go from risking your fortune at the casino to sampling a variety of Balkan and Mediterranean cuisines at any number of its excellent restaurants.

The **Plitvice Lakes** are about 85 km (50 miles) inland from the coast. One of the great natural wonders of Eastern Europe, the Plitvice Lakes National Park is a particular favourite with Croats, who come here to celebrate the beauty of the scenery and admire the power of nature. An 8-km (5-mile) sequence of 16 crystal-clear lakes are linked together by a multitudinous cascade of waterfalls, some of which, such as the Plitvice, Veliki and Sastavci, are especially spectacular. For maximum drama, visit in the spring, when the mountain snows melt and the torrents increase in force. There's an exhilarating walking trail on wooden boards that takes you along the rivers and around the falls. Within the National Park, hikers will also enjoy Čorkova Uvala in the northwest, the remnant of a primeval forest.

Without a vowel to its pithy name, **Krk**, at some 410 sq km (158 sq miles), is the biggest Croatian island. Offshore from

Crikvenica, it was connected to the mainland in 1980 when a 1,039-m (3,409-ft) bridge, incorporating one of the world's longest concrete arches, was opened.

Krk island holds a special place in Croatian culture. One of the cornerstones of Croatian literature, the "Baška Inscription", was found here, dating back to 1100 and written in the old Slav Glagolitic alphabet. The village of **Baška** at the southern end of the island is especially attractive, with picturesque scenery and good places for swimming. There are many ancient Croatian churches here; the Chapel of St John *(Sveti Ivan)*, set on a hillside, has a superb panorama of the wide bay and village.

The Romans settled in what is now Krk town 2,000 years earlier, and, being people who liked their comforts, built thermal baths decorated with mosaics. A cathedral was constructed over the baths in the 12th century, and the mosaics can still be seen from one of the side-chapels. Notice also the silver Gothic screen showing the Virgin Mary. Reached by a small arched passageway from the cathedral, the 10th-century Basilica of St Quirinus *(Sveti Kvirin)* is topped by a later Romanesque church and bell tower complete with onion dome. Krk was a centre of the medieval Frankopan dynasty, and

istockphoto.com/Antica

Boardwalks cross over the many lakes of Plitvice.

their indomitable castle stands at the waterfront entrance to the town, offering lofty views of the surrounding area.

A short ferry ride from Krk, **Cres** is a wild and barren island, home to a colony of white-headed griffon vultures. Its neighbour **Losinj** is noticeably greener and gentler, with woodland, holiday resorts and popular beaches. Bottlenose dolphins swim in the seas around the islands.

Rab, a rocky island south of Krk has a split personality; barren and windy to the northeast, lush and pine-forested to the south-west. Coveted by successive larger powers ever since the Greeks, it's now a popular resort, with the delightful old walled town of Rab as its centrepiece. Built on a steep promontory, the town was a Venetian stronghold for centuries, as the grand patrician houses testify. The highest of the three parallel main streets, ulica Rade Končara, has a row of splendid Romanesque church towers that dominate the terra-cotta roofs of the city skyline. The 27-m (88-ft) campanile attached to the 12th-century St Mary's Cathedral is said to be the finest example of Romanesque architecture on the Adriatic, and the views from the top are tremendous. Further along, the Church of St Justine contains a small collection of religious art.

Zadar

The Illyrians first settled here in the 9th century BC, but it was the Romans and the Byzantines who really developed the town. Situated on a narrow peninsula and bordered on three sides by water, Zadar enhanced its natural defences in the 16th century with massive walls to keep out the Turks. The worst attack came from the air, however, when in 1943–44 Allied bombers destroyed three-quarters of the buildings. To the dismay of its citizens, Zadar was shelled again in the winter of 1991 by the National Army, damaging the cathedral and houses.

Start your tour in the east part of the city near the ancient **tower** *(Kopnena vrata),* a triumphal arch with a lion of St Mark. The exquisitely crafted silver sarcophagus at the nearby church of **St Simeon** *(Sveti Simun)* dates from the 14th century. The remains of St Simeon are said to be inside; they attracted pilgrims from all over medieval Europe.

A litle further, the Museum of Ancient Glass presents a collection of 2000 objects found in the region, dating from the 1st century BC to the 5th century AD.

Heading towards the tip of the island, you will reach **Narodni trg** (People's Square) in the centre of town. On the west side is the renovated 16th-century watch-tower; the loggia opposite, also dating from the 16th century, now houses a **Museum of Art**. To the north, next to the Fanfogna and Guerini palaces, is the 12th-century **St Chrysogonus** *(Sveti Krsevan),* and the **National Museum** with displays, paintings and models depicting the history of Zadar and the coastal towns.

Walking westwards, you will come to the most impressive of Zadar's many churches, the circular **St Donat's** *(Sveti Donat),* built by the Byzantines in the 9th century on the old Roman forum. Much of it was recycled from the stones of existing Roman structures. The area around the church is still covered with the forum's poignant ruins. Not far from here is the **archaeological museum**, with as good a collection of Roman antiquities as you might expect in such a town. Next door, the **Benedictine monastery of St Mary** contains a museum of church art.

Just across the forum from St Donat's, the 13th-century Romanesque **Cathedral of St Anastasia** (*Sveti Stošija*) was badly damaged during World War II. Inside, look for the superb baroque altar and Gothic choir stalls.

Continue from here to the seafront at the tip of the peninsula to listen to the **Sea Organ** set in the steps, and the nearby **Greeting to the Sun**, made up of photovoltaic cells set into the paving, which make a spectacular light show at night.

Off the coast of Zadar is a clutch of islands large and small (the Zadarian Islands), ranging from **Dugi Otok** (Long Island) with its west coast facing the sea, sheltering the smaller **Ugljan** and **Pašman** islands closer to shore, and a host of islets. Cruise ships spend time in the secluded anchorage of Dugi Otok's **Triluke Bay** where the waters are ideal for scuba divers. You can explore the nearby fishing and farming villages or enjoy the natural landscape of medicinal and aromatic herbs, vineyards, olive groves and pine forest.

Kornati Islands

South of the Zadarian islands, the Kornatis make up the largest archipelago in the Mediterranean. Most of them are wild, deserted slivers of windswept rock—created by God, according to legend, out of boulders left over after the creation of the world—although the uninhabited Kornat Island itself is all of 35 km (21 miles) long. Humpbacked and dotted with salt lakes, the islands are fringed with sheer cliffs that emerge dramatically from the limpid Adriatic. The 89 southernmost islands are protected as a national park.

Šibenik

Perfectly located, Šibenik looks out across an azure lagoon towards the Kornati Islands. It was first mentioned in a royal document in 1066, and served as a fortress guarding the mouth of the Krka River on which it lies. The town flourished after the Venetians took control in 1412, and thanks to its mighty fortifications held off several attacks by the Turks.

The 12th–13th-century **Fortress of St Anne** (*Tvrdjava Sveti Ana*) still dominates the ancient town's maze of houses and alleyways and surrounding bay. Jutting up from the red rooftops, the magnificent **Cathedral of St Jakov** *(Sveti Jakov)* was begun in 1431 and took over a century to complete. Built entirely of stone, the church has withstood the dangers of fire, flood and bombshell with ease. The cathedral is the masterpiece of Juraj Dalmatinac, a sculptor and architect from Zadar who was asked by the Šibenik authorities to take over the design of the building in 1441. The neat trefoil façade, the barrelled roof and dome are especially striking, constructed from huge stone slabs. Most impressive of all, though, is a marvellous frieze of 72 remarkably lifelike sculpted heads lining the outer walls of the apses. Inside the church there are some fine Gothic columns, above which can be seen Dalmatinac's trademark acanthus leaf design in a double row. To the right of the choir, his exquisite little **baptistery**, with superb lacy stonework and pretty shell motif, is one of the highlights of Croatia's church interiors.

Dalmatinac is celebrated by a statue in front of the church sculpted by the modern Croatian sculptor Ivan Meštrović.

The square outside St Jakov's is a great spot to sit and enjoy a drink. Apart from the church to admire, there's also the Renaissance **town hall** and arcaded loggia, now a restaurant, and the **Prince's Palace**, dating from the Venetian era and housing the city museum.

Šibenik is filled with old churches linked by an intricate web of narrow medieval streets. During the 15th and 16th centuries, the city was a centre of Croatian culture and scholarship; many of the nation's most famous composers, artists, scientists and writers lived here. The 14th-century **Franciscan monastery** *(Sveti Franjo)*, to the south of the old town, was one of the most important focal points of the Dalmatian renaissance and today has a large collection of valuable manuscripts from the period.

From Šibenik, be sure to take a trip out to the powerful **Krka Falls**, 15 km (24 miles) upriver. Here, the Krka River comes crashing over a series of limestone barriers covered in lush foliage. Near Skradinski Buk, the most beautiful of the falls, there's a pool for bathing. You can visit the small rustic museum, and the laundry where you can see how the force of the water was exploited for washing clothes, cleaning carpets and fleece, and milling grain. Further upriver, a 15th-century Franciscan monastery sits on a small river island at the point where it widens to form a lake. You can reach it by boat.

Split

This is probably the only city in the world that started as a retirement home. A common soldier turned emperor, Diocletian became the first sovereign to resign voluntarily, when he abdicated in AD 305. With a vast empire to choose from, he picked this splendid bay on the south side of the Split peninsula to build his sumptuous palace.

It found a new lease of life more than 300 years later, when marauding Avar tribes sacked the provincial centre of nearby Salona and refugees sought shelter in the great palace here. They took over the cellars and the imperial apartments, rebuilt, settled in, and eventually spread beyond the massive outer walls. **Diocletian's Palace** is today the extraordinary old town of Split — to the bafflement of many a tourist who wanders about inside the palace asking the way to it.

The palace, covering an area of about 27,000 sq m (32,292 sq yd), has a simple rectangular layout with main streets crossing in the centre and leading to gates in the middle of each wall. Diocletian's quarters were located in the seaward half; the palace staff and legionaries used to live in the northern part.

Start at the waterfront. The emperor used to admire the sea view from between the columns

Huber/Fabijanic

Ancient doors make an appropriate setting for traditional costume.

of a covered pavement, up above. From here you can enter the palace by the southern **Bronze Gate** (*Mjedena vrata*), which leads down to the **basement** (*Podrumi*). The deliciously cool vaulted halls used to be directly below the imperial apartments. They now contain souvenir stalls and some archaeological finds, and are used for temporary exhibitions.

Continue along the passage to the Palace's centrepiece, the **Peristyle** (*Peristil*). Bordered on three sides by immense Corinthian columns, this sunken courtyard has defied time to continue its original function as a meeting place and open-air festival hall (the site of the Split Summer Festival in July). This is the perfect spot to sit on the steps and contemplate seventeen centuries of history in evidence around you.

Behind the stairs to the south of the Peristyle, a monumental portico leads to the circular, now domeless **vestibule**, the waiting room for visiting dignitaries.

Walk back across the Peristyle and down an alley bordered by medieval buildings to an ancient house of worship. Originally sacrifices to Jupiter were performed here, but early Christians turned it into a **Baptistery of St John** (*Sv. Ivan Krstitelj*). A headless black sphinx keeps vigil in front of the entrance.

The outside of the **Cathedral of St Domnius** (*Sveti Dujam*), formerly the emperor's mausoleum, has not changed since Diocletian's time, although it is ironic that the last resting place of such an avid persecutor of Christians should become a church. A black Egyptian sphinx guards the entrance, and 24 columns surround the octagonal structure dominated by its medieval tower, which is worth climbing for a marvellous view of the old city. On the **main doors**, the carved panels representing scenes from the life of Christ are a masterpiece of 13th-century art. Inside, look up to see the sculpture of Diocletian's head set within a stone wreath, in a medallion just below the dome. And don't miss the beautifully carved choir stalls.

Behind the cathedral, the **Ethnographical Museum** (*Etnografski muzej*) at Iza Vestibula 4 displays collections of costumes, jewellery and musical instruments.

The wide thoroughfare leading east from the Peristyle takes you to the **Silver Gate** (*Srebrna vrata*), the site of the colourful and lively flower market. From there, walk through the warren of medieval streets leading in a northwesterly direction to the **Golden Gate** (*Zlatna vrata*). On the way look into the flamboyant, Gothic **Papalic Palace**, now the city museum with a fine collection of early weapons, paintings and other artefacts.

Outside the Golden Gate, pause to rub the toe (for luck) of the **statue of Bishop Gregory of Nin** (*Grgur Ninski*)—a 10th-century Croatian bishop honoured for asserting the right to say mass in Croat. The statue was sculpted by Ivan Meštrović in 1929.

A street along the west wall takes you to **People's Square** (*Narodni trg*), an early evening meeting place for young and old. On the northeast side of the square stands the Venetian former town hall, *Vijećnica*, with three Gothic arches.

From Braće-Radića Square, with its monument to the poet Marko Marulić (by Ivan Meštrović), you reach the **Port Gate** *(Hrvoje Kula)*, flanked by two imposing towers remaining from the fortifications the Venetians built to hold off the Turks in the 15th century.

On the north side of Split, at Frankopanska 25, is an **archaeological museum**, whose fine exhibition of Roman and early Christian pieces from nearby Salona was first put together at the start of the 19th century.

Ivan Meštrović's former summer residence near the tip of the peninsula now houses the **Meštrović Museum**, displaying more of his works. He designed the building himself, intending it to be his retirement home. But he spent his last days elsewhere, emigrating to the US after World War II, where he lived till his death in 1962. In the Kastelet, a small 16th-century castle on the coast, you can see his cycle of *The Life of Christ*, carved in wood on four walls. A nearby **archaeological museum** features fragments taken from medieval Croatian churches.

Split's landmark, beloved of all its citizens, is wooded **Marjan Hill** where Diocletian once hunted. A climb up the steps near the Meštrović Museum to the terrace will reward you with views of the city and its surroundings.

Rainer Hackenberg

In Trogir most windows are ornate, like those of Čipiko Palace.

Trogir

Along the coast north of Split lie the **Seven Castles** *(Sedam Kaštela)*—a string of villages along the curve of a bay, built around the castles of medieval landlords. The old coastal road leads past them to Trogir, rising out of the sea on its own island. This ancient town, founded by the Greeks, is a delight. It's a pleasure simply to walk through the intertwining streets broken by steps and vaulted passages. Don't miss the Venetian **Cathedral of St Lawrence** *(Sveti Lovro)* with its carved Romanesque portal flanked by statues of Adam and Eve, dating from the 13th century. The interior has many fine features, including the superb Renaissance Chapel of St Ivan, a pulpit supported by eight columns, and the ciborium, a canopy over the main altar. Climb the clock tower for a splendid view of the city.

Opposite the cathedral on the main square, the **Čipiko Palace** is a lavishly decorated 15th-century mansion. The nearby **town hall**, built in the 1470s by Donatello's student, Nicholas of Florence, has served as law court, prison and public forum.

Brač

The island of Brač has been coveted for its natural riches for 2,000 years. It was here that the stone for Diocletian's palace was quarried, and a long procession of subsequent invaders have shown a marked taste for its bountiful crop of figs, wine-grapes, olives and almonds. A 45-minute ferry ride from Split, Brač is a delightful haven for beach-lovers, hikers and anyone wanting to flee city life.

On the south side of the island, the medieval port of **Bol** has fine beaches nearby, such as the Golden Horn (*Zlatni Rat*), a striking sandy promontory jutting into the clear waters of the Adriatic. If

Ahead by a Neck.
Croatia has made an indelible mark on the world's neckwear. The cravat is actually a French pronunciation of *hrvati*, the Croat word for—Croatian. The most likely reason is that the scarves worn by Croat mercenaries who served in Louis XIV's army became fashionable among the French troops. The cravat now graces stylish necks around the globe.

the landscape looks different from any photographs you might have seen, don't be concerned— the Golden Horn is constantly changing shape due to the effects of the wind. Bol is also well placed for hiking to old villages and Vidova Mountain, the highest peak in the Adriatic islands.

Hvar

A short distance further, Hvar is often spoken of as the loveliest Dalmatian island, which is helped by it also being the sunniest place in Croatia. The town of Hvar, surrounded by fields of lavender and gardens overflowing with semi-tropical flowers, retains its medieval charm. **St Stephen's Cathedral** looks out on the main square (*Trg Svetog Stepana*). At the other end, there's the Gothic **Arsenal**, with its great arch facing the harbour. On the second floor is a real surprise—Europe's earliest **municipal theatre**, built in 1612. Southeast of the city, the 15th-century **Franciscan monastery** contains a good museum of Venetian paintings. Overlooking the town and its harbour, a **Venetian fortress** from the mid-16th century offers panoramic views. If you need a refreshing dip in the sea after all this, the best places for bathing are the sandy beaches of the **Pakleni islets** just offshore.

Stari Grad, 20 km (12 miles) east of Hvar, was originally founded by the Ancient Greeks as a *pharos*, or lighthouse. It was the island's capital until the 14th century, and boasts many fine old streets. You can also see the 16th-century mansion of Croatian poet Petar Hektorović, with its fish pond and garden.

Korčula

Tradition has it that Korčula was founded by the Trojans in the 12th century BC, but in fact it was their old enemies, the Greeks, who colonized the island, calling it Korkyra Melaina (Black Korčula) because of its dark forests. Korčula is a famous wine-producing island, and while you're here be sure to try some Grk, which is one of the best wines in Croatia.

Situated on a headland at the eastern end of the island, **Korčula town** is a tight cluster of narrow streets on a herring-bone pattern, old churches and red-roofed houses, overlooked by the round towers of the ancient city walls. The buildings are made from a honey-coloured stone that dazzles at noon and changes to a rich golden hue with the sunset. Korčulans say that the famous traveller Marco Polo was born here, but sceptical visitors will find it hard to believe he would ever have wanted to leave this most beautiful of Dalmatian cities.

Until the mid-19th century, the town was completely enveloped by a wall, built originally to defend it from Turkish invaders and marauding pirates. The remaining parts date mostly from the 14th–16th centuries. The towers are in particularly good condition. Dominating the port, the square **Revelin tower** dates from 1495. Look out also for the superb main **town gate**, built by Korčula's noblemen in 1650 to celebrate the victory of the Venetian governor, Leonardo Foscolo, over the Turks. The grand **town hall** just inside the gate perfectly illustrates the city's eminence under Venetian rule.

The town's architectural masterpiece is the splendid **St Mark's Cathedral** *(Sveti Marko)*. Construction began in the early part of the 15th century and took 150 years

istockphoto.com/Kabakovitch

The old town of Korčula is embraced by ramparts.

to complete, incorporating on the way a change in styles from Gothic to Renaissance. Its finely carved portal, rose window and remarkable gables are testament to the skills of the island's masons, renowned throughout Europe at the time. In the interior you will find a Gothic baptistery, complete with 13th-century fonts. There are also some fine art works, including an altarpiece painting of St Mark, the work of Tintoretto.

Near the cathedral, the 14th-century **Abbot's Palace** now houses a fine display of art and antiquities, with a collection that varies from ancient church robes to contemporary Croatian art.

Across the square, next to the Arneri Palace with its fine interior courtyard, the **municipal museum** is located in the 16th-century Gabriellis Palace. The displays are dedicated to local history and culture, especially the traditional

Korčula industries such as shipbuilding and stonemasonry.

Another museum well worth visiting is housed in the **Guildhall**. There is a splendid collection of Cretan icons here, as well as a 4th-century Madonna. It also allows access to the adjoining **All Saints' Church** (*Svi Sveti*), which has an 18th-century wooden Pietà by the Austrian artist Georg Raphael Donner.

By far the oldest church in Korčula, **St Peter's** (*Sveti Petar*) started as far back as the 10th century. The Renaissance porch is a 15th-century addition. Not far from the church is a tall building advertised as **Marco Polo's birthplace**, although there's not a shred of evidence to support the claim. Polo is a common surname on Korčula. Nevertheless, the view of the town from the tower is worthwhile.

The town was built out of stone quarried from the attractive nearby island of **Vrnika**. Used since Roman times, the island's clean white stone also contributed to such distant buildings as the St Sofia basilica in Istanbul, the parliament in Vienna and even Stockholm's town hall.

Mljet

Located between Korčula and Dubrovnik, this island is popular with day-trippers from both places. But Mljet more than merits a longer stay. Indeed, legend has it this was Ogygia, where Odysseus dallied for seven years here on his way back from the Trojan Wars, captivated by the charms of the nymph Calypso.

The entire western part of the island is a national park, that can be visited on foot or by bicycle. Don't miss the 12th-century Benedictine monastery in the middle of **Veliko jezero** (Great Lake), a picturesque salt lake. The monastery is set on a delightful islet, covered in Mljet's famous Aleppo pines and also with good beaches for bathing. The lake shore itself provides an excellent spot for walking and enjoying the island's natural beauty.

One thing you won't have to worry about as you explore Mljet is bumping into a snake. At the beginning of the 20th century, the authorities introduced the mongoose to the island. Today there are no snakes but a lot of mongooses.

Dubrovnik

In the Middle Ages, Dubrovnik's sophisticated diplomacy made it an independent city state rivalling Venice in the extent of its maritime trade. Indeed, such was the size and fame of its fleet that the word "argosy", deriving from the city's former name of Ragusa, became a synonym for a merchant treasure ship. Entering the medieval walled old town from the new Dubrovnik is like travelling back into that golden past. For here, the ancient paved stone streets, churches and palaces retain their ageless beauty.

On the menu

Brodet – fish soup
Cevapčići – spicy meatballs
Dalmatinski pršut – raw ham
Djuveč – goulash
Gavrilovićeva salama – salami
Istarski – smoked, dried ham
Jastog – lobster
Manistra od bobića – bean soup
Paški sir – cheese, served as an appetizer
Pljeskavica – hamburgers
Punjene paprike – stuffed peppers
Ražnjići – brochettes
Roštilj – grilled meat
Sarma – stuffed cabbage

istockphoto.com/ShyMan

Despite coming under intense shellfire from the Yugoslav National Army during the war of the early 1990s, Dubrovnik repaired the damage as quickly as possible. The city is still as rewarding a place as ever to follow your instinct and simply wander through the maze of steep sidestreets, with their outdoor markets, little cafés and all but hidden gardens, churches and mansions.

The best place to get an overview of the whole rich pageant is from on top of the magnificent **city walls**. Some 2.5 km (over a mile) in circumference, the fortifications date mainly from the 15th and 16th centuries and include fifteen towers, five bastions, two corner towers and a fortress. In some places they are up to 6 m (20 ft) thick—enough to withstand both the earthquake of 1667 and the bombardment of 1991. The best panorama is from the highest tower, **Minčeta**, at the northern corner of the wall. This great round fortress, begun in the 14th century, symbolizes the power of the ancient city state. One of the most exhilarating walks anywhere in the country is to go on a complete circuit of the ramparts, starting inside the **Pile Gate**, the main entrance to the town, which you reach by a wooden drawbridge. You will be rewarded by unforgettable new perspectives over the terracotta

The best buys
Dried figs and fig cakes *(hib)*
Embroidery
Home-made spirits
Lace
Lavender oil from Hvar
Local wines
Moor's-head earrings from Rijeka
Naïve paintings
Pottery
Woodcarvings

roofs of the city and the sparkling waters of the Adriatic.

Notice the statue of St Blaise above the Gothic arch of the Pile Gate, one of a number of portrayals of the saint who is venerated locally for having helped repel a Venetian attack a thousand years ago.

Immediately in front of you is **Onofrio's Great Fountain**, dating from the 15th century and named after a Neapolitan architect, Onofrio della Cava. He specialized in fountains, and this handsome, 16-sided reservoir is the biggest of his many waterworks. The water was supplied by a system he designed using an 11-km (7-mile) aqueduct starting in the mountains.

Facing the fountain, the tiny **Our Saviour's Church** (*crkva Sveti Spas*) has a Renaissance façade and a Gothic interior. Remarkably, it escaped destruction in the 1667 earthquake that damaged much of the city. It is now used as an art gallery.

Next to Sveti Spas, and overshadowing it, the church of the **Franciscan monastery** is entered through a richly decorated main portal. The monastery complex was originally built in the 14th century and acted as a defensive watchtower for the Pile Gate, as well as a house of worship. In its delightful gardened cloister, a **chemist's shop** dating from 1317 has been restored down to the last apothecary jar, mortar and pestle.

The **Placa** (pronounced *platsa*), heading east from here, is old Dubrovnik's great, straight main thoroughfare. The architecture on either side is a model of harmony, where the houses —all of them four storeys high with arched doorways—are of the same light-coloured stone as the street itself. Their unpretentious baroque façades are an afterthought, added after the devastation of the 17th-century earthquake. The Placa is still the ancient city's most animated artery. During the day, it's alive with the bustle of busy shops, pavement cafés and restaurants, while around sunset the street fills with families enjoying the traditional *korzo*, the Mediterranean style of evening promenade, as clouds of swallows swoop and dive overhead.

Reconstructed in 1929, the municipal **clock tower** at the far end of the Placa has been tolling the hours since the 15th century. Striking the bell, the bronze clappers in the form of soldiers are symbols of Dubrovnik, known as the "green men". In the centre of the square, **Orlando's Column** dates from 1419. Proclamations used to be read from the top by the town crier, while the base was the place for punishing criminals.

Built from 1516 to 1522, the **Sponza Palace** is an elegant example of Gothic and Renaissance architecture. This was the republic's customs house and mint, and now contains the state archives. Behind the palace, the huge **Dominican monastery** once protected the city's eastern gate. It's worth seeing the fine collection of religious art in its museum. In the cloister, the hollows in the ledge between the columns were scooped out by Napoleon's soldiers as mangers for their horses which were stabled there.

Back on the Placa, the small **Church of St Blaise** *(Sveti Vlaho),* just south of Orlando's Column, is a 20th-century successor to the 14th-century church, which had suffered much damage. Inside the church, look out for the image of St Blaise, Dubrovnik's patron saint, holding a model of the walled city as accurate as a modern map.

Dubrovnik's most impressive building, the Gothic **Rector's Palace** is now a museum. The building dates from 1441 and was designed by the fountain man, Onofrio della Cava. Here the city state's supreme leader received petitioners and foreign diplomats. The grand staircase, leading from the perfectly proportioned courtyard inside the entrance up to an arcaded balcony, is particularly fine.

The baroque **cathedral** replaced a 12th-century church destroyed in the 1667 earthquake. It contains some interesting art works inside, including a large polyptych of the Assumption by Titian. The treasury features a 12th-century Byzantine crown said to contain a relic of St Blaise himself.

A gate in the city wall between the cathedral and the palace leads to the **old harbour**, where warships and treasure ships used to bob at anchor in the republic's heyday. In the 16th century it became so crowded that the principal port was moved a couple of miles to the west at Gruz. From the old harbour, you can take a ferry across to Lokrum Island for an afternoon swim, hire a boat for Cavtat or Mlini, or just sit at the outdoor café and enjoy the little port's pleasing hubbub.

On the southern hook of the old harbour, there's an aquarium in **St John's Fortress** and, keeping up the aquatic theme, a maritime museum above it, concentrating on Dubrovnik's 16th-century Golden Age.

Lokrum

A stone's throw from Dubrovnik, this tiny island packs in a lot of history. It was off Lokrum that Richard the Lion-Heart was in danger of shipwreck when he returned from the Third Crusade in 1192. It's said that in gratitude for his rescue, he contributed towards Dubrovnik's cathedral. The **Benedictine monastery**, located back from where the Dubrovnik ferry docks, was founded in the 11th century. The monks brought many exotic flora with them, a tradition that continues at the nearby **Botanical Garden**, where plants and trees from Australia and South America are testament to the sultriness of the climate.

Lokrum also has a French-built **fortress** from the time of Napoleon's Illyrian province, which has great views across to Dubrovnik, and a mansion constructed for the Habsburg Archduke Maximilian in 1859. He was crowned Emperor of Mexico in 1864, only to face rebellion and execution three years later.

The atmosphere in Lokrum is surprisingly "back to nature", with pleasant pine woods for shady walks and rocky beaches, including an FKK (nudist) beach.

PRACTICAL INFORMATION

Banks. Generally open Monday to Friday 7.30 a.m.–7 p.m. and Saturday 7.30 a.m.–1 p.m. Hours may be more flexible in coastal tourist resorts. Keep your receipt when you change money as you may need to show it in order to change Croatian money back again.

Climate. Croatia's Adriatic coast has a Mediterranean climate with an annual average of 2,600 hours of sunshine. Summers are hot, dry and mostly sunny. Spring is warm, cooled by the maestral winds, while autumn temperatures are pleasant, with warm seas. Winters are generally mild and wet.

Credit cards. Increasingly accepted in hotels, restaurants, shops etc., and can also be used at exchange bureaux and most banks.

Currency. The Croatian *kuna* (HRK) is divided into 100 *lipa*. Notes range from 10 to 1,000 kuna, and coins from 1 lipa to 5 kuna. Euros are welcome in many places.

Electricity. The standard is 220-volts AC, 50 Hz.

Emergencies. Police, 92; fire, 93; ambulance, 94, or the general European number 112.

Language. Croatian is a Slavic language but written in the Roman, as opposed to Cyrillic, alphabet. Due to the traditional influence of Germany in the region, German is widely spoken. English is increasingly popular, especially with young people.

Post office. Open Monday to Friday 7 a.m. to 7 p.m., Saturday to 1 p.m. In tourist resorts during high season, post offices and exchange bureaux may also be open until 10 p.m. as well as on Sundays.

Telephone. For calls from public telephones, phonecards can be purchased at post offices, newspaper kiosks and tobacconists. The outgoing international code is 00. Country code for USA and Canada is 1; UK 44. To make a call via the operator, dial 901.

Time. Croatia follows UTC/GMT +1. Daylight saving comes into operation in March, when clocks are put forward an hour.

Tipping. A service charge is usually included in restaurant bills and taxi fares.

Water. Local tap water is safe to drink, but visitors can choose bottled mineral water.

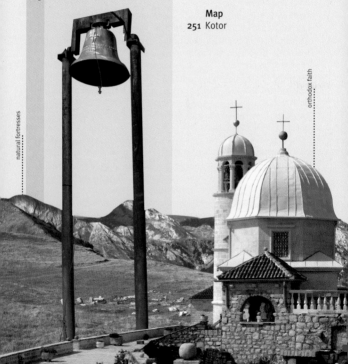

discreet charm

SIGHTSEEING

natural fortresses

orthodox faith

MONTENEGRO

The sharply indented coastline stretches over 293 km (182 miles), alternating cliffs and beaches of sand or pebbles. At the centre is the jewel of Montenegro's bays, Boka Kotorska. The Kotor fjord extending inland is Europe's southernmost, a UNESCO World Heritage Site. The coastal towns radiate a delicate charm, marked by features of the Venetian Renaissance and Austrian baroque. Along their narrow streets, the palaces are surrounded by small gardens scented by fragrant mimosa and oleander.

Kotor

The main tourist area of Montenegro extends around the wonderful Kotor Bay *(Boka Kotorska)* which thrusts 28 km (17 miles) inland, forming a butterfly-winged fjord hemmed in by tall limestone cliffs. The shelter offered by the Boka to shipping has managed to attract since ancient times the attention of merchants and invading conquerors. Indeed, a navigator's guild was created there in the 9th century. But it is the crystalline beauty of its waters that attracts visitors today: a whole universe of islands, mountain peaks reflected in the deep blue water and, from one harbour to the next, from one village to the next, a series of coves with their profusion of oleander, palms and mimosa. The penetration of the Adriatic deep into the mountainous interior gives the region a delightful microclimate.

At the very rear of the bay, the little town of Kotor backs onto tall cliffs crowned by a fortress. Its medieval centre, typical of the cities that grew up on the shores of the Adriatic between the 12th and 14th century, has been completely restored following a devastating earthquake in 1979. It is now a UNESCO World Heritage Site. The maze of lanes and small squares are protected by formidable city walls with foundations dating back to the Byzantines. Fortified by the Venetians (who called the town Cattaro), they are in places 16 m (52 ft) thick and 20 m (66 ft) high. The aim was to defend this prosperous port-town, bastion of the southern Dalmatian coast, against the covetous eye of the Turks.

The historic centre is quite small and can easily be visited on foot. The main entrance is through the **Sea Gate**, built in Renaissance style in 1555, one of three gateways originally built in the walls facing the harbour. It opens onto the **Trg od Oruzija** (Armoury Square), an elegant esplanade dominated by the sturdy **Clock Tower** (1602), the city's landmark. At its foot, criminals were once put in the stocks where pleasant open-air cafés now have their tables.

From the square, a lane lined with Venetians' Renaissance palazzi leads to a second square and the two dissimilar towers of the Roman Catholic **St Tryphon Cathedral** (*Sveti Tripun*). Consecrated in 1166, but frequently hit by earthquake and reconstructed, it has largely retained its Romanesque appearance. Legend has it that the choice of its patron saint was due to chance when, in the 9th century, the citizens bought his relics from a Levantine ship seeking shelter in the port. They are still kept in the crypt, and Tryphon duly became the patron saint of the Guild of Kotor Bay Navigators. His votive offerings are displayed as part of the sacristy's treasure. Behind the ciborium see the superb gilded silver bas-relief by a 15th-century Swiss master.

Strolling around the lanes, you will come across many Gothic or baroque palaces from the town's Venetian or Austrian era, notably the 14th–15th century Drago Palace on St Tryphon Square. The 18th-century Grgurina Palace today houses the **Naval Museum** whose collections trace Kotor's long maritime history and colourful traditions. One of its most precious documents is the Guild of Navigators charter, emphasizing the "mutual aid and solidarity" expected of all seamen. A little further on is the small Romanesque **Basilica of St Luke** (*Sveti Luka*) where for many years both Catholic mass and Orthodox rites were conducted. It possesses some murals dating back to its late 12th-century origins.

On a narrow nearby square, the 17th-century wrought-iron **Karampana Well** was for long a rallying point for popular demonstrations.

Embracing the whole hillside on which Kotor is built, the old city walls cover a distance of nearly 5 km. A long stairway leads up to the **Sveti Ivan Citadel** on the hilltop, 260 m up. Most of the edifice is 16th-century, erected on the site of an ancient Illyrian fortress. The climb (one hour up and down) is rewarded with a superb view of the town and the bay. Halfway up, you will pass by the little Chapel of Our Lady (*Gospa od Zdravlja*), built in 1572 by plague survivors.

Around Kotor Bay

The bay's ports, each possessing its own commercial fleet, have always enjoyed considerable autonomy, expressed in their distinctive and often splendid architecture. This is true of **Perast**, today a rather sleepy little town 14 km northwest of Kotor. When Peter the Great was building the Russian fleet in the 17th century, he sent a group of young nobles to attend the Naval Academy here. A baroque charm still pervades the waterfront, the main square dominated by the 17th-century church of St Nicholas and the sea captains' homes, some clinging to the hillside, others surrounded by gardens. The Bujovic Palace today houses the **town museum**, which displays period costumes, paintings, ship models and other memorabilia recalling the sailors' heyday on the Adriatic.

Facing the harbour, the **Church of Our Lady of the Rock** (*Gospa od Škrpjela*) rises from an artificial isle of rocks and ballast piled up by sailors over the years. It was

Huber/Grandadam

On the menu

Cicvara – mashed potatoes and polenta with *kajmak*
Čorba – thick soup
Čorbast pasulj – bean stew with smoked chops and sausage
Hljeb – bread
Japraci – veal stew with rice and *rastan*
Kajmak – thick fresh cream
Kačamak – polenta, usually served with *kajmak*
Kuvani brav – lamb stew
Pastrva – trout
Popara – a mixture of bread, milk, oil and cheese
Popeci – deep-fried veal rolls with ham and *kajmak*
Prljo – cheese aged in a leather bag
Pršut – smoked ham
Raštan – a vegetable of the cabbage family, cooked with potatoes and generously seasoned
Sarma – cabbage leaves stuffed with a mixture of rice and minced meat
Supa – bouillon

built in the 15th century to honour an icon of the Virgin Mary
found here and believed to have
miraculously cured one of the
sailors. The original chapel was
replaced in 1630 by a baroque
sanctuary which has kept the icon
along with 200 ex-votos and a
collection of paintings by Tripo
Kokolja, a renowned 17th-cen-
tury local artist.

Nearby, on **Sveti Juraj**, St
George's Island, stands a Benedictine abbey founded in the 11th
century. Its church was rebuilt in
the 17th and 18th centuries.

A few kilometres to the west,
Risan is the oldest town on the
bay. Founded in the 3rd century
BC, it was the vital centre of the
Illyrian state before falling to the
Romans. A Roman villa has been
excavated with fine geometric
mosaics from the 2nd century, as
well as a rare depiction of Hyp-
nos, the god of sleep.

From Kotor, the bay's very
narrow coastal road passes by
Tivat, the ferry-landing for trips to
Herceg-Novi. The town has preserved some handsome dwellings
originally used as summer residences by Kotor's upper classes.
It also has two beaches blue-
flagged safe for swimming, Plavi
Horizonti and Kalardovo, and a
new marina.

Keeping guard over Boka Kotorska at its western end, **Herceg-
Novi** is a health resort reputed for

The best buys
Carved wooden objects: salad bowls, figurines, flutes etc.
Colourful embroidery
Copper coffee mills
Hand-painted multicoloured pottery
Leatherware
Petit-point lace
Turkish tea sets

its high sunshine-rate, mellow climate and lush vegetation of
palms and mimosas, the latter
earning their own annual festival
in late January. The town became
important in the 14th century
with its development by the then
powerful kings of Bosnia, one of
whom gave it his name, Herceg
Stjepan. Parts of the city-walls
are still intact, along with several
bastions: Kauli Kula (the Bloody
Tower, 1483), a Turkish prison
now serving as an open-air theatre; the Spanish Citadel (1538,
rebuilt by the Turks); and the
Venetian Forte Mare (1687). The
heart of the old town, climbing
the hillside, is accessible through
a Turkish gate crowned by a
17th-century Venetian clock
tower. Up there on a little square
is the church of St Michael, surrounded by open-air cafés.

Outside the town, **Savina
Monastery** is worth the short trip.
Founded around 1030, it was

rebuilt in baroque style in Venetian times. Its church treasures include a crystal cross encrusted with gold, silver and rubies.

The resorts of Porto, Dobreč and Cuba Libre all have pretty blue-flagged **beaches**, good for swimming.

South Coast

The little port of **Budva**, 23 km (14 miles) south of Kotor, claims to be one of the oldest settlement in the Balkans, tracing its foundation the son of the mythical Phoenician King Agenor, while written testimonies date it to the 5th century BC. Today, it is the most important beach resort on the Montenegro coast, particularly lively in summer. The picturesque old town, entirely rebuilt after the earthquake of 1979, clusters on a small peninsula surrounded by 15th-century ramparts—the walk along the battlements makes an almost complete circuit. Several city gates lead to a labyrinth of lanes and cobblestoned squares, with four churches, the oldest dating back to the 8th and 9th centuries. Among the old limestone dwellings, handsome palaces have been restored to house galleries, restaurants and shops. A large summer arts festival is held with open-air theatre and concerts. Budva is also a very popular health resort, proud of its 17 **beaches**, notably Mogren, Ocaso, Sveti Toma and, finest of all, Bečići, once voted the most beautiful beach in Europe.

A few kilometres to the south, **Miločer** is an old summer resort once favoured by the Serbian royal family. Its pretty little Queen's Beach is half hidden among the lush vegetation and the cliffs. After this, the coastal road presents an impressive view over **Sveti Stefan**, an extraordinary fortified fishing village. Founded in the 15th century on a peninsula linked to the continent by a simple causeway, it was completely transformed in the 1960s into a luxury hotel. Actors, film directors, princes and other greats of this world all used to stay here, before the Yugoslav wars broke out. Visitors can tour the peninsula and use its two beaches of brick-coloured sand.

A little further along the mainland coast, **Petrovac** offers more fine beaches as well as a 16th-century Venetian fortress.

Bar, Montenegro's most important modern port, has a ferry link to Italy. Forget the rather grim architecture of the new town, a legacy of the Communist era, and take a look at the remains of the old upper town, **Stari Bar**, a few kilometres away up on the slopes of Mount Rumija, 1,593 m (5,226 ft). Once known as Antibari, it seems to have been founded back in the 9th century and has retained an ensemble of partly abandoned medieval buildings. Among the town's "treasures" is a 2,000-year-old olive tree. Along the coast near Sutomore you will find several long beaches of sand and pebbles.

On the other side of Mount Rumija, **Lake Skadar** *(Skadarsko jezero)*, the largest lake in the Balkans with an area of 368 sq km (142 sq miles), is shared between Montenegro and Albania (where its name is Shkodër). Fed by a large number of springs, its waters are astonishingly clear but shallow, averaging 6–7 m (19–22 ft). The lake is surrounded by reed marshland and has become one of Europe's most important nature reserves for waterfowl. Among the 270 identified species you can see heron, black ibis and the lake's emblematic rare curly-feathered Dalmatian pelican. Boat cruises are organized from the information centre at Vranjina and from several fishing villages on the south bank, such as Murići. On nearby isles Orthodox monasteries were built in the 15th and 16th centuries.

The last stop on the Montenegro coast before reaching the Albanian border is the hillside town of **Ulcinj**. It rivals Budva for the title of the country's most ancient city. Its slightly oriental atmosphere is perceptible at once thanks to its tall slender minarets, in particular that of the Pasha Mosque (1719). Only two gateways provide access to the old town on its promontory, one down by the sea, the other up on the heights, reached by a long sun-drenched ramp. On the outskirts of the town, to the right, you will see the old **Sveti Nikola Monastery** surrounded by olive trees. Its church, transformed into a mosque under the Turks, was reconstructed in 1890. Bombardments at the time of fighting between Montenegrins and Albanians devastated much of the upper town. However, a nicely restored Turkish fountain (1749) is still in place on one of the squares, and a little **museum** displays Montenegrin costumes and old tools. Approaching the sea and its rocky islands, you reach the Sea Gate which opens out on to the shore and the pretty **Mala Plaža** beach, which becomes a colourful forest of parasols in summer. To the east, **Velika Plaža** is said to be the Adriatic's longest beach, 13 km (8 miles). It ends opposite the estuary of the River Bojana, in the middle of which is the sandy island of **Ada Bojana**, much appreciated by nudist bathers. The island formed around the wreck of a ship sunk here in the 19th century. The seafood restaurants around here have a good reputation.

PRACTICAL INFORMATION

Banks. Open Monday to Friday 8 a.m.–7 p.m. and Saturday 8 a.m.–1 p.m.

Climate. On the coast, the climate is temperate, with long, dry summers. The most pleasant months for travelling are May, June and September. The sea temperature varies between 25 and 28 °C.

Credit cards. The major international credit cards are generally accepted in shops and the bigger hotels and restaurants but sometimes you will be told that the machine has broken down. Cash distributor machines can be found in most towns.

Currency. The unit of Montenegro currency is the Euro (€), divided into 100 centimes.

Electricity. The current is 220 volts, 50 Hz; plugs are the European kind with two round pins. Power cuts occur, especially in the south.

Emergencies. The European emergency number is 112. You can also dial 122 for the police, 123 for the fire brigade and 124 for an ambulance.

Language. The Montenegrin language is very close to Serbian. Some English is spoken in resorts.

Museums. Almost all museums close Monday.

Photography. Avoid taking photos of buildings guarded by the police.

Shops. Open in general 9 a.m.–9 p.m., some groceries from 6 a.m., sometimes until midnight in touristic areas, in summer. Some shops also open Sundays.

Time. UTC/GMT +1, advancing one hour for daylight saving time in summer to UTC/GMT +2.

Tipping. It is customary to give waiters a tip of 10 to 15 per cent of the bill. Taxi drivers and hotel staff (porters, chambermaids) will also appreciate a tip.

Tourist information. See www.montenegro.travel or www.visit-montenegro.com.

Water. In principle, tap water is drinkable, but sometimes supplies are scarce and it is best to buy bottled mineral water.

land of the eagles

folk music

SIGHTSEEING

valiant people

the memory of stones

strategic location

ALBANIA

Today's Albanians are strongly rooted in the Mediterranean world, experiencing the influence of all the great civilizations on its shores: Greek, Roman, Byzantine and Ottoman. All these powers battled to control the highly strategic land, its hilly and mountainous terrain forming a natural Balkan gateway to the heart of the European continent. They all left their mark on Albania's coasts and its interior so that the country today abounds in archaeological treasures.

Only 20 per cent of Albania's 28,748 sq km (11,000 sq miles) is suitable for farming, in an area concentrated in the coastal plain on the Adriatic and further south on the Ionian Sea. The seacoast, with its numerous beaches, stretches over 362 km (225 miles) with a hinterland of many vast lakes. Shared with neighbouring Montenegro, Lake Shkodër is the largest in the entire Balkan region, home of the rare grey-feathered Dalmatian pelican (*Pelicanus crispus*).

Durrës

Albania's main commercial port, Durrës is one of the country's most ancient towns. It was founded by Greek colonists from Corfu and Corinth in 627 BC with the name of Epidamnos. From its long history, the town preserves a somewhat disparate collection of archaeological remains, though most are still buried under the houses in the city-centre. As testimony to its revival in the Roman era, the **amphitheatre** (2nd century AD) was the largest in the Balkans, seating 15,000 spectators. An Early Christian crypt can be seen there, with quite remarkable mosaic decoration. In antiquity, the town owed much of its importance as the land terminus of the Via Egnatia route linking Rome and Byzantium, but several earthquakes left it in ruins. From later period, Durrës has preserved the **Byzantine forum** (6th century) and part of the city-walls with a fine Venetian watch-tower near the waterfront. Ancient history buffs will enjoy the **Archaeology Museum**, exhibiting mosaics, sculptures and burial stones. Also worth a look is **King Zog's summer palace**, built on a hilltop in the 1930s. The village of **Arapaj**, 5 km (3 miles) to the southwest, is known for its exceptional 9th-century Byzantine mosaic in the Basilica of Saint Mehill, depicting two herdsmen surrounded by a flock of animals.

In recent years, Durrës has been developing the attractions of its **beaches**. Many townspeople from Tirana head out here at the weekend and new apartment buildings have been sprouting along the sandy sea front. Pollution has been an occasional obstacle to bathing; it's best to enquire at the local tourist office about rapidly changing conditions. One sightseeing attraction along the beach is the series of bunkers erected by Enver Hoxha—now popular as castles for the kids.

Shkodër

Passing through the coastal plain, the first-rate national highway links up with the main town in the country's north, Shkodër, 120 km (75 miles) from Durrës. One of the oldest cities in Europe, it was inhabited by the Illyrians around 500 BC. It was built on the shore of the vast lake to which it gave its name—the Montenegrins, who possess its western half, call it Lake Skadar. The largest lake in the Balkans at 368 sq km (142 sq miles) is quite shallow and attracts a great number of wildfowl, migratory and otherwise. The rare Dalmatian pelican makes its nest there.

At the entrance to the town, overlooking the lake, is the old citadel of **Rozafat**, stronghold of King Genthios who fought valiantly against the Romans in the 2nd century BC. The Venetians added to its fortifications and it was occupied by the Turks until independence in 1912. You get a superb view from its bastions to the east down over the beautiful **Leaden Mosque**. Built in 1773, the shrine was spared but abandoned after the cultural revolution of 1967. In front of the main domed house of worship is a square roofed forecourt covered with 15 smaller domes. In town, the great modern **Sheik Zamil Abdullah Mosque** was built in 1995 in the Turkish style, with two tall minarets. Nearby is the **History Museum**, with exhibits devoted to archaeology, weaponry, painting and historic photographs. A few kilometres to the north is the attractive 18th-century stone **Mesi Bridge** spanning the River Kir.

Shkodër makes an excellent base from which to explore the **Albanian Alps**, especially the splendid artificial Lake Fierza formed by a dam on the River Drin. Its steeply sloping shores are scattered here and there with Ottoman-style *kule,* fortified tower houses. A ferry plies its waters as far as the town of Fierza, from where you can continue to Tropojë and **Valbonë**, a hill resort once popular with members of the Albanian Communist Politburo.

Albanian Riviera

Full of the promise of living up to its ambitious new name, Albania's relatively undeveloped south coast stretches over 100 km (60 miles) between Vlorë and the Greek frontier across from the island of Corfu. The coast is blessed with a typical Mediterranean landscape of heath, cliffs and secluded coves of sandy or pebble beaches and translucent water. The region is served by just one road, with a few hair-raising bends in places.

Gateway to the Albanian Riviera is the port-town of **Vlorë**, the country's second in importance and just 123 km (77 miles) south of Durrës, at the heart of a very large bay. The cape sheltering it separates the Adriatic to the north

Ottoman houses of the 17th and 18th centuries, with slate roofs. | **The ruins of the old Greek city of Apollonia.** | **The theatre of Butrint is remarkably well preserved.**

Huber/Pavan Aldo

Corbis/Poole/Robert Harding World Imagery

Corbis/Setboun

from the Ionian Sea to the south. From here Italy—the Cape of Otranto—is just 75 km (47 miles) away as the crow flies. It was at Vlorë in 1912 that Albania declared its independence, an event commemorated both by the Independence Museum and a formidable monument standing on Flag Square (Shashi I Flamurit). Today it attracts visitors to its pine-shaded **beaches**, several of which can be found on the bay south of town. Its most venerable edifice is the **Murad Mosque** (Xhamia e Muradi), built in 1542 by Mimar Sinan, Ottoman architect of Suleiman the Magnificent. A few kilometres to the south is the **Kanina fortress**, an important stronghold in Vlorë's past.

Near Fier, 40 km (25 miles) to the north, the ancient Greek city of **Apollonia** is the first to bear the name of the god of poetry and music. Founded in 588 BC by settlers from Corinth and Corfu, it was the most important Greek colony on Albanian soil, probably numbering some 50,000 inhabitants. Located 8 km (5 miles) from the coast, it was linked to the sea by a river port. It made its fortune from agriculture and bitumen. It was abandoned in the 5th century AD, probably after a violent earthquake.

Protected by a double walled perimeter, the site, scattered with olive trees, has some superb edifices dating back to its revival under the Romans in the 2nd century AD. Among them is the assembly hall (bouleuterion), a monument to the Agonothetes who presided over the town's sacred games. There's also a great portico with 17 niches facing the terraced seating of an odeon theatre, and a monumental fountain. In the 12th century, the **St Mary Monastery** recycled the ancient masonry for its building in the middle of the site with a vast courtyard surrounding the Byzantine church (now a museum).

Some 8 km (5 miles) from Fier, the **Orthodox Monastery of Ardenica**, founded in 1474, witnessed the marriage of Skanderbeg to the Byzantine princess Donika Comnenus. It has been restored and partially transformed into a hotel. The church retains some superb frescoes from the 18th century.

Further inland, the site of **Byllis** was the capital of the Illyrian tribe of the same name. Laid out on a vast plateau, it has kept a monumental central area bearing witness to the important Greek influence—its agora (market place), theatre, stadium and great colonnades. Many Early Christian basilicas were erected there in the 6th century.

South of Vlorë Bay, the road begins its climb to the Llogara Pass, 1,027 m (3,369 ft), offering some stunning views over the coast. A series of hairpin bends leads down to **Dhërmi**, a town squeezed in between the mountains and the seashore. It is known for its beaches, seafood restaurants and two Byzantine churches, St Stefan and St Mitri, from the 12th and 14th centuries. Beyond, cliffs, beaches and seaside villages are gradually awakening to their tourist potential, notably **Vunoi**, **Jali** and **Himarë**. Nestling in a charming bay, **Porto Palermo** has kept a fine castle built by Ali Pasha on a peninsula.

Built as an amphitheatre on the north side of a bay at the beginning of the Straits of Corfu, **Saranda** is a modern town, enjoying a mellow climate. Its great attraction is the sea-front promenade lined with palm trees and small cafés. Near the town is the site of the ancient Illyrian port of **Onchesmos** where foundations and wells have been excavated, along with an Early Christian basilica from the 6th century, with fine mosaic paving. Other mosaics are displayed in the museum.

From Saranda, a small road leads 18 km (11 miles) to the site of **Butrint**—ancient Buthroton—a city founded by Greek settlers from Corfu between the 7th and 5th centuries BC. Conquered by the Romans in 167 BC, the city was rebuilt and became a major focus for the Romanization of the region. Its prosperity endured in Byzantine times and was then abandoned at the end of the Middle Ages, a victim of earthquake and the encroaching sea. Laid out on a short peninsula, the city occupied a strategic position at the end of the Vivari Canal linking the Ionian Sea to Lake Butrint, a lagoon renowned for the abundance of its fauna and flora.

istockphoto.com/Long

On the menu

Byrek – cheese pasties

Fërgesë – a dish of tomatoes and peppers with cheese sauce

Hoshaf – figs cooked in curds

Qofte – meatballs with garlic, onion and spices

Romsteak – minced meat

Tavë dheu – chopped liver with ewe's cheese, eggs, yoghurt, tomatoes, onions and garlic

Tavë kosi – leg of lamb with yoghurt, flavoured with saffron and garlic

istockphoto.com/Long

The best buys
Agricultural implements
Carpets
Copper coffee sets
Crafts inspired by ancient Illyrian
  and Byzantine designs
Embroidery
Filigree jewellery
Flea market finds
Lace
Snuff boxes
Traditional costumes
Wooden kitchen utensils

The fortification enclose an area of 16 ha divided into two unequal parts: the **acropolis** and, at its foot, the lower town. The former, perched on a rock 42 m (138 ft) up, is protected by a wall of megaliths 3.5 m (11 ft) thick in places. On its slopes, the splendidly preserved **theatre** (3rd century BC) has terraced seating for just 1,500 spectators hewn from the bedrock, with the stone scenic wall built by the Romans in the 2nd century AD. Notice how the VIP seats in the front row are decorated with carved lions' feet. A modern arts festival is held there now.

The Roman era left **public baths**, a **gymnasium** and, closer to the canal, the **Triconch Palace**, a vast villa frequently expanded. But the highlight of the visit is the **Early Christian Baptistery**, largest of its kind after Istanbul's St Sophia. Built at the end of the 6th century inside antique public baths, its floors are paved with a superb series of mosaics decorated with geometric and floral motifs, with birds and fish here and there. Remains of a basilica from the same era can be seen nearby, as well as an ancient nymphaeum.

The Venetians built a massive, well-preserved **tower** close to the entrance to town and just beyond it, on the opposite bank of the Vivari Canal, a triangular **fortress**. For their part, the Turks have bequeathed the **Castle of Alia Pasha**, built at Vrina at the beginning of the canal in 1814 to counter the English presence on Corfu.

Syri i Kaltër, 18 km (11 miles) from Saranda, the "blue eye" spring, in the shade of venerable old oak, trees gushes from a deep natural well. The deep blue waters feed the River Bistrica.

PRACTICAL INFORMATION

Banks. Open generally Monday to Friday 8.30 a.m.–2.30 p.m.

Climate. The Albanian coast enjoys Mediterranean weather—hot summers and rainy but mellow winters. The mountainous hinterland has a more continental climate with greater variations and extremes in temperature.

Electricity. The current is 220 volts, 50 Hz; plugs are the standard European type with two round pins. Power cuts are quite frequent.

Emergencies. Dial 129 for the police, 127 for medical emergencies and 128 for the fire brigade.

Entry formalities. Residents of the EU can enter Albania with a passport or identity card valid at least 3 months after date of arrival. No visa is required but there is an entry tax of 10 Euro.

Health. To avoid intestinal problems, it's best not to drink the tap water. Bottled mineral water is available.

Language. The official language of the country is Albanian, but Greek is also spoken in the south. It is quite easy to communicate in Italian and, to a lesser extent, in English, German and occasionally in French. Place names have two forms, indefinite (used on signs and maps) and definite. For the sake of simplicity we have preferred to use the indefinite forms.

Money. The unit of currency is the *lek* (ALL), in coins from 1 to 100 *Lekë* and banknotes from 200 to 5000 *Lekë*. Euros and US dollars are easily changed if the notes are reasonably new. Old and crumpled notes are not usually accepted, not even in banks. Credit cards are rarely accepted.

Safety. The tense political and social situation has improved and along with it, the level of personal safety. Albania is still a poor country, don't tempt providence by exhibiting your jewels and other signs of wealth.

Tipping. Service is included in restaurant bills. You do not need to leave an extra tip but many people leave 5 to 10 per cent more.

Tourist Information. www.albaniantourism.com

majestic colours

SIGHTSEEING

in the shade of the olive groves

ancient sites

local crafts

GREECE

Everything begins and ends at Athens: spreading around the Acropolis, the eternal city is the perfect introduction to the treasures of this appealing country, land of the gods. From there, reach out into Attika and the Peloponnese, the seat of heroes and site of the first great cities of continental Greece. North of the Gulf of Corinth is Delphi, the shrine of Apollo, while the surrounding seas are dotted with islands large and small: Corfu and the Ionian isles, the Sporades, the Cyclades centred on Delos, Crete in the Aegean, Rhodes and the Dodecanese near the Turkish coast.

Piraeus

One of the largest Mediterranean ports, Piraeus has served as the gateway to Athens since it was founded by Themistocles in the 5th century BC. A generation later, Pericles connected it to Athens via the fortified "Long Walls", though nowadays the same has been achieved by the capital's suburban sprawl and the opening of a direct metro line from the centre.

The typical seediness of a major port—seamen's cafés, harbourfront bars frequented by salty characters—has gradually been replaced by marble-clad banks catering for big shipping and oil clients. But you can still find plenty of local colour, especially on the eastern side of the city, at

Zea Marina and around the little port Mikrolimano, where you can eat at one of the many fine seafood restaurants ringing the waterfront.

Antiquities dredged up from ancient shipwrecks in Piraeus's harbours fill its Archaeological Museum. Look for the huge, hollow statue of Apollo dating from 520 BC and an exquisite bronze Athena with owls and griffins on her helmet. The Hellenic Maritime Museum covers the history of the Greek navy from Themistocles to the present day, and will fascinate fans of all things nautical.

Athens

Athens became the capital of independent Greece and royal city of King Otto I in 1834, from which date a new town was laid out in strict grid pattern, enhanced by several impressive neoclassical buildings. The two great squares, elegant Syntagma and dowdier Omonia, still give a good idea of the grandiose plans of that time, despite suffering from a surfeit of traffic and some less than sensitive modern development. Linked directly by two major streets, Stadiou and Venizelou (or Panepistimiou), they are about a ten-minute stroll apart.

Syntagma is at the heart of the city's business district and filled with modern buildings housing banks, airline offices and international business concerns. The vast neoclassical royal palace on the east side of the square has been the seat of the nation's **Parliament** since 1935. *Evzones* in traditional uniform guard a memorial to Greece's unknown soldier in the forecourt, and perform the complicated ceremony of the Changing of the Guard every hour. The adjacent **National Garden**, once the private garden of the palace, is a peaceful oasis of exotic plants, ornamental ponds and shady paths.

On Vasilissis Sofias 22 is the **Byzantine and Christian Museum**. Covering the period between the fall of the Roman Empire (5th century) and the rule of Constantinople (1453), with a futher department documenting the 15th–20th centuries, the museum's collection illustrates the emergence of the Byzantine era. The exhibition brings to the fore the specific rôle of Athens, a centre of pagan thought for at least two centuries before the advent of Christianity. See in particular the section of Coptic art, the treasure from Mytilini, icons, frescoes from the Episkopi church of Evrytania (9th–13th centuries) and superb illuminated manuscripts.

A few streets north of Omonia stands the world-famous **National Archaeological Museum**, with its unparalleled collection of Mycenean, Cycladic, Minoan and Classical Greek art. You won't regret devoting at least half a day to its treasure-trove of sculpture, frescoes, vases, cameos, jewels, coins and countless other items. The museum's most precious object, in room 4, is perhaps the gold death mask of Agamemnon, discovered at Mycenae in 1876 by the German archaeologist Heinrich Schliemann. In the same room is another important find from this period, the magnificent Warrior Vase. Visitors should also be sure to see the Minoan frescoes recovered from the island of Thera (Santorini), estimated to be some 3,500 years old; the Poseidon poised to hurl his trident (room 15) and the superb Jockey of Artemision with his steed, both in bronze (room 21); and the exquisite marble head of Hygeia, thought to be the work of Praxiteles.

The oldest quarter of Athens —and by far the most charming—is the **Plaka**. People have lived continuously for more than 3,000 years in this picturesque maze huddled against the northern slope of the Acropolis, though the layout mainly dates from the Turkish era. Ancient ruins and Byzantine churches, shops, cafés, restaurants, bars and nightclubs are packed into this small area. In the labyrinthine— and largely car-free—lanes you'll stumble upon attractive 19th-century houses with ochre-coloured façades, green shutters and balconies, their courtyards splashed with bougainvillaea and hibiscus.

Ancient Athens

The **Acropolis**, a 4-ha (10-acre) rock rising 90 m (300 ft) above the plain of Attica, was the focal point of ancient Athens. Battered and incomplete though it may be now, the Acropolis possesses such majesty that it still ranks among the world's true wonders. The name means "high town", from the Greek *acro* (highest point) and *polis* (town or city). Alternatively it means "citadel", a rôle it fulfilled during the Bronze Age and even more so in the Mycenean era.

The visitors' entrance is the **Beulé Gate**, a Roman addition of the 3rd century that's named after the French archaeologist who discovered it in 1852. Six fluted Doric columns mark the **Propylaea**, a monumental archway to the Acropolis. The central and largest of the gateways was for chariots and approached by a ramp; steps lead up to the four other entries destined for pedestrians.

High on a terrace off to the right of the Propylaea perches the elegant **Temple of Athena Nike**, the work of architect Callicrates in 421 BC. It enjoys a glorious panorama of the sea and distant mountains. Remarkably, the temple is a piece-by-piece modern reconstruction of what remained after the Turks tore down the original in 1687, again restored in recent years.

Passing through the Propylaea, you emerge onto the great sloping esplanade of the Acropolis, with a first breathtaking view of the beautiful white marble Doric **Parthenon** (Temple of the Virgin). During the heyday of the Acropolis, 2,400 years ago, the immediate foreground was dominated by a gigantic bronze statue of Athena under another guise— Athena Promachos, the Defender. This statue of the city's presiding goddess holding shield and spear was created by Phidias to honour

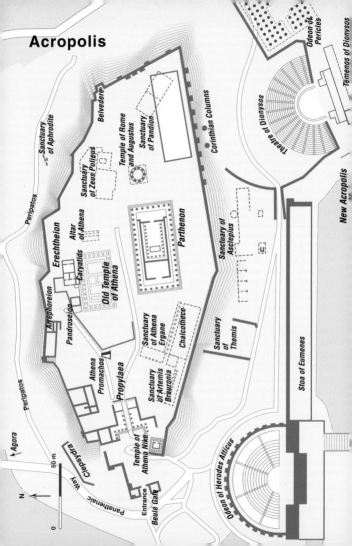

the victory at Marathon in 490 BC. It stood here for a thousand years, until it was carted off to Constantinople in the 6th century.

The temple's exterior columns rise 10 m (34 ft), each consisting of about a dozen fluted marble drums placed one above the other.

Across the plateau at the northern wall stands the **Erechtheion**, the last temple to go up on the Acropolis. Construction took 15 years, with dedication in 406 BC. The north porch is an architectural marvel, with a dark-blue marble frieze (removed), panelled ceiling and distinguished Ionic columns. Holding up the roof of the south porch are the famous Caryatids, six larger-than-life figures said to represent enslaved widows from the city of Caryae. These days copies stand in for the originals.

From the south wall against the old museum, you'll be treated to a fine perspective of the **Theatre of Dionysos**. The huge 17,000-seat auditorium is a 5th–4th-century BC construction on top of a much older theatre. On this site were held the first performances of tragedies by Sophocles, Aeschylus and Euripides and Aristophanes' comedies.

At the southern base of the Acropolis hill stands the marble, concrete and glass **New Acropolis Museum**, designed by Swiss-born architect Bernard Tschumi. The displays comprise an outstanding collection of sculpture and reliefs found at the site.

Down from the Acropolis, the **Temple of Olympian Zeus**, the largest temple in ancient Greece, reflected an appropriate reverence for the ruler of the gods. However, legend has it that the tyrant Peisistratos conceived of the monumental project to keep the population too busy to plot against his rule. For once, the Greeks over-estimated their architectural skills: the building wasn't completed till AD 132. At that time it had 104 Corinthian columns, each 17 m (56 ft) high and more than 2 m (7 ft) thick. Today only 15 remain upright.

In the hollow of Arditos Hill, the modern **Panathinaiko Stadium** is on the site of the stone original built by Lycurgus in 330 BC. In the 2nd century, Hadrian introduced Rome's favourite sport here, importing thousands of wild animals to be pitted against gladiators. The new stadium was built for the first modern Olympics in 1896 and seats 70,000 people. It was renovated for the 2004 Olympics and was the arrival point of the marathon.

The **Agora** is almost as old as Athens itself. Originally the word meant "a gathering together", later the place where people met and conducted business. It was in fact the earthy, secular counterpoint to the high-blown world of the Acropolis. Sprawling under the northern walls of the Acropolis, it was the beating heart of the ancient city, its marketplace and civic centre.

Overlooking the Agora, the Theseion, or more correctly the **Temple of Hephaistos** has a fine set of Doric columns in pentelic marble and friezes of marble from Paros.

At the other end of the Roman agora, the octagonal **Tower of the Winds** served as a weather vane, compass, sundial and water clock rolled into one. It was designed by Andronicus, a Macedonian astronomer of the 1st century BC, and built in white marble. Each side has a superbly carved relief representing one of the eight winds, beneath which can be seen traces of the original sundials.

Sounion

The imposing Temple of Poseidon crowns this spectacular promontory 70 km (45 miles) south of Athens. Overlooking a precipice, it's a wondrous place to watch the sun rise or set.

The grey-veined marble temple, with 16 of its original 34 Doric columns now standing, was built about 444 BC. An earlier one made of stone had been started in this commanding location, but the Persians destroyed it in 490 BC. Marvellous though the setting is, the temple is famous as much as anything for a piece of aristocratic graffiti. Lord Byron swung by here in 1810 and couldn't resist carving his name on one of the columns. Years later Sounion was still in his thoughts when he made a stirring reference to its "marbled steep" in his epic poem, *Don Juan*.

Aegina

Most boats anchor on the west coast, in the pretty **port of Aegina**, which has nothing left to show that it was the first capital of Greece in the throes of retrieving its independence. Fishermen mend their nets in view of the tourists sitting on the café terraces or riding past in carriages. Just back from the waterfront, the pedestrian street is full of shopping opportunities. At the northern exit of town, the **archaeological site of Kolona** has little to show but a few meagre remains of a temple to Apollo (5th century BC). The Archaeological Museum displays objects excavated from the site.

Corinth Canal

Until sturdy ships were built in the 13th century, the easy way to get from the Ionian Sea to the Aegean was by portage across the isthmus of Corinth. The ships were loaded onto carts and trundled over a paved way, the *diolkos*, with ruts 150 cm apart to guide the wheels. From as far back as the 7th century BC, this route avoided a dangerous 185-mile sea journey around the peninsula of the Peloponnese.

Periander, Tyrant of Corinth around 600 BC, toyed with the idea of digging a canal, but he never made any headway. Alexander, Julius Caesar, Caligula, Hadrian and Herod Atticus also weighed up the possibilities—Caligula even sent an engineer to survey the site. But the first to begin work on a waterway was Nero, in AD 67. Vespasian dispatched 6,000 Jewish prisoners of war from Judaea as a workforce, and Nero himself dug out the first clod of earth with a golden shovel. The enterprise was well under way when Nero had to transfer his attention to quashing an insurrection in Gaul. After his death, the project was abandoned. A little figure of Hercules carved into a rock marks the spot where the prisoners and legionnaires downed tools.

In 1882, a French company revived the project of building a waterway through the isthmus, following the same route as planned by Nero. Even this undertaking was not immediately destined for success: the firm went bankrupt. The canal was finally completed by a Greek company in 1893. An awe-inspiring feat of engineering, the canal

Claude Hervé-Bazin

Passing through the Corinth Canal is a fascinating experience.

reaches from the Gulf of Corinth at its north-west extremity to the town of Isthmia and the Saronic Gulf at its southeast end, about 6 km (almost 4 miles). Its depth is 7 m (23 ft) below the water, with a width of 21 m (69 ft) at the bottom and 25 m (81 ft) at land level. The walls rise steeply on each side, up to 70 m (over 285 ft) high. As you sail along the canal (a journey of 2 to 3 hours), the passage seems incredibly narrow—but little Greek tug boats guide the big ships through without a scrape.

Peloponnese

Surrounded by water: the Gulf of Corinth in the north, the Ionian sea in the west and the Aegean in the east, the Peloponnesian peninsula is attached to mainland Greece by a narrow isthmus divided by the Corinth Canal. The three long fingers of the Southern Peloponnese are a tourist's dream: scenic seascapes, historical sites galore and picturesque towns where time seems to have stood still.

Mycenae

Even on a blisteringly sunny day, the ruins of this once-regal ancient city are invested by a brooding sense of darkness and horror. It was here that Orestes committed the heinous crime of matricide, winding up a gory succession of family atrocities perpetrated by the members of the House of Atreus, the legendary rulers of Mycenae. Mythology attributes the foundation of the city to Perseus, son of Zeus, with the help of cyclopes, the one-eyed giants who were the only beings thought capable of moving the colossal blocks of stone that make up the massive walls.

Enter the acropolis through the **Lion Gate**, a colossal limestone tympanum flanked by two standing headless lionesses of impressive dimensions. This is Europe's earliest known monumental

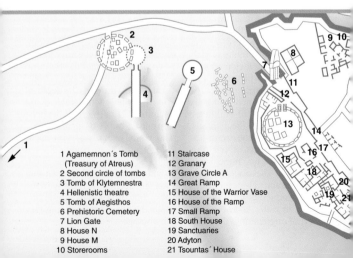

1 Agamemnon´s Tomb
  (Treasury of Atreus)
2 Second circle of tombs
3 Tomb of Klytemnestra
4 Hellenistic theatre
5 Tomb of Aegisthos
6 Prehistoric Cemetery
7 Lion Gate
8 House N
9 House M
10 Storerooms
11 Staircase
12 Granary
13 Grave Circle A
14 Great Ramp
15 House of the Warrior Vase
16 House of the Ramp
17 Small Ramp
18 South House
19 Sanctuaries
20 Adyton
21 Tsountas´ House

sculpture. Through the gate you'll find the concentric stone circles that form the royal tombs of **Grave Circle A**, in which 19 skeletons were found. These six tombs are dated to around the end of the 16th century BC. The shaft graves also yielded furnishings, gold treasures and other burial objects.

Proceeding upwards to the peak of the hill on the royal road or Great Ramp (a tarmac path today), you reach the remains of the **Atrides Palace**, burnt down at the end of the 13th century BC and partially reconstructed afterwards. The great courtyard, open to the sky, leads into the *megaron* or inner royal chamber, where you can still see the bases of wooden columns which once supported a roof.

Downhill from the Lion Gate are several beehive tombs. **Clytemnestra's Tomb** is so-named for convenience. It's a 14th-century BC construction in the typically Mycenaean "beehive" shape used for several royal burials.

Heading back towards the village, you come to the **Treasury of Atreus**, also known as Agamemnon's Tomb, dated at around 1300 BC. You enter through the *dromos*, the typical Mycenaean long stone funnel leading deep into the hillside. The *tholos*, or circular interior, is reached through an impressive portal with a lintel of colossal monolithic

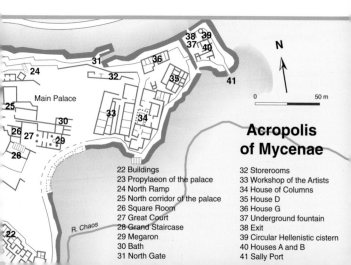

Acropolis of Mycenae

22 Buildings
23 Propylaeon of the palace
24 North Ramp
25 North corridor of the palace
26 Square Room
27 Great Court
28 Grand Staircase
29 Megaron
30 Bath
31 North Gate

32 Storerooms
33 Workshop of the Artists
34 House of Columns
35 House D
36 House G
37 Underground fountain
38 Exit
39 Circular Hellenistic cistern
40 Houses A and B
41 Sally Port

R. Chaos

The famous Lion Gate marks the entrance to Mycenae. | Nafplion: the Bourdzi Fortress stands opposite the harbour.

stone blocks, one of them weighing nearly 120 tons. Remarkably, the vault built in gradually diminishing circles of breccia stones — an amalgam of pebbles — was so perfect that no mortar was required to join them.

Nafplion

This scenic city is a favourite stop for visitors to the Peloponnese. It stands on its own rocky peninsula jutting into the shimmering bay of the Argolic Gulf, with two citadels and a fortified island brooding over the harbour. The old town is full of intriguing corners and byways, imprinted with the memories of ancient conquerors, Francs, Venetians and Turks. In the 19th century, Nafplion was the headquarters of the Greek and Allied forces struggling for Greek independence. In 1829 it was proclaimed the first capital of the liberated country, before Athens was designated five years later.

Attractive, clean and airy, **Sintagma Square** in the centre of the old town is an ideal starting point for a tour of the city. It is surrounded by shops and tavernas and framed by old façades. The **Archaeological Museum**, built as a naval arsenal by the Venetians in 1713, stands out as the most striking building on the square, with arcades in golden stone.

The **waterfront** is a pleasant place to linger, lined with outdoor cafés with comfortably cushioned seating. Out in the bay lies the fortified islet of **Bourdzi**, built by the Venetians in 1471 and modified several times since then. From there, a promenade partly cut from the base of the cliff goes all round the Akronafplion promontory as far as a small pebble beach. Above it looms a formidable rocky peak topped by Fort Palamidi. Local families meet up here at the end of the day for the *volta*, the evening promenade.

Epidaurus

Located on the sleepy, pine-scented Argolis plain, 30 km (19 miles) from Nafplion, Epidauros is the legendary home of Asclepius, the great healer. This pastoral place does seem to exude a healthy aura, although the ancient town and spa have long since been reduced to ruins.

A cult devoted to the gods of healing seems to have been implanted here way back in prehistoric times. Apollo was worshipped at first, but he was gradually replaced by Asclepius in the 6th century BC, when his sanctuary was founded. It became wealthy thanks to crowds of pilgrims, and two centuries later the complex was much expanded. Despite various hardships, the renown of Epidaurus survived several centuries until it was pillaged by Barbarians in 395.

The semi-circular **theatre** is one of the great marvels of Greece and one of its best-preserved monuments. Perfectly proportioned, it was constructed on a majestic scale by the architect Polykleitos the Younger in the 4th century BC. The theatre, which can seat 14,000 spectators and is made up of 55 rows intersected by aisles to produce a "pie-wedge" effect, was built according to the golden rules of acoustics. Speaking or humming in a normal voice from the orchestra, you can still be heard perfectly by someone on the top row — 22 m (74 ft) higher up.

Sparta

Today's Sparta (pronounced *Sparti* in Greek) has little in common with its belli-cose ancestor, although there is a

A Spartan Existence. The rigorous training imposed on young Spartan men had one aim: to toughen them up and build an invincible army. The State decided at birth whether a boy was fit for military training; if not, he was left to his fate on a mountain top. At the age of seven his training began in earnest with a harsh regime of exercise and military drill. Only when he reached 30, if he survived the discipline and initiation ordeals, did a Spartan become a fully-fledged soldier fit to fight for his fatherland. Not only did this Spartan life produce good results on the battlefield, the fit young men also excelled in the sports arena. The first recorded Spartan victory at the Ancient Olympic Games was around 720 BC; during the next hundred years, Spartans athletes carried off over half the honours.

big army base on the plain nearby. Situated under the Taigetos peaks on a broad plain in Laconia, it's a modern city of 14,000 inhabitants. From the 9th to 4th centuries BC, the city was ruled by warlords, whose sole duties were to defend their homeland and spread its influence.

The **Archaeological Museum**, in a peaceful, quiet garden setting, contains local finds, such as Archaic bas-reliefs, notably one of Helen of Troy and Menelaus, and a good head of Apollo Dionysus from the 4th century BC, discovered in 1978.

To the north of town lie the vestiges of an **acropolis** hidden away in an olive grove. The small site features a ruined 1st century temple, a 2nd-century BC theatre, the foundations of a temple toå Athena and remains of a 10th-century Byzantine monastery standing among pine and eucalyptus trees.

Mistra

This splendid Byzantine city perched on a steep hill 6 km (4 miles) from Sparta, was founded as a defensive castle in the middle of the 13th centuy by William II Villehardouin, Frankish prince of Achaia. It came into the hands of the Byzantine emperors of the Palaeologus dynasty, who transformed it into a magnificent city that ruled over most of the Peloponnese for nearly two centuries. A lower town developed on the slopes of the promontory crowned by the original fortress, and a multitude of domed orthodox churches were built. Their scalloped tile roofs contrast strikingly with the green, grassy slopes.

The site is divided into three sectors, linked by foothpaths; the fortress (kastro), the aristocratic Upper Town and the monasteries and museum of Lower Mistra. It's best to start at the top and work your way down.

The visit of the Upper Town starts down below at the church of **Agia Sophia**, founded in the 14th century. It is an elegant example of Greco-Byzantine architecture, with its arched walls and windows and square colonnaded bell tower. Down a small signposted path stands the **Palace of the Despots**, actually two palaces.

The **Monemvasia Gate** marks the entrance to the lower town with, first right, the **Pantanassa Monastery**, still inhabited by a few nuns. Take a minute or two to relax and enjoy the view from the arcaded portico-gallery. There are some 14th- and 15th-century frescoes inside, the most impressive being the *Entry into Jerusalem*, to the west of the apse, and the *Raising of Lazarus*.

Downhill, past the balconied mansion of Frangopoulos and

through a stone gateway, **Peri-vleptos Monastery** is a pretty pink-ish stone and brick church dating roughly from the 13th and 14th centuries; its typical octagonal tiled dome nestles under the rocks, giving it a cave-like impression. Its frescoes representing scenes from the New Testament are the best-preserved in Mistra.

The highlight of the visit is the Cathedral of Agios Dimitrios or **Mitropolis**. In the flowered courtyard, take a look at the fountain, installed in the 19th century even though the town was soon to be abandoned, and the ancient sarcophagus. Inside the cathedral you can see a remarkable fretwork marble arcade over the iconostasis, and a double-headed marble eagle on the floor. Some historians claim it signifies that Constantine Paleologus was crowned emperor here in 1449.

Past the 14th-century cross-shaped Evangelistria Church, you come to the **Monastery of Vronto-chion**, the wealthiest of Mistra. Its two churches are Agii Theodori (1296, restored in 1932) and the more noteworthy Afendiko, also called Odigitria, a cruciform basilica with several domes built in the 14th century.

Monemvasia

You'll be absolutely enchanted with this medieval fortress-island that can only be entered across a causeway built on the foundations of an ancient bridge. Indeed, the town's "only entrance" (the literal translation of its name: *mono emvasis*) no more discourages modern visitors than it put off the numerous invaders of its troubled past. Originally founded in the 6th century and fortified by Byzantinum during Slav incursions, Monemvasia was held in turn by the Franks, Venetians and Turks, who all left architectural signs of their presence.

Gradually abandoned during the 20th century, the town now is home to a mere 100 souls (a far cry from the 40,000 of its heyday). Its flower-bedecked, pedestrian-only streets are largely taken over by tourists.

Of Monemvasia's original 40 churches, unfortunately only a handful remain standing today. Try to visit the largest, **Elkomenos Christos** (Christ in Chains). Built by the Byzantines and restored by the Venetians, it is noted for its original Byzantine bas-relief of peacocks strutting above the porch, as well as some interesting icons.

Don't be put off by the stiff 10-minute climb to the **citadel**, or *kas-tro*, in a wilderness of shrubs, olives and fig trees, rewarded by magnificent views over the town and out to sea.

Along the cobbled path you'll come to the 12th-century **Agia**

Sophia church, with its specially elegant brick and stone exterior and fine fragments of ancient frescoes.

Kythira

Easily reached from Monemvasia, this small island is linked administratively to Attica but belongs the the Ionian archipelago. It has none of the pleasant green areas so often found on the Greek islands. Instead, it is an arid, windswept piece of land. **Agia Pelagia**, the chief arrival point, boasts the island's main beaches, and also the ruins of (yet another) Byzantine city founded around the early 12th century and later razed by the infamous pirate Barbarossa. Another ruined city at inland **Mylopotamos** shows distinct Venetian influences, and on the south side of the island the capital **Chora**, or Kythira, has a Venetian castle and excellent views of the offshore islet of Avgo.

Githio

This lively little seaside town and fishing village on the Mani peninsula serves as a base for excursions around the region. Don't miss the action at sunset when the garden square and picturesque quayside are filled with Greeks and tourists gaily streaming in and out of shops or perching at tables by the water to eat the delicious fresh fish, admiring the view of the island of Kythira in the distance.

In Spartan times, Githio was a major trade centre and naval base, especially during the Peloponnesian War. Today, houses fronted by wrought-iron balconies climb up the lower slopes of Mt Koumaros, 183 m (600 ft), which was named Larysion in ancient times. A few ruins can be seen at the top. The little island of **Marathonisi**, connected to the mainland by a minuscule causeway, is graced by a peaceful pine grove, a small white chapel, an ancient tower, converted into a museum, and a lighthouse.

Kalamata

This port town on the Gulf of Messinia is a significant trade and communications hub. It was destroyed by the Turks during the War of Independence, and again by an earthquake in 1986.

The old town, set back from the seafront, has a lively bazaar and some old restored houses. The **Benaki Museum** displays finds from local excavations tracing the region's history from the Bronze Age to Roman times. The **Church of the Apostles** dates from 1626. Overlooking it all, the **Kastro**, built on the site of the ancient acropolis, stands as a reminder of times when the Franks ruled the region. Part of the 13th-century keep can still be seen.

Messini

The ruins of ancient Messini, beneath Mt Ithomi, surround the modern village of Mavromati, some 25 km northwest of Kalamata, and are not to be confused with the modern town of the same name on the coast. The 4th-century **city walls**, 9 km long, were pierced by four gates with bastions between them. The northern section is the best preserved, with the **Arcadia Gate** and its two separate entrances. You can also see the remains of a semi-circular temple and a small, well-restored theatre that was part of a shrine of Asclepius. A small archaeological museum displays funerary objects excavated on the site.

Methoni

From Koroni, a little road leads to this pleasant resort in the southeast of the westernmost peninsula of the Peloponnese.

Guarding the port, the 13th-century **fortress** is surrounded on three sides by the sea. Linked by a causeway is a little islet bearing the **Bourdzi Tower**, built by the Turks. The ramparts used to enclose an entire city, with its cathedral, houses and public baths. Here and there you'll notice sculpted lions, the symbol of Venice and a reminder of Methoni's significance for the Venetian fleet; it was on the pilgrim route to the Holy Land.

Pilos

Pilos is probably the most beautiful town on the west coast of the Peloponnese. Of strategic importance on this vital part of the coastline, the area has been inhabited since the mists of time, although the modern town dates from 1829, when it was built by the French after the Battle of Navarino in the Greek War of Independence, won by the combined armada of British, French and Russian forces in 1827. In the town's main square a monument to the three admirals commemorates this important victory.

The harbour is still guarded by two fortresses. A 30-minute walk from the centre of Pilos, **Neokastro**, the newer castle, served until quite recent times as a prison and has been harmoniously restored. You can see the fortifications, a mosque converted into the Church of the Metamorphosis and a small museum devoted to Greek independence. Enjoy the magnificent views over the bay and the small island of Sfaktiria, which can also be visited by boat.

On its inhospitable promontory and generally reached by boat, **Paleokastro**, the older castle, valiantly defended the area from the 6th century onwards, under many different masters. Down below, evidence of king Nestor is to be seen in **Nestor's Grotto**, full of stalagmites and stalactites.

Nestor's Palace

Of the previous inhabitants of the region, the most famous was surely Nestor, an early Greek king and henchman of Agamemnon, to whom he gave a hand in the Trojan campaign. The king lived to a ripe old age in his palace, situated some 17 km (10.5 miles) north of Pilos. Discovered only in 1939 by the US archaeologist Carl Blegen, this palace was once a large and imposing complex which unfortunately suffered considerable damage from fire in 1200 BC. Visible today are the remains of spacious coutyards and workshops, elaborate royal apartments, complete with terracotta bath, and scorch marks of the flames. The most noted find was the Linear B tablets, the palace accounting records, which provided clear evidence that the Peloponnese of the Mycenean age had used an early form of Greek.

Olympia

Gateway to the site of Olympia is the port town of **Katakolon**. A major attraction is the ingenious Museum of Ancient Greek Technology, a short work from the pier. Also worth visiting, in the same building, is the Museum of Ancient Greek Instruments, displaying more than 40 working instruments reconstructed from literature and vase paintings.

In a lush, green valley, where the Alpheios and Kladeos rivers meet, Olympia is one of Greece's glories, a truly appropriate choice of the ancients for the worship of their greatest god and goddess, Zeus and Hera. Here, in the 8th century BC, were inaugurated the Olympic Games.

Immediately after the entrance to the site, you'll see, to your left, the remains of **Roman baths of Kronos**, with vestiges of mosaics. The path passes the east wing of the **Gymnasium**, a quadrangle with two rows of capitals and column bases still in place. From here head for the **Palaestra**, or wrestling school, a splendid square formed by a 19-column Doric colonnade.

Beyond the Palaestra, you reach the remaining brick walls of the **Workshop of Phidias**, where the Golden Age sculptor is said to have worked on the huge chryselephantine statue of Zeus (one of the Seven Wonders of the World) that stood in the temple here — an inner core of wood covered with ivory and gold.

On the other side of the central pathway, the Sanctuary, or **Altis**, is the high point of any visit. The 5th-century BC Temple of Zeus has only one column standing, yet it's a stunning sight, with the drums and capitals of Doric columns tumbled down like a house of cards — the result of an earthquake in the 6th century.

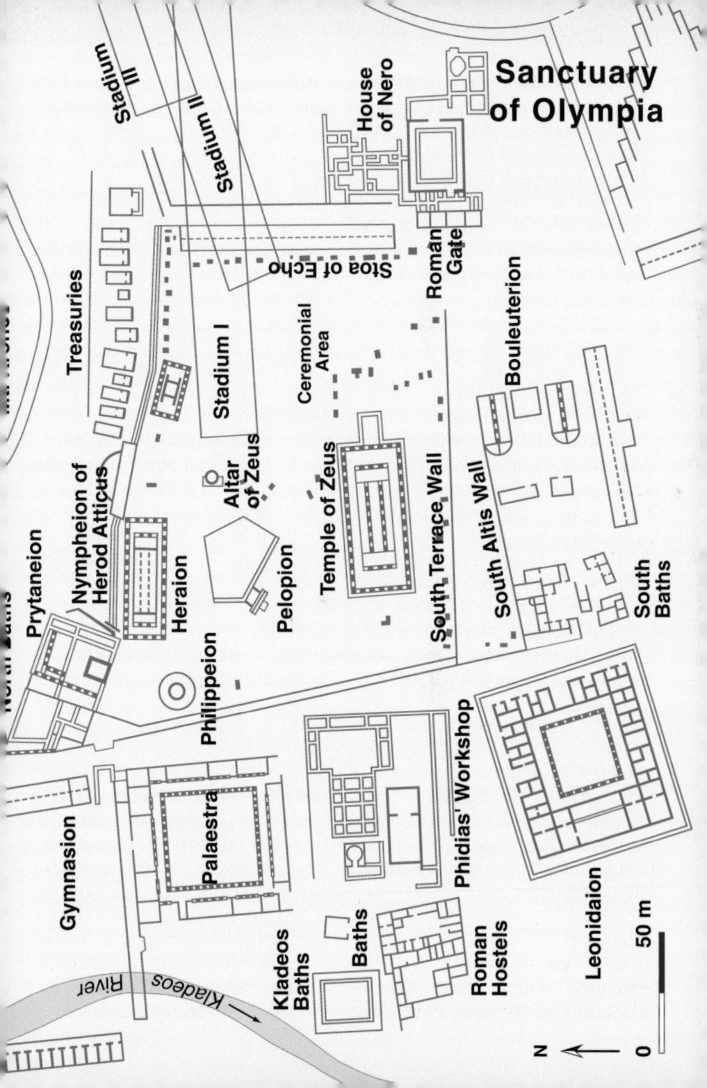

Sanctuary of Olympia

Stadium III

Stadium II

House of Nero

Roman Gate

Stoa of Echo

Treasuries

Stadium I

Ceremonial Area

Bo   Baths

Nympheion of Herod Atticus

Altar of Zeus

Temple of Zeus

Bouleuterion

Prytaneion

Heraion

Pelopion

South Terrace Wall

South Altis Wall

South Baths

Philippeion

Gymnasion

Palaestra

Phidias' Workshop

Kladeos Baths

Baths

Roman Hostels

Leonidaion

Kladeos River

N

0   50 m

The **Heraion** or Temple of Hera was built in typical Archaic style around 600 BC at the foot of Mt Kronos; several of the fluted columns have been expertly restored to standing position. The temple, 50 m (164 ft) long, contained many effigies of the goddess and Zeus, plus a famed statue of Hermes by Praxiteles.

Continue to the **Nympheion of Herod Atticus**, a rich Athenian who built it in AD 160; once encircled by colonnades and statues, it consists of a semi-circular fountain surrounded by ponds, where water was collected from the springs on Mt Kronos. Next to it stand the ruins of 12 Doric-columned **treasuries** or "chapels", which were erected by various Greek cities and colonies as votive offerings to the gods.

The **Stadium** was the world's first. The main entrance is a restoration of an arched passageway, originally built in the 4th century BC; the archway was added in the 1st century BC—only athletes and judges were allowed to enter at this point. The Stadium could accommodate up to 45,000 spectators; on the right of the entry were marble seats reserved for the judges.

Patras

Patras, largest city of the Peloponnese with a population of 162,000, is the hub of maritime traffic between Greece and Italy and between the Peloponnese and the Ionian islands. Rebuilt after the Turks took their vengeance on it, Patras divides into a lower and an upper town. The lower part is distinguished by the imposing **Agios Andreas** church, dedicated to Patras's patron saint Andrew and treasuring his skull as its most precious relic—it was returned to Patras in 1964 after reposing in St. Peter's in the Vatican for 500 years. Take time to meander amidst the town's pleasant green squares and lively streets, where you'll discover some handsome neoclassical buildings as well as three museums, one devoted to archaeology, the second to ethnology and history, and the third, outside the centre, to folk art.

Delphi

Basking in a setting of unparalleled beauty on Mount Parnassus, Delphi is the most famous classical site in Greece. For the ancient Greeks it was the "navel" of the earth—the spot where two eagles let loose by Zeus had flown from opposite ends of the world and met. Apollo slew the dragon Python when he took over the precinct from the earth goddess Gaia and her daughters. The oracle he founded here, in a cleft on the rock face, was the religious and moral capital of the classical world for centuries.

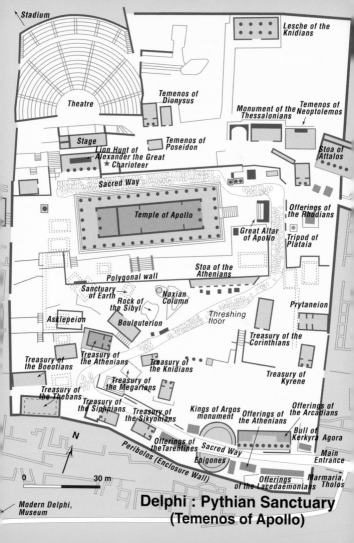

Delphi : Pythian Sanctuary
(Temenos of Apollo)

In reality, Delphi's power was based on prodigious wealth: city-states and islands stretching from Syracuse in Sicily to Lydia in Asia Minor vied with each other, trying to offer the oracle the richest gifts. Wars were fought for it. And no important decisions of state were taken without first seeking the advice of the sacred oracle.

The **sanctuary** and springs lie at the foot of two scarred crags called the Phedriades (Shining Rocks) soaring over 1,200 m (4,000 ft) above sea level. In ancient times, blasphemers were hurled off the edge if found guilty of disrespect towards the oracle. The **Kastalian Spring** emerges from the ravine between the rose-coloured rocks; all who came to consult the oracle had to bathe ritually in it.

You enter the site by the **Agora**, where the merchants of the temple were gathered in Roman times. Leading from there, the **Sacred Way** was once lined with votive monuments and treasuries built by the important cities, islands and colonies of ancient Greece to house offerings made by their citizens. That of the Athenians (5th century BC) has been restored.

The road curves round as it nears the foundations of the **Temple of Apollo**, the holiest place in Delphi, its stones meticulously fitted together. It is 83 m (272 ft) long and carved with inscriptions made by former Athenian slaves who had to explain why they had deserved freedom. In the innermost shrine, the oracle held forth.

Up the mountainside, the 2nd-century BC **theatre** is still used for summer festival performances. Looking down to the blue bay of Itea, you'll feel Delphi's magic. The **stadium** here used to hold 7000 spectators during the Pythian Games.

The Delphi **museum** contains an outstanding selection of classical and archaic pieces. Top honours go to the world-famous bronze statue of the Charioteer (*Iniochos*). This 5th-century BC treasure was unearthed in 1896 after lying under rubble from an earthquake for more than 2,000 years. Astonishingly lifelike, the charioteer is heading into his victory lap: note the look of calm pride on his face and his eyes—made of onyx—still intact.

Preveza

At the mouth of the Ambracian Gulf (Arta), the port was founded in the 3rd century BC by king Pyrrhus. It witnessed the naval battle of Actium (Aktio) in 31 BC, when the forces of Octavian (the future Augustus) defeated those of his enemy Mark Antony and Cleopatra, ensuring him domination over the Roman world. The resort is lively and cheerful, with some attractive Ottoman houses, a Venetian clocktower and plenty of welcoming clubs, taverns and cafés. It is linked to Aktio on the southern shore of the gulf by an undersea tunnel which opened in 2002 and is the only one in Greece.

Nikopolis, 8 km (5 miles) north of Preveza, was built by Octavian to celebrate his victory in the battle of Actium. The odeon has been well restored, while the theatre was probably redesigned. During the first millennium the city flourished under the Byzantines who erected several buildings: the Alkyson basilica was one of the most important.

Parga

This charming seaside town sprawls across the neck of a rocky promontory that juts out into a pretty bay down the mainland coast of Epirus, south of the island of Corfu. With an old Venetian fortress at its highest point, the headland divides the bay into two harbours. The narrower one is lined with boutiques, tavernas and lively cafés overlooking several rocky islets; the other has a handsome broad sweep of sandy beach. For the resident population of 2,500 Parganiotes, trade in olives and olive oil is, after tourism, their major source of income.

Behind the harbour with its waterfront cafés and tavernas, the town's narrow lanes and alleys climb the hillside to the green and silver backdrop of olive groves and orchards. The fortress, or **Erimokastro**, originally built for the Parganiotes by the Normans in the 14th century, stands on the summit. The winged Lion of St Mark adorning the main keep is the emblem of the Venetians who expanded the fortifications in 1401, bringing in 20 cannons. Beyond the monumental entrance gate built in 1764, the lower terrace affords a splendid view of Parga and the coast of Epirus.

A 20-minute walk southwest of the town-centre (faster by water-taxi), Parga's main beach at **Valtos Bay**, of white shingle and golden sand, is framed by olive groves with villas tucked away among the trees and a few tavernas right on the waterfront. Also within walking distance east of town, **Krioneri Bay** is more popular with families. It has a lovely view of Agios Nikolaos church amid its pine trees on Panagia Island.

Some 3 km (2 miles) southeast of Parga, **Lichnos** beach is best reached by car or water-taxi. At one end of the beach, the sea has carved out several caves and grottoes among the red rocks, the best-known being the Cave of Aphrodite, big enough to be explored by boat.

The Nekromanteion

A visit to the Nekromanteion is a good day-trip to combine with swimming at Lichnos. On the Acheron river near Ammoudia are the excavated remains of this ancient Greek Oracle of the Dead, posted at the gates of the Hades underworld. The ruins include arched stone doors that lead to dark labyrinthine corridors and a central room where the Oracle used to put visitors in touch with their dearly departed loved ones. Also serving as a sanctuary for Persephone, its layout reflects the circumstances of Homer's story in Book X of *The Odyssey* when his hero paid just such a visit to the dead.

Volos

An industrial and commercial town, Volos, with over 80,000 inhabitants, is Greece's third-largest port. It is set on a wide bay on the east coast. Much of it was ravaged by earthquake in 1955, and so today it looks fairly modern. There are several good hotels and a splendid seafront promenade. The region has been occupied since the Stone Age and has its roots in mythology, for it's believed that Jason set out with his Argonauts from the neighbouring port of Iolkos (where the remains of a Mycenaean fortress have been excavated) on his quest for the Golden Fleece.

The **archaeological museum** in Volos displays vases from Iolkos together with artefacts found in various prehistoric and Mycenaean tombs. The site of **Demetrias**, to the south of Volos, turned up a superb collection of some 300 painted tombstones dating from the Hellenistic period.

Meteora

Weathered monasteries perch like giant eagles' nests on a collection of barren rocks in the Valley of Meteora. The very name speaks of things beyond, hovering in the air, otherworldly. The origins of monastic life at Meteora go back to the 9th century, when hermits lived in caverns at the foot of the rocks. Later they were driven to seek refuge from the Turks and Albanians on the heights. By the 16th century, there were 24 monasteries. Only six are inhabited today, reminders of a faith and an asceticism so strong that it is hard for a modern visitor to comprehend.

Largely rebuilt after World War II, the town of **Kalambaka** makes a good base for visiting the high monasteries of Meteora (the name means "high in the air". Its cathedral is worth a visit for its 12th- and 16th-century frescoes and unusual marble pulpit which, like the hexagonal ciborium, dates from early Christian times.

The first of the monasteries after Kastraki, on the left-hand side of the road, is **Agios Nikolaos Anapafsas**. The tiny church has a superb series of frescoes dating from the early 16th century by Theophanes the Cretan, who also worked on Mount Athos. The *Last Judgment*, on the screen separating the narthex from the choir, is particularly striking.

The little monastery of **Roussanou** clings to a narrow spur reached by a suspension bridge. Its setting is spectacular: in the background you see an impressive group of rocks sculpted by erosion, a stone forest mysterious by day, enormous and eerie by night. The area is much appreciated by rock climbers.

Further on, the road divides into two. The left-hand branch takes you to the 16th-century **Varlaam**, set on a narrow piece of land on the edge of a plateau. You mount 130 steps and pass through a gateway into a sunny courtyard, overlooked by the church. Inside are more Byzantine works. Pause for a moment at the picture of a holy man lamenting earthly vanity over Alexander the Great's skeleton. See the beautiful fresco of the *Last Judgment* on the wall near the choir.

Megalo Meteoron or Metamorfosis (Monastery of the Transfiguration) was founded by Athanasius the Meteorite in the

Claude Hervé-Bazin

The monastery of Agios Nikolaos Anapafsas is one of the smallest of the Meteora.

14th century and was the first to be built. It crowns the highest of the rocks, a flat-topped giant 613 m (2,011 ft) high. To reach it, you first have to go down 106 steps, then climb up another 192. In spite of the catastrophes the monastery has suffered, it still preserves many beautiful works of Byzantine art, including ecclesiastical embroidery and wall paintings. The wooden iconostasis in the lovely main church is rich with jewel-like gilded icons. You can also visit the old refec-

Claude Hervé-Bazin

commons.wikimedia.org

Thessaloniki: the Byzantine church of Panagia Chalkeon; a mosaic in the church of Agios Dimitrios representing the saint himself.

old refectory has been converted into a museum, the best of the Meteora, displaying icons, religious vestments, illuminated manuscripts and embroidery. The only accessible church dates from the 18th century.

Thessaloniki

The port city of Thessaloniki (or Salonika) is the capital of Macedonia and all Northern Greece. Second only to Athens in size, Thessaloniki is as modern as concrete, plate-glass and thriving commerce can make it. Yet the town has a past as old as that of Byzantium itself, and some of the gilded dust from that stronghold of Eastern Christianity still powders it.

Thessaloniki rises like an amphitheatre from its bay to the spur of Mount Chortiatis. The city's longstanding commercial importance results from its favourable situation on the Thermaic Gulf. Not only does it have a natural outlet to the sea, but it is also logically placed for serving the needs of the hinterland. For many visitors it is also a good base for excursions into the Chalkidiki region and its fine beaches.

The wide seaside promenade, Leoforos Nikis leads directly to the symbol of Thessaloniki, the **White Tower** (*Lefkos Pirgos*), dominating the waterfront. The tower,

tory, the kitchen with its soot-covered walls, several rooms with displays illustrating the way the monks used to live, and the ossuary with heaps of skulls. There's a splendid view of neighbouring Varlaam from the balcony.

Today a convent and orphanage, **Agios Stefanos** is notable for its views of the town of Kalambaka, glimmering in the distance like an oasis, and the wide plain of Thessaly stretching ahead. The built under the Turks in the 15th century by Venetian engineers, originally formed part of Thessaloniki's old sea wall. One of its names, "Tower of Blood", referred to its use as a prison. In the final years of the 19th century, the Turkish Sultan ordered the tower whitewashed, hoping to erase the unhappy memories it represented. Now the White Tower looks down on the sunset-hour promenade. A museum of Byzantine culture has been set up inside it.

Picturesque houses and small, tangled gardens dot Thessaloniki's **acropolis**, situated towards the north near the Turkish quarter. You can inspect the remains of the old ramparts *(kastra)* that once enclosed the city and look out over Thessaloniki to the bay. The castle in ruins at the top is called the **Eptapirgia**. Nowadays the historic structure houses a prison.

Like its counterpart in Constantinople, **Agia Sofia** was constructed in honour of the wisdom *(sofia)* of God. The church is thought to have been erected some time in the 8th century. Note the unusual design of the acanthus leaves on the capitals, probably taken from an earlier building.

A few streets away is **Panagia Achiropiitos** (or Agia Paraskevi), one of the earliest examples of Christian architecture in Thessaloniki. On the site of a Roman villa, it was built in honour of the Virgin after the Council of Ephesus recognized her as the Mother of God in AD 431.

Panagia Chalkeon is located on a corner of the Platia Dikastirion, in the centre of town. The small brick church was one of the first in Thessaloniki to be constructed in the cruciform style (1028).

Overlooking Platia Dikastirion, **Agios Dimitrios** is the largest Byzantine church in Thessaloniki, with Roman columns incorporated into its structure. In the crypt you will see the remains of the original shrine built over the tomb of Saint Demetrius, a Christian noble martyred at the command of Galerius, the ruins of the Roman baths where he was confined and killed, a well as a splendid baptistery.

Near the White Tower and the main entrance of the grounds of the International Trade Fair, the **Archaeological Museum** shows finds from all over Northern Greece, including weapons, pottery, jewellery and carvings from Neolithic to Byzantine times. The highlight of the display is a collection of funerary objects found in Macedonian tombs. The collections are constantly increased as new finds are unearthed.

It is also worth spending some time in the **Museum of Byzantine Culture**, housed in a modern building

The monks who reside on Mont Athos perpetuate a tradition hundreds of years old.

south of the International Trade Fair. It illustrates the importance of Thessaloniki from early Christian times to the Turkish era. Icons are displayed along with sculpture, jewellery, mosaics, medieval embroidery and old stone carvings.

Chalkidiki

Thessaloniki is gateway to the Chalkidiki region, like a great fist plunging into the Aegean with three finger-like peninsulas, Kassandra, Sithonia and Agio Oros (the seat of an autonomous theocratic republic on the slopes of Mount Athos). The region is blessed with superb sandy beaches and a spectacular coastline.

The closest to Thessaloniki, the most densely populated and most well-developed is **Kassandra**, linked to the mainland by a narrow isthmus. Near to it lie scattered the ruins of **Olynthos**, an old Athenian colony set out on a grid plan. You can still see some of the mosaics that covered the floors of the villas.

Wilder and covered with pines, the peninsula of **Sithonia** has a rugged coast indented with countless sandy creeks. The coast road offers a multitude of beautiful views, especially on the east side overlooking Mount Athos. The best beaches are at **Toroni** and **Porto Koufos** in the west, **Kalamitsi** and **Sarti** in the east. Off the resort of Neos Marmaras, Turtle Island, named because of its shape, is surrounded by crystalline waters that are perfect for swimming.

Several resorts spread around the base of **Agio Oros**, the easternmost of Chalkidiki's peninsulas, which is mostly occupied by the autonomous territory of **Mount Athos** (meaning Holy Mountain), whose sheer slopes tumbling spectacularly into the sea are covered with forest. About 20 Orthodox monasteries have been built on the peninsula, dating back to the 10th century. Most of them are Greek, but some are home to Russian, Serbian or Bulgarian communities. Some 1,500 monks live there. Some of them have chosen to live as hermits in lonely caves. Very strict rules are applied for anyone wanting to visit the monasteries—only a dozen people are allowed each day—but it can be seen from a boat. Women are not allowed to set foot on the Mount.

At the bottom of the eastern coast, the Great Lavra is the oldest and biggest of all the monasteries. It was founded in 963 by Saint Athanasius at the foot of Mount Athos. About a hundred monks live there. The library is renowned for its collection of 5000 ancient tomes, some of them illuminated.

Kavala

Kavala, Macedonia's second-largest city (population 55,000) rises in tiers from the waterfront up the slopes of Mount Simvolon. People here have a happy way with colour. Buildings sparkle, boats are gay combinations of red, yellow and blue—even the sky seems to have just been given a fresh coat of paint. In St Paul's time, Kavala was known as Neapolis. It was the port for nearby Philippi and the usual landing for travellers from the Levant. Later it was called Christoupolis, for St Paul began his European mission here. The town was burned by the Normans, controlled by the Venetians and occupied by the Turks. Not until after World War I was it incorporated into Greece, along with the rest of Western Thrace—which goes to explain why so many of its buildings have an Oriental appearance.

On the west side of town, the **Imaret** is a 19th-century group of courtyards, terraces and domes that served as an almshouse. The inmates enjoyed free food and exemption from military service, which caused the place to be known as the "Lazy Man's Home". It was financed by Mohammed Ali, founder of the modern Egyptian dynasty that ended with King Farouk.

From the old Turkish district, go up to the Byzantine **fortress**. Its ramparts were renovated in the 16th century and give you a wonderful view of the town and harbour. Also of interest is Kavala's worthy **Archaeological Museum** (*Archeologiko Mousio*) on the waterfront in the newer part of town. Finds from the city and nearby Amphipolis, Philippi and Abdera include carved stone tombs, Ionic capitals from the temple of Athena, gold Hellenistic jewellery, figurines and pottery.

Thassos

Ferries leave Kavala several times a day for the island of Thassos. Famous in antiquity for its gold and marble, the island is almost circular in shape, clad in pines, chestnuts and silver-green olive trees and surrounded by a golden ring of beaches. In the centre, the marble mountain Ypsari rises to 1,000 m (3,290 ft).

On the northeast coast, **Limenas** has retained many reminders of the island's heyday in the 7th–5th centuries BC when it ruled part of the Macedonian coast, including Kavala and Salonica.

Philippi

The town Philip II named after himself, once he'd conquered it in 358 BC, lies just 15 km (9 miles) northwest of Kavala. Its historical associations are mainly Roman and early Christian. It was here that Caesar's assassins, Brutus and Cassius, were defeated by Octavius and Antony in the famous battle that ended the Roman Republic in 42 BC. The victors elevated the town to a Roman colony where the Latin language was spoken and Roman law enforced.

The excavations lie on either side of the modern road to Drama. On the north side, in an elevated area near the Byzantine walls, is the **theatre**, dating back to the 4th century BC, but twice altered. Across the road is the forum, its outline still clear, and the unfinished **Basilica of the Pillars**. Adjoining it is an ancient and impressive **lavatory** with marble seats still in place.

Corfu, Ionian Islands

Corfu (Kerkyra) really is an emerald isle on a turquoise sea. And this greenest of Greece's islands, the second-largest of the Ionians, is arguably the prettiest, as well. Almost 500 years of Venetian, French and British occupation have left their mark. Italian was once the official language here, and the place names are still bilingual. Since union with the mainland in 1864, it has proudly styled itself Greece's western gateway, its entry to the Adriatic.

Corfu Town

Bustling, elegant, sometimes bewildering, often charming, this improbable port town is the island's proud capital. A large green swathe separating the Old Fort from the rest of town, the **Esplanade** (Spianada) was the Venetians' parade ground. Running along the west side is the **Liston**, a graceful, arcaded row of buildings erected by the French during their brief occupation of Corfu.

The **Palace of St Michael and St George** (1819), fronted by a colonnade, sprawls across the north side of the Esplanade. The imposing and unmistakably English building originally housed Britain's high commissioners, then the Ionian senate and later the Greek royal family. In the state apartments you'll find the splendid collections of the **Museum of Asian Art**.

Down through the centuries, the **Old Fort** (*Palaio Frourio*), a crumbling Venetian citadel, was always the bastion of Corfiote defence. Festivals and concerts are held here in summer.

West of the Liston is the **Old Town** or Campiello, a fascinating maze of narrow medieval streets, steep stairways and arched alleys wedged between the two forts, old and new. The **New Fort** (*Neo Frourio*) was begun by the Venetians in 1576 and later completed by the French and English.

Within the Old Town are two churches much esteemed in Corfu. The solemn **Agios Spyridon** houses the richly ornamented silver coffin of the island's beloved patron saint. The other church is the marvellously cool **Mitropoli**, the Orthodox cathedral of Corfu, dating from 1577. Inside are the headless remains of the island's second saint, Theodora.

North of the cathedral, a small restored 16th-century basilica houses the **Byzantine Museum**, which displays a magnificent col-

The island of Vlacherna and its monastery are linked by a causeway to Corfu town. | **The streets of the Old Town, filled with flowers, are a charming place to stroll.**

lection of icons dating from the 13th to 17th centuries.

South of the city walls, in the airy and modern **Archaeological Museum** you'll see remnants of antiquity discovered in the area around Corfu Town. The main attraction is the Gorgon Pediment of the Temple of Artemis, a monumental work of Corinthian sculpture over 2,500 years old.

At Anemomilos you'll find the villa of **Mon Repos**, the birthplace of Prince Philip, Duke of Edinburgh. The house was built in 1831 as a summer residence for the British high commissioner and subsequently became the property of the Greek royal family.

The **Achilleion** at Gastouri is the most controversial sight on the island. The chronically morose Empress Elisabeth of Austria built it in the 1890s. She wanted a palace that would be worthy of her hero Achilles, but neither she nor her architects had a very clear idea of the harmonies of antiquity; what they turned out is a neoclassical hodge-podge. German Kaiser Wilhelm II bought it in 1907 as a base from which to pursue his hobby of archaeology. The palace functioned for a while as a casino, but it has now been renovated and opened to the public as a small museum filled with the original furniture and mementoes of Elisabeth.

Lefkas (Lefkada)

Of all the Ionian Islands, Lefkas is the most hilly and the least fertile. Once a peninsula, Lefkas is now linked by bridge to the mainland over a narrow canal, probably first dug in the 7th century BC by Corinthians wishing to avoid the long and dangerous detour by sea, and fitfully re-excavated ever since as it silted up. The land in between is marshy and uninviting, but in view of its strategic importance, the Franks built the fort of **Agia Mavra** on the mainland, redesigned by the Venetians and later the Turks.

The capital, **Lefkas**, has Turkish-style wooden houses but there are several good Italian churches, erected in gratitude when the Turks were finally ousted at the end of the 17th century.

Nydri on the east coast is the main resort, very busy in summer, while **Vlicho Bay**, to the south, is popular with yachtsmen. Offshore, the island of **Skorpios** belongs to the Onassis family.

Cephalonia (Kefallinia)

Shaped like a complex piece of a jigsaw puzzle, the largest of the Ionian Islands possesses a distinctive grandeur inspired by its mountainous scenery, jagged coastlines and dark forests of the cedar-like firs that are unique to Cephalonia. Underground caves and lakes, and quaint villages with picturesque churches also add to its charm. The capital, and a good base for exploring, is **Argostoli**, a lively town set on a lagoon on the southwest coast that's large by Ionian standards. Many Venetian buildings were destroyed in the 1953 earthquake, so go to the **Corgialenios Museum** to see get a glimpse of what the island must have looked like before tragedy struck.

For those seeking sea and sand, nearby **Lassi** has some excellent beaches. Other good, albeit small, resorts are **Lixouri**, **Poros** and **Skala**. If you venture to the northernmost tip of the island, you can relax on one of the most beautiful beaches in all Greece, **Myrtos**. The pretty villages of **Assos** and **Fiskardo**, nearby, are also worth a detour. Assos lies at the base of a promontory beneath a mighty Venetian fortress. At Fiskardo, a pretty fishing port, you can see the distinctly Norman-style church built by crusader and invader, Robert Guiscard, supposedly housing his own tomb.

On the other side of the bay, the remains of a Venetian stronghold are worth the climb. Among other monasteries and ruins on the island, the 13th-century Venetian **Castle of Saint George** overlooking the Livatho plain is the most impressive. And don't miss the famous underground lake of **Melissani**: the sunlight shines through a hole in the roof and highlights its turquoise waters.

Ithaca (Ithaki)

This tiny island's claim to fame is, of course, that it was the home of Odysseus (Ulysses). The legendary Greek hero took a decade to sail back here after many years' absence, in order to rescue his more-than-patient wife Penelope from her suitors. The name might be the same as Homer's Ithaca, but no real archaeological proof has ever turned up, and understandably other islands try to cash in on the act.

Wherever you go, you will find reminders of Homer's hero. The **Nymphs' Grotto**, the hiding place for his treasure, is said to be located at Marmarospilia, on the Bay of Dexia, his alleged landing place. Further south, a pleasant walk takes you to **Arethusa's Fountain**, and in the northern part of the island, on the hill of Pelikata near Stavros, you can visit "**Odysseus' Palace**" and its small museum, in fact the ruins of the city of Alalkomenes.

Odysseus apart, the island is worth a visit in its own right. Its capital **Vathy**, with 2,000 inhabitants, is a picturesque port of gleaming white houses hugging the bay in the shelter of wooded hills. Its quay doubles up as main square, and is particularly lively in the evening. The **Archaeological Museum** is also the cultural centre, with occasional lectures on Homer.

Zakynthos (Zante)

Called "Flower of the East" by the Venetians who appreciated its fertile fields and temperate climate, the island will enchant you as much as it did Renaissance Italians. Olive groves, colourful and fragrant orchards of oranges, lemons, peaches and melons, and vineyards producing the island's famous currants stretch as far as the eye can see.

As is usual in Greece, both island and capital bear the same name. The port of **Zakynthos** is unmistakably Venetian in character, with arcaded streets, spacious squares, churches and a typically Italian campanile; many buildings were reconstructed as close to the original as possible after devastating earthquakes in the 19th and 20th centuries. Beautiful frescoes from the 16th–18th centuries and icons rescued from damaged churches are now housed in the **Museum of Byzantine Art**, whereas the **Dionysios Solomos Museum** is devoted to Greek heritage and honours the locally-born poet who composed the Greek national anthem. If you can make the trip up Strani hill behind the town to the **Venetian citadel**, you'll enjoy a superb view over the Peloponnese, just across the water.

Crete

Serving throughout history as Crete's main bastion of resistance to the many foreign invaders, the capital, **Heraklion**, is still known to older islanders as *megalo kastro* (great fortress). This aspect of military defence remains in evidence in the old **Venetian harbour**. Located on the quay, across the

street from the harbour authority, are the huge arcades and store-rooms of the 16th-century **Arsenali**. Here, the Venetians performed ship repairs and refitting for trade and warfare in the Mediterranean.

Take a walk along the top of the **Venetian ramparts** which extend some 4 km (2.5 miles) and provide interesting views of the city's old historical core. On the walls' south side is the Martinengo Bastion where one of Heraklion's great heroes is buried, 20th-century writer Nikos Kazantzakis (1883–1957), famous for his novel *Alexis Zorba*.

The **Venetian castle**, still known by its Turkish name, Koules, fulfils anyone's notion of a romantic castle. The thick, golden stone walls, erected between 1523 and 1540, are pierced by arched windows; from the battlements you have a fine view of the harbour and the sea. In the 17th century, the Venetians waged a 21-year, ultimately unsuccessful battle to hold onto the fort. On three of the outside walls you can still see the sculpted lions of St Mark.

Agios Titos is the church of the patron saint of Crete. Each occupying power built onto the original Greek Byzantine church, concocting an architectural medley of the island's history.

The **Morosini Fountain** (1628), named after a Venetian governor-general, stands in the middle of Venizelos Square (Platia Venizelou). The 14th-century lions supporting the fountain were taken from an earlier one.

Opposite stands the basilica of **Agios Markos** (St Mark). It was built under the Venetians in 1239, rebuilt after an earthquake in 1303, repaired after a second earthquake in 1508, turned into a mosque under the Turks and finally restored to its Venetian character in the 1960s. The basilica's greatest attraction is a series of reproductions of frescoes from Cretan churches.

The 19th-century cathedral dominates another square, Platia Agias Ekaterini. But the real reason for coming to the square is to see **Agia Ekaterini** (St Catherine's Church), built in the 16th century and enhanced a century later with such features as the beautiful entrance. It harbours a fine collection of frescoes, carvings and other art from Cretan churches.

The famous **Archaeological Museum** is being modernized and expanded; until it re-opens a small temporary exhibition displays the 400 most important pieces of the collections in a specially designed room on the north side. One of the highlights is the **Phaistos Disk**, with its inscrutable spiralling message. The collections include several beautiful frescoes taken from Knossos—

Bernard Joliat

hemis.fr/Slatter

Reconstruction of the northern entrance of the palace at Knossos, and one of the frescoes, to be seen in the Archaeological Museum.

the almond-eyed Minoan woman, known as La Parisienne, the Prince of the Lilies and the acrobatic bull-leapers.

Knossos

To do them justice, the fascinating excavations at Knossos need a full morning (perhaps followed by a short afternoon siesta). The palace of King Minos is a ten-minute ride south of Heraklion. A walk beneath an appropriately festive arcade of bougainvillaea brings you to the west court where archaeologist Sir Arthur Evans is honoured by a bronze bust. The stone walls on this side still bear blackened traces of the fire possibly caused by an earthquake that destroyed the palace in 1500 BC.

The royal residence at Knossos numbered a total of 1,200 rooms, arranged around a maze of corridors, stairways, narrow passages, hallways, small and large courts.

With the bust of Sir Arthur Evans behind you, turn right to the **Corridor of Processions**, with replicas of frescoes now in the Archaeological Museum. A slight detour off the corridor leads to the **Horns of Consecration**, the Minoan symbol, which perfectly frame a view of Mount Giouktas.

Past the horns and the partially restored South Propylaeum (containing a replica of the Cup Bearer fresco) one comes not to the expected central court but to a flight of broad stairs leading to the upper storey, or piano nobile. The walls here are adorned with reproductions of frescoes. From the balcony you can look down on the **central court**, which is reached by several entrances. Facing south, ceremonial rooms go off to the right and royal living quarters to the left. Surrounding the court is a honeycomb network of other sacred rooms, zigzag corridors, lustral (ceremonial washing) chambers and storerooms containing tall *pithoi* (clay jars).

In the **throne room**, off the central court, frescoes of griffins guard a small gypsum throne. It may have been the ritual chair of the high priestess known as the

On the menu

Choriatiki salata – Greek salad

Chtapodi – octopus

Dolmades – stuffed vine leaves

Kleftiko – mutton baked with vegetables

Loukanika – small sausages

Melitzanosalata – aubergine purée

Mezedes – selection of appetizers

Pastitsio – stodgy baked macaroni

Saganaki – breaded and fried cheese slices

Stifado – a tasty stew of beef, veal or rabbit, with lots of onions

Taramosalata – fish roe paste

Tzatziki – yoghurt with cucumber and mint

Lady of the Labyrinth, with the sunken lustral area in front used for purification rites.

Going down the grand staircase to the left of the central court, you come to the suite of rooms Evans designated as the **royal chambers**; they may have been embalming rooms. In any case, they are among the best preserved parts of the palace, intricately connected and illuminated by a remarkable device — light wells (air shafts, open above, that carried light to lower floors). Double axes incised in stone and enormous shields in a figure-eight shape mark the men's quarters; frescoes of blue dolphins, rosettes and dancing girls decorate the women's. The famous flush toilet connected to a vast drainage system is also located here.

Excursion East

Occupying a promontory jutting out into the graceful curve of the Gulf of Mirabello, **Agios Nikolaos** has almost everything you could wish for in a modern resort town. The year-round climate is a delight, very warm but dry in summer, blessedly mellow in winter. The town is well equipped for all the latest water sports, cheerful and hospitable. The Municipal Beach is located south of the bus station.

The harbour is linked by a channel in the rock to the pretty little lagoon of **Lake Voulismeni**. In ancient times, its waters — 64 m (210 ft) deep — were thought to take you straight down to hell. In the other direction, take the road up to the top of the inland cliff for a heavenly panorama across the lagoon and harbour.

In the **Archaeological Museum** on Odos Paleologou, the town has assembled in seven rooms a small collection of Minoan gold and ivory jewellery, bronze weapons, carved shells, terracotta figurines and stone and ceramic pottery from nearby excavations.

Excursion West

An atmosphere of old-fashioned elegance continues to pervade the streets of **Rethimnon**, a town that is still a favourite among Crete's small but honourable band of writers and artists.

Starting on the east side of the town's historic centre, the **Venizelou Promenade** follows the gentle curve of the sandy municipal beach. It is lined with boutiques, open-air restaurants and cafés. At the end of the day, everybody makes their way to the **Venetian Harbour**, where an old lighthouse looms up from the jetty.

Crossing the promontory of the town's historic centre, Melissinou Street leads west from the rear of the harbour to the Venetians' imposing 16th-century **Fortezza**, built and constantly reinforced to resist repeated Turkish assaults, until it was captured in 1646. The old Venetian prison near the Fortezza serves now as Rethimnon's **Archaeological Museum**. Its impressive prehistoric collection includes Stone and Bronze Age jewellery, statuary, tools and funeral ornaments.

Inland from the harbour, the combined Venetian and Turkish influences on Rethimnon can be seen in the handsome houses along Arkadiou Street—now mostly shops or cafés. On Petikhaki Square, the Venetian-Turkish marriage of styles can be seen in the **Rimondi Fountain**.

Chania, the town that was capital of Crete from 1898 to 1971, stands on the site of Kydonia, an ancient Minoan city mentioned in the stone tablets of Knossos as being founded by Kydon, the grandson of King Minos. In the graceful sweep of its old harbour, Chania can claim perhaps the most attractive waterfront on the island. At the west end of the Outer Harbour, the **Firkas**, part of the Venetian fortifications, has been restored to house the **Maritime Museum of Crete** tracing Greek maritime history with models of ancient triremes and a 20th-century submarine. Opposite, the Tourist Information Centre has set up shop in the town's oldest surviving Turkish building, the **Janissaries' Mosque** of 1645.

In the narrow streets behind the maritime museum **Topanas**, the main Turkish neighbourhood, is apparent from the "oriental" wooden balconies and mansards built onto the stone houses of the Venetians.

The **Archaeological Museum** occupies the Venetian church that was part of a Franciscan monastery. Its chief interest is in the ongoing finds of Minoan material from ancient Kydonia.

On the southeast outskirts of town, on Sfakianaki Street, the **Historical Museum** contains some fascinating Venetian maps, documents and furniture but constitutes in the main a patriotic homage to Greek, and more particularly Cretan, struggles for independence. A formidable array of weapons accompanies portraits of the island's heroic fighters against both Turks and Germans. Pride of place is accorded to the city's most venerated son, Eleftherios Venizelos. A separate room is set aside for this Greek prime minister born in Chania in 1864.

Aegean Islands

Whether they are arid or green and lush, like the Sporades, white as in the Cyclades or, as in the Eastern Aegean, drenched in luxuriant vegetation, each of the islands has its own special charm and timeless atmosphere.

Skiathos

Skiathos is blessed with more than its fair share of natural splendour. For the best view and a good photograph of the caïques and yachts bobbing at the quayside in **Skiathos Town**, take a late afternoon stroll up the cobbled street just to the south and out onto the Bourdzi promontory in the middle of the harbour.

Apart from the short road to the airport, there is only one paved route on the island—leading along the southern coast for about 12 km (7 miles). If you want to escape for a while, hire a moped and follow this route— likely as not you'll find an inviting, deserted stretch of beach.

On the rocky northernmost headland perch the remains of the old capital, **Kastro**. If you climb to the top of the rugged path, past grazing goats, you'll see wildly beautiful, heart-stopping drops to the blue-green sea far below.

The beaches on the western side include **Keria** hemmed with olive and pine trees, and the famous **Mandraki**, backed by reddish cliffs. More crowded is the so-called "Banana Beach", formally **Krassa**, close to the southwestern corner of the island. Around the tip lies **Koukounaries**, a long sandy crescent stretching below low trees and a bay where you'll be able to water-ski or hire a boat.

Skopelos

Triangular-shaped Skopelos has been inhabited since ancient times. The main port and capital is also called **Skopelos**, on the east coast. Its dazzling white houses clustered below a 13th-century Venetian castle are distinguished by roofs of blue slate or grey stone tiles, most with little balconies and gardens full of flowers. On the beach close to town you can see the scant remains of the 4th-century BC temple of Asclipio.

The **tomb of Staphylos**, one of the first Cretan settlers, was discovered 4 km (2.5 miles) from town; it hoarded a fabulous treasure which was transferred to the museum of Volos, on mainland Greece. The beach near here is one of the island's best.

The landscape is dotted with monasteries and more than 350 churches. Of particular interest, all within easy reach of Skopelos town, are the 17th-century **Monastery of Panagia Livadiotissa**, 18th-century **Evangelistria** (both with remarkable icons).

On **Mount Delphi**, in the centre of the island, are two more monasteries, and in the rocks at **Sentoukia** you can see some ancient tombs excavated in the rocks.

Near Loutraki, a port on the west coast, the picturesque mountain village of **Glossa** affords a fine sea view.

Rural life on the peaceful island of Skyros.

Huber/Huber

Alonissos

In the north of the island, a succession of hills stretch to the sea where they form steep cliffs, while the south is covered in pine forest. The west coast is rugged and wild, but the east coast, especially in at the southern end, is dotted with attractive pebble beaches, like those of **Milia Ialos** or **Agios Dimitrios**. Agriculture—figs, almonds and olives—is well developed, and grapes are grown for wine.

The old village of **Alonissos**, on the southwestern heights, has

been the island capital since the Middle Ages. It was destroyed by an earthquake in 1965 and the inhabitants had to move to the nearby port of Patitiri. In the meantime it has been restored, with its dazzling white and blue houses, its narrow winding streets, its sunny squares and views over the sea.

Skyros

The quietest and largest of the Sporades, Skyros covers 210 sq km (81 sq miles). It is sparsely populated, most of the inhabitants living in the capital. Here and there you'll find workshops where artisans produce traditional pottery, embroidery and wood-carvings. The northern part of the island has a mild climate, and there's a whole succession of fine beaches in the neighbourhood of the main town, Skyros, including the longest in the whole Sporades, 4 km (2.5 miles) from end to end. A road links the town to the pretty harbour of **Linaria**, which nestles in a sheltered bay on the west coast. The southern part of the island is stony, treeless and barren.

Andros

The second-largest of the Cyclades, with an area of 304 sq km (117 sq miles), Andros stretches off the south coast of the big island of Euboea (or Evia), just off the Attika coast. Crossed by steep mountains, it has a rocky coastline with high cliffs and, here and there, sandy beaches. The central valleys are planted with terraces where figs, olives and lemons are grown, around sleepy villages and ancient dovecotes.

The two main resorts are in the northwest: **Gavrio**, nestling in a protected bay, where the boats from Attika land, and the little port of **Batsi** a little further south, very busy in summer. It has one of the prettiest beaches of the whole islands, but there are others on each side of the two towns.

The main archaeological sites are south of Batsi, but they consist of a few meagre ruins scattered over the meadows. On a promontory overlooking the sea, **Paleopolis** was capital of the island from Antiquity to Byzantine times. Beyond it is **Zagora**, where archaeologists have found many significant vestiges dating from the Geometric period.

Today's capital, and the second-largest port is Chora, built in the Middle Ages on a rocky tongue of land on the east coast, separating two of Andros's liveliest beaches: **Nimborio** and **Paraporti**. This last, is a pretty little stepped town with neoclassical mansions and white houses, hilly streets, churchs and picturesque squares. A ruined 13th-century Venetian

kastro defends the town from its rocky islet linked to Andros by a stone arch. Objects found in excavations are displayed in the Archaeological Museum, but the Contemporary Art Museum is more interesting; it was founded by the local Goulandris family of shipowners.

From Chora, the road parallels the coast at a distance, to the village of Sineti. Further south, in the heart of a wide, protected bay, the fishing port of **Ormous Korthiou** resembles a resort in summer.

Inland, the **Korthi Valley** is scattered with countless dovecotes and chapels.

Tinos

The island is famous for its venerated icon of the Virgin Mary, attracting thousands of pilgrims on March 25 (Annunciation) and August 15 (Assumption). Visible from afar, the pilgrimage church of Panaghia Evangelistra (or familiarly "Tiniotissa") dominates the island capital **Chora** (or Tinos Town). The Tinians' jewel was built between 1823 and 1830 on the place where, according to legend, the miraculous icon was found. From the harbour, a broad processional avenue climbs up to the basilica. In the lanes running parallel, little specialist shops sell the pilgrims their candles, medallions, small gourds and icons. The marble for the quite palatial sanctuary, with its two levels of colonnades surrounding a vast courtyard, was quarried locally and imported from Paros. A large stairway leads up to the forecourt which offers a view back over the harbour and in the distance to the islands of Mykonos, Delos and Syros. The sanctuary includes a crypt with a sacred spring and 120 whitewashed cells surrounding the courtyard with its marble decoration, cypresses and palms.

At the bottom end of the processional avenue, the Archaeological Museum traces the island's past in classical antiquity. Its collections include huge vases with carved reliefs from the 7th and 8th centuries BC as well as statue fragments from the Temple of Poseidon and Amphitrite at Kionia, as well as from the Temple of Demeter on the slopes of the granite crag of Exobourgo.

Outside the capital, the island roads take you to a succession of peaceful villages, many of them encircling Exobourgo, or scattered in the north, where the tradition of marble quarrying continues. In the south, Tinos culminates at Mount Tsiknia, refuge of Aeolus, god of the Winds. On the lower slopes, low stone walls surround the arid fields, brightened up by chapels, mills or the famous square dovecotes built by the Venetians, for which the island is famous.

Mykonos

In the 1980s Mykonos became a popular destination with the international jet set, royalty and ship-owners, and today it is still the most cosmopolitan of the Greek islands. Unlike most Aegean towns, the island capital, Chora, does not spread around the slopes of a hill or on an outcrop looking out over the sea. Instead, it sprawls lazily along the coast. Boats sail into the harbour passing white houses with blue or red doors and shutters. In the narrow streets—deliberately laid out in a labyrinth to confuse medieval pirates—tiny squares and staircases alternate with bars, tavernas and souvenir shops.

Brightly painted fishing boats bob up and down in the port, jealously guarded by pink pelicans, the successors of Petros I who was the island's mascot. Set back from the harbourside, the small Archaeological Museum displays a collection of antiquities discovered on Delos and the neighbouring island of Rhenia.

Cats slink around the alleys of the old town or snooze in shafts of sunlight. You'll come across a chapel, then another, and yet another. They say there's one for every day of the year.

An old brass cannon and sculpted marble doorway herald the fascinating Naval Museum on Enoplon Dinameon street, behind the church of St George. It relates the history of navigation between the islands and in the eastern Mediterranean.

West of the port, the Captain's Houses, with wooden balconies and bow windows, are built along the sea front. Because of their presence, the district is called **Little Venice** (Venetia). In the background, five of the island's famous thatch-roofed windmills are lined up on a ridge. Three of them have been restored as private houses.

The island's most famous church, the 16th-century **Panagia Paraportiani** looks like a miniature fortress. Its name means "little door", referring to the one that gave access to the original building, around which several chapels were built in later years. Quite close by, the **Folk Museum** has been set up in an old Captain's House.

Chapels, isolated houses and prickly pears are scattered over the otherwise desolate inland area, while the shores are indented with creeks and hemmed with superb beaches, some with fine golden sand, others with a coarser variety, but all bathed by irresistible crystalline turquoise waters. In summer many of them are linked to Chora by boat. They tend to get crowded, like Paradise Beach. For somewhere quieter, try Agios Ioannis in the southwest, Agios Sostis and Panormos

Author's Image

Windmills are the first things you see when you sail into Mykonos.

Delos

The island of Delos ("luminous") was first devoted to the worship of a Mycenian goddess then, from the 2nd millennium BC, to that of Apollo. It is here, the ancients believed, that Apollo was born, with his twin sister Artemis. That made the rocky, wind-lashed island sacred, and powerful rulers, warriors and pilgrims came in order to consult its oracle, carrying gifts and treasure as tribute. They contributed to the wealth and development of the political and commercial power

istockphoto.com/Sorrie

istockphoto.com/Hollitzer

Archaeological marvels discovered at Delos: one of the famous lions and terracotta jars.

of the island. Delos became cosmopolitan, populous and prosperous as a grain port and slave market. Sometimes as many as 10,000 human beings would be sold in a single day. But in 88 BC, Mithridates, king of Pontus, sacked the island and killing half the population. The island was raided again 20 years later, and the last inhabitants were murdered or sold as slaves by the pirate Athenodorus.

The first excavations were undertaken in 1873 by the French School of Athens and still continue. Spreading up from the ancient harbour, the extensive ruins make fascinating wandering. The visit begins on the west coast, on the site of the sacred port.

From behind the Agora, the Sacred Way leads to the **Sanctuary of Apollo**, where you can see the remains of four temples. Of the colossal statue of the god that once stood here, only a huge pedestal remains. The site of the Bulls' Shrine by the beautiful frieze that adorned its capitals. Near to the museum, the small shrine of Dionysus is heralded by two amazing phallic stones. On the northwest corner is the little shrine of Artemis, with an Ionic temple devoted to the goddess.

The most dramatic sight is to the north, beyond big agora, with the Portico of Antigone. On the famous **Terrace of the Lions**, five beasts remain of the original nine or more carved of Naxos marble in the 7th century BC. Only two are complete (and one is in Venice, near the Arsenal). Alert on their haunches, mouth open in roaring fashion, the lions guard the Sacred Lake. For more than 2,500 years, until half a century ago, there was an oval pond here in which swans associated with shrine rituals once swam. It was deliberately dried up in the 1920s for sanitary reasons.

At the House of Dionysos, you can see a mosaic of the god with staff and tambourine sitting on a sharp-clawed panther. This is in the theatre district where fine mosaic flooring survives in many houses, along with marble doorways, urns and some cavernous old wells. The **theatre** itself was built before 250 BC for about 5,500 spectators. Higher up, past the so-called "Hôtellerie", with a huge well, the largely restored House of Masks has carefully sheltered mosaics of theatrical masks and one showing Artemis riding a panther. Next door, the impressive **House of the Dolphins** is named for its mosaics of dolphins ridden by cupids.

A pathway climbs from here to the summit of **Mt Kynthos**. From a platform halfway up, you can see the whole sanctuary, and from the summit, the view looks out over all the islands that paid allegiance to Delos. Around 700 BC, a one of the first temples on the island was built here, dedicated to Hera, goddess of marriage.

Syros

A trading centre since the 19th century, then administrative capital of the province, Syros is small but one of the most densely populated islands of the archipelago, home to a quarter of the inhabitants. Like many other islands, it was colonized by the Venetians and remains one of the bastions of catholicism in the Aegean Sea (40 per cent of the population). It was long known as the Pope's Island, and was protected by the kings of France in the 17th century. Although it has now lost its economic importance, it remains an important maritime crossroads, ensuring ferry transfers to neighbouring islands.

Mostly rocky and mountainous, especially in the north, Syros is produces fruit and vegetables in the south. Its rugged coast forms two wide gulfs. That of Ermopouli, the capital, has pleasant beaches.

Paros

With some 3,000 inhabitants, **Parikia**, the pretty little capital in a protected bay on the west coast, can hardly be said to be overcrowded, but it is certainly cluttered. Its narrow, winding streets are crammed with tiny whitewashed houses and those typically Greek shops selling a fascinating jumble of goods. Bougainvillaea, honeysuckle and hibiscus flowers brighten the buildings. Old churches and 18th-century fountains casually stand at street corners as life goes on.

The ruins of the local **Kastro** (castle) stand on a promontory close to the port. The builders of this 13th-century Venetian fortification recycled marble col-

Paros reveals its charms: the port of Naoussa; Panagia Ekatonta- piliani, the oldest church in the Cyclades.

umns and other bits of an ancient Greek acropolis that once stood there, creating an interesting combination of styles. Above the castle you can see a very photogenic blue-domed church, as well as the meagre ruins of an ancient temple to Apollo. The views are memorable, too.

The jewel in the crown of this majestic little island is undoubtedly the Church of a Hundred Doors, **Panagia Ekatontapiliani**, on the square to the east of the port.

One of the best examples of Byzantine art in all the Greek islands, the church is built on the site of an earlier sanctuary, supposedly founded in the 4th century by St Helen, mother of Constantine, the first emperor to be converted to Christianity.

The three-naved building owes much of its interior beauty to the local white marble, especially the bishop's throne, the Byzantine capitals on the pre-Christian columns and the sunken font in the 6th-century baptistery to the right of the church. In the right wing, the small **Ecclesiastical Museum** has an exceptional collection of icons from the 15th to 19th centuries.

Behind the church, the **Archaeological Museum** houses a fragment of the famous Parian Chronicle, brought to light at the end of the 19th century. The rest, discovered in 1627, is in the Ashmolean Museum in Oxford. This old marble slab records Greek history in the 4th century BC.

Antiparos

Across a narrow strait on the western side of the island lies Antiparos, the little sister of Paros. Anti here means opposite, not opposing. With some 800 inhabitants, Antiparos is the largest of the islands in the region and is reached by taking a scenic 40-minute boat trip from Parikia, or by the shorter ferry from Pounda (to which a bus runs from the capital). Its most interesting feature is a grotto, situated 175 m (550 ft) above sea level, on Mt Agios Ilias. If you can manage the 400 steps leading down, you'll find a spacious cave adorned with a generous ration of stalactites and stalagmites.

Naxos

Approximately in the centre of the Aegean, Naxos is the most fertile and largest of the islands. It was here, they say, that Theseus abandoned Ariadne after defeating the Minotaur. One of the main centres of the Cycladic culture, the island was part of a Venetian county in the 13th century. Some of the mansions and the ruins of the kastro are decidedly Venetian in style.

Naxos Town (or Chora), is laid out in a semi-circle on the site where an earlier town (Grotta) was settled in Late Mycenaean times (12th century BC). Testifying to its illustrious past is the Palatia islet at the entrance to the harbour, with a giant **marble gateway** from the vestibule of the Temple of Apollo (6th century BC), destroyed by the Persians. A causeway now links it to the island mainland.

The harbour, always lively in the summer, is the starting point for a walk through the narrow lanes with their clusters of white box-like houses up to the **Venetian Citadel** (Kastro) from the 13th century. Within its walls are the convent of the Ursulines and monastery of the Capuchins, the Catholic **cathedral** with a façade and tower entirely covered with slabs of marble, as well as some fine medieval patrician houses.

Not far from the Catholic cathedral, the **Archaeology Museum** exhibits the island's excavation finds: ceramic vases and other objects of everyday life from the Mycenaean period, some splendid Cycladic figures marble vessels and fine Roman glassware.

Amorgos

The easternmost island of the Cyclades at the very heart of the Aegean stretches its long, mountainous silhouette towards the Southern Sporades. Behind the cliffs of the coast lie the dazzling white houses of villages where the cats are kings. Another king, Minos of Crete, is said to have retired here from the cares of state. Three thousand years later the peace and quiet are still there—despite the transient celebrity of the island after Luc Besson used it as a location for his film *The Big Blue (Le Grand Bleu)*.

In the northwest, the port of **Katapola**, uniting three towns, nestles in a bay known for its blessedly sheltered situation. A shady promenade leads along the seafront where the typical little boats of the Aegean are moored. The town itself spreads out at the foot of a hill where the remains of Minoa, one of three ancient independent cities, have been excavated. The site, reachable along a stony path, was inhabited from the Stone Age till the Roman era. It offers a fine view along the coast.

Chora, the island capital, lies roughly in the centre, built high up on a bare hill. It leans against a peak shaped like a sugarloaf where you will find the remains of a castle occupied successively by the Byzantines, Venetians and Turks. On the heights, you can also make out the ruins of some old windmills. A maze of lanes, stairways and arched passages winds among the white cube houses. The **museum** in an 18th-century house exhibits finds from the island's excavations — a reminder that Amorgos played an important role in the development of the Cycladic civilization.

On the slopes of Mount Profitis Ilias east of Chora can be seen, 300 m above sea level, the gigantic white walls of the **Panagia Chosoviotissa Monastery**, clinging to the rock. According to legend, its site is where an icon of the Virgin Mary was found, brought in by the sea, miraculously intact again after it had been broken in two by heathens. History's version has monks fleeing persecution in Palestine in the 9th century and choosing this spectacular site because it reminded them of where they had built their original rock-hewn monastery near Jericho. Today the monks grow fruit and vegetables on a few narrow terraces below the monastery.

Santorini

The southernmost island of the Cyclades, said to be the legendary Atlantis, is the most spectacular and fascinating of all Aegean islands, perhaps of the whole Mediterranean. When ships enter the harbour, the remains of the ancient submerged crater, passengers are filled with admiration at the sight of the landscape, like the birth of the world. Cataclysmic red and black rocks rear high above the waves.

Some 3,500 years ago a great explosion blew up the island and its volcano. A cloud of ash and pumice, 40 km (25 miles) high, was formed, coming back to earth in a thick hail and accumulating in some places to a depth of 40 m. The sea rushed into the crater through a gap pierced in its wall, while burning clouds destroyed every living thing on the island. When it was all over, the island had been transformed from a circle to a wide crescent of cinder and lava surrounding a bay, so deep that boats have never been able to anchor there.

The island continues to incur the earth's fury. In 1956, in just one minute, hundreds of houses were destroyed, especially in the village of Ia, and around 50 people were killed. In the middle of the harbour, in the shade of the island of Thirasia, the black and ochre Kameni islets remain as a reminder that the volcano is not dormant.

Of late the island has officially reverted to its ancient name of Thira, or Thera. But it's also called Santorini, the Italian version of its patron saint, Irene. The capital **Fira** (or Thira, just to complicate matters) is perched on a rocky precipice and offers spectacular views of the harbour, Santorini's west coastline and the neighbouring islands. Its narrow, cobbled streets, fine craft shops and barrel-vaulted houses give it a unique character.

In the **Archaeological Museum** you can see an interesting collection of geometric and 5th-century red-black figure vases discovered on the site of Ancient Thira.

The **Gyzi Cultural Centre**, also called the Megara Gyzi Museum, maintains the island's memories. On display is an impressive collection of photographs showing the extent of the damage caused by the 1956 earthquake, as well

Huber/Gräfenhain

Be kind to the overloaded donkeys, and let the cable car hoist you up to Fira.

as an icon-painting workshop. Temporary exhibitions are held here, but the centre is only open during the summer.

Following the same street upwards then an alleyway to the left, you will reach the Catholic church, recognizable by its pink bell-tower, and opposite, the Dominican convent. Higher up, the **Petros M. Nomikos conference centre** holds summer exhibitions displaying copies of the Akrotiri frescoes from the site in the south of the island.

Fira spreads northwards to the district around Agios Minas church, sparkling white and blue-domed, overlooking the bay. From there, carry on to **Imerovigli**, clinging to the highest rocky promontory of the island. At the foot of the houses, the cliff drops vertically into the sea, 350 m (1,148 ft) below.

The beautiful village of **Ia**, in the north, nestles on the edge of the caldera. The most handsome houses, perched over the void, were built by sea captains at the end of the 19th century, when Ia had a big merchant fleet, which is documented in a small museum. The village was entirely rebuilt after the 1956 earthquake. The little hamlet is quieter than Fira and has plenty of café terraces perfectly sited for watching the sun sink behind the horizon.

The **ancient site** of Thira, set on a high promontory on the east coast, can be reached by a road full of hairpin bends from Kamari, or by footpath from Perissa (an easy 30- to 40-minute climb). Most of the relics found here date back to the 3rd and 2nd centuries BC, when the Ptolemies of Egypt conquered the southern Aegean and set up a garrison in Thira. From the wide terrace where rites were celebrated to Apollo in ancient times, you can see the whole southern tip of Santorini.

Ios

Between Naxos and Santorini, the mountainous island was long isolated from the rest of the world. Its superb beaches are lapped by crystalline water; some of them are easy to access, others can only be reached by boat, which only enhances their charm. The inhabitants call their island Nio; it attracts a lot of young visitors who invade the beaches and discos in summer. Inland, the island is as quiet as ever, amid meadows and clumps of olive trees, and countless chapels.

Boats land in the port of **Ormos**, at the end of a wide fertile valley dotted with blue beehives and outlined by terraces and low walls. From there, a road leads to the capital, **Chora**, where most of the islanders live. The little town occupies the site of an ancient city, spreading around a rocky outcrop topped by a trio of white chapels. Opposite, on another hill, stand several windmills and the ruins of a medieval castle. The view over the town, the sea and the island of Sikinos is superb.

In high season, Chora sees many tourists. Its narrow streets are lined with bars, souvenir shops and nightclubs. On summer nights the whole town is transformed into a disco.

Take advantage of the early hours to stroll around—you're

likely to have the town to yourself. Climbing one staircase after another, you will reach the church of **Panagia Gremiotis**, topped by a blue dome and belltower. From the courtyard and its two palm trees, the view lingers over the maze of rooftops. A paved track leads up to the top of the hill, where you can see old icons in the neighbouring chapels.

Sikinos

Perhaps the wildest and least visited of all the Cyclades, this little mountainous island, with fewer than 300 inhabitants, will charm anyone searching for absolute calm and authenticity.

The only road in the island links the port of Alopronia to the delightful village of **Sikinos**, dominating the north coast. It is composed of the old Cycladic town of Chora, and Kastro. Clinging to a rock on the heights, the monastery of **Zoodohos Pigi** ("source of life") looks like a fortress.

An hour's walk westwards will take you to another monastery, **Episkopi**, long abandoned. The ancient church incorporates various elements of what was probably a mausoleum, built in the 3rd century.

Folegandros

Its name, derived from the Phoenician, announces it bluntly; this is the "rocky island". Despite the stones, despite the aridity, Folegandros is undoubtedly one of the most beautiful islands of the Cyclades. Floating in the deep blue sea between Sikinos and Milo, it has just 600 inhabitants and covers 32 sq km (12 sq miles). In days gone by, Folegandros was a place of political exile. Today, anyone in search of calm and nature is glad to discover the wild beauty of its landscapes, dotted with huge craggy rocks and sandy beaches, pathways beneath the cliffs and orchards with espaliered trees.

Built on a plateau overlooking the sea, with the port of Karavostassis in the distance, the capital, **Chora**, is one of the most handsome villages in the Cyclades. Its white cubic houses, with pretty flower-filled balconies and blue doors and windows, huddle together, forming a rampart around the central core of the ancient castle built by the Venetians in the 13th century. There are several churches to visit, including the Panagia, which affords a splendid view over the town and port from the square outside the main door. Over the centuries the houses have gradually spread outside the walls, creating a new district just as charming as the original, threaded with narrow streets dotted with more churches and pleasant little squares shaded by trees.

What remains of the famous Venus of Milo.

Milo

Halfway between the Peloponnese and Crete, Milo (or Milos) developed under the dual influence of the Minoan and Mycenean civilizations. Known thanks to the statue of Venus that was discovered in 1820 by a farmer working his fields, the southernmost of the Western Cyclades is an island with a rich history and varied landscapes, revealing its volcanic heritage. The indented shores of black, white and red cliffs, are riddled with countless caves, bays and creeks lined with a multitude of deserted beaches where pirates once came ashore. In the hollow of its bay, the submerged crater of an ancient volcano, the island shelters one of the safest natural ports in the Aegean: **Adamas**, where most of the tourist facilities are grouped. From there, a road climbs gently to **Plaka**, the island capital. The town clings to a peak crowned by a Venetian fortress in ruins, a sentinel watching over the entrance of the deep bay of Milo at the northeast. The site, close to the fertile plain, was chosen by the Ancients for its springs and strategic location. The last battle, which saw the demise of the islanders, allied with Sparta, against the Athenian armies in 416 BC, was fought here.

From the main square, take the narrow stepped streets, adorned with colourful flowers, between the white houses with wooden gates and blue-painted doors and windows. As you climb, you'll notice churches here and there, all with blue-painted domes. From the summit, you get a fantastic view over the bay, all the way round from the northeast tip of Milo and over the nearest Cyclades. You will also see the sandy arc of Plathenia beach.

Near the church of **Panagia Korfiotissa**, its terrace hanging out over the void, the **Folklore Museum** reveals the daily life of the islanders and their history. You will note, in particular, the importance of embroidery in their traditions.

Lower down in the village, on an acacia-shaded square, the little **Archaeological Museum** is set in a neoclassical house. There's a plaster replica of the Venus of Milo (the original is displayed in the Louvre Museum in Paris), and a small selection of objects discovered during excavations of the Phylacopi site.

Venus was discovered in 1820, in the terraced fields below the village of **Tripiti**, near Plaka. The first excavations, undertaken 23 years later, revealed the existence of an ancient city built on a site inhabited since Neolithic times: **Melos** or Archaeio Klima. The city flourished from the Cycladic era thanks to the trade in obsidian, carved into arrowheads and cutting tools, exchanged all over the Aegean and part of the eastern Mediterranean. It was destroyed by the Athenians and rebuilt in Roman times. Temples, now in ruins, date from the Roman era, as do the gymnasium and baths, scattered around the fields, as well as one of the most handsome ancient monuments in the whole of the Cyclades: the **Roman theatre** nestling on the slope of a hill, facing Adamas Bay. The terraced slopes are planted with olives; dog daisies and poppies flower in spring. In summer, plays and recitals are held here. The friezes and pediments, carved in a marble imported from Asia Minor, give you a glimpse of the theatre's former splendour.

A short walk away, underground, spread vast **catacombs**, second in size only to those of Rome. Used in the 2nd to 5th centuries, the corridors tunnel some 200 m (650 ft) into the soft rock. Each of the alcoves could hold five to six tombs, totalling almost 2,000 in all. You can only see a small part of the immense network.

A path winds down from the catacombs to the little port of **Klima**, dating from Antiquity. It backs onto a hillside and is composed of row of fishermen's cottages, their wooden doors, blinds and balconies painted blue, green and red.

Kimolos

Boats make regular trips from Pollonia to the mountainous island of Kimolos, located just on the other side of a narrow strait. Inhabited since the Mycenean era, the island, with its numerous grottoes, was also a pirates' hideout in the Middle Ages. Its chalky cliffs now have a more peaceful role: they are exploited today for their white clay and loamy earth. Far from the madding crowds, Kimolos has several lonely beaches. The capital, **Chora**, is an attractive fortified village above the port of Psathi; most of the population of under 1000 is gathered there.

Sifnos

The island lies in the middle of the triangle formed by Milo, Serifos and Paros. When you approach by ship, you see only grey cliffs dotted with the occasional white church or monastery; the sight belies the fertile interior of the island, bedecked with olive groves. Thanks to the colours of its clay, it has always been known for its pottery, which now fuels the tourist market.

A road from the port at **Kamares** leads to the capital, **Apollonia**, a town spreading over several hills. Most of the population is concentrated here and in the neighbouring villages of Artemonas, Exambela, Kato and Pano Petali. Among the dazzling white houses stitched together by narrow stone steps, are several beautiful churches—the island is said to have 365 in all. That of Agios Sozon has a fine carved wood iconostasis, and higher up, Panagia Ouranofora is well worth the climb. There's a small Folklore Museum on the main square.

Near Exambela, the big white **Kyria Vryssi** monastery has fortified walls, dating from 1642. It houses a Liturgical Museum.

The best buys

Amulets against the evil eye
Ceramics from Lindos
Filigree jewellery
Honey, olive oil, nougat, Turkish delight (loukoum)
Leatherware
Natural sponges
Olive wood items
Replicas of Cycladic statues
Rugs

Serifos

Its name means "bare", but the arid mountains of Serifos shelter little green valleys, dotted with pleasant villages and opening into wide bays.

Boats anchor on the east coast at the port of **Livadi**, hidden away at the end of a very deep bay. Several beaches will delight swimmers: Livadakia and Avlomona, but also Karavi and Psili Ammos in the north (you can walk there in 20 to 30 minutes).

Dominating the port and visible from afar, the white houses of the capital **Chora**, a village built on terraces, cascade down a steep hill topped by the ruins of a Venetian fortress and two chapels. A road leads north to **Panagia**, site of a 10th-century Byzantine church that is adorned with faded 13th-century wall paintings. Beyond, at the village of Galani, stands the proud **Moni**

Taxiarchon, a monastery built in 1660 and fortified to resist pirate attack. Known for its rare manuscripts, it also has fine 18th-century frescoes.

Kea

Sometimes called Tzia, the island is the closest to the tip of Attika, not far from Cape Sounion. It is covered in mountains carved with green valleys of orchards and terraces of olive trees. On the northwest side is the ferry port of **Korissia**. A road goes up from there to the island capital at **Ioulis**. Built like an amphitheatre, the town is located on the same site as the ancient city of the same name. Meander through its labyrinth of cobbled streets, lined with houses with tiled roofs, and old churches. Steps will take you to the Kastro district, where once the acropolis stood. The view over the town, the west coast and the tip of Attica is magnificent. Apart from the Archaeological Museum, displaying a collection of objects from island excavations, you can also see the famous **Lion of Kea**, an enormous and indolent animal carved into the rock in the 5th century BC.

Limnos

The jagged teeth of a sprawling ancient fort gape along the hilltop above the island's capital, **Mirina**. The citadel, a Venetian and Turk-ish project in the Middle Ages, involved recycling the massive stones of walls going back many more centuries. The hill itself is also menacing in its steep, rocky abandon. But the town of Mirina below, also known as Castro (meaning "castle"), has a friendly charm. The fortress walls are illuminated at night. By day you can explore the ruins, from which the views are splendid; when the sky is clear you can see the sacred Mount Athos on the horizon.

The unspoiled town along the twin-harboured waterfront has enough shops, cafés and restaurants to meet your needs, and there's a tourist information office in the town hall building. Mirina also has a significant **Archaeological Museum**, featuring relics from Poliochni, on the east coast of Limnos. The stone tools and pottery go back as far as 4000 BC, and visitors are fascinated by some petrified figs of about the same age. Other exhibits are items unearthed at sites around the island, including Mirina itself. From Hephaïstia come figures of bird-women.

Mudros Bay, on the south coast, is a grand natural harbour. From here British and French forces departed on their ill-fated Dardanelles expedition in the First World War. The event is recalled in a well-kept British military cemetery and a French monument. Excavations here have revealed stone tools from the 12th millennium BC.

On the east coast, **Poliochni** was founded even before Troy, according to the Italian archaeologists who began excavations there between the world wars. The most ancient part of the site — on the bottom level — goes back some 6,000 years. Other levels show ever more sophisticated cities, rebuilt after each major natural disaster. You can see vestiges of the town walls, of houses and baths.

Samothrace

Green and wooded, with luxuriant valleys irrigated by countless streams, Samothrace (Samothraki) is dominated by the mighty **Mount Fengari**, at 1,611 m (5,285 ft), the highest peak in the whole of the Aegean. Inhabited from Antiquity, it was home to the temple of the Great Gods, mysterious divinities who preceded the gods of Olympos.

It's on the site of the temple, not far from **Paleopolis** on the northwest coast, that the famous winged statue of Athena Nike, the Victory of Samothrace, was discovered in 1863. Today it stands in the Louvre Museum in Paris.

The little port of **Kamariotissa**, on the northwest coast, is the gateway to Samothrace. A few kilometres inland, the capital, **Chora**, is built on steep hillsides covered with pines and clad with red-tiled houses along narrow paved streets.

Lesbos

The Turks called it the Garden of the Aegean. Third-largest of the Greek islands, after Crete and Evia, with an area of 1,630 sq km (630 sq miles), Lesbos is very diverse; you can laze on its beautiful beaches or make long hikes into the mountainous interior, covered in pine forest and olive groves.

Mitilini has been the island's capital ever since the days of Pittacus in the 6th century BC. Julius Caesar is supposed to have excelled himself in battle here, when he personally led the storming of the city, earning a crown of oak leaves for bravery. Situated on the southeast side of Lesbos, Mitilini overlooks the shores of Asia Minor, only 15 km (8 miles) across the strait. In a 19th-century mansion near the shore is the **Archaeological Museum**, displaying early Bronze Age vases, terracotta funerary figurines from the 4th century BC, and some beautiful Roman mosaics.

Perched on a rocky promontory partly covered by forest, the well-preserved **Genoese Fort** was built on the site of a 6th-century Byzantine fortress, itself constructed on the ancient acropolis. It was transformed into a sturdy castle by the Gattilusi in 1373 using material from the older buildings.

Another relic of antiquity is the **Hellenistic theatre** near the chapel of Agia Kiriaki. It was one of the largest in ancient Greece, and apparently Pompey admired it so much that he had a theatre built in Rome on the same plans.

Chios

This beautiful Aegean island, 840 sq km (324 sq miles) in area, is full of scenic surprises. Barren, mountains areas in the north contrast with fertile plains in the south where citrus and olive trees, vines and mastic bushes abound. Rocky cliffs suddenly give way to sheltered coves and inviting beaches; inland, half-deserted villages contrast with the modern tourist facilities of the coast.

Arriving by sea, you discover the superb panorama of the wide harbour, with mountains in the background.

Capital and principal port, Chios Town, or **Chora**, is a bustling picturesque place, full of pretty, colourful houses with latticed windows and balconies. Social life centres on either the port area or the main square, **Vounaki**, which has a public garden and a lovely Turkish fountain dating from 1768. The bronze

Two facets of Chios: a lentisk plantation and façades decorated with sgraffiti at Pirgi.

statue is of Constantine Kanaris, hero of the 1822 uprising, when he blew up part of the Turkish fleet. The former Great Mosque on one side of the square is now the setting of the **Byzantine Museum**, which has some lovely old mosaics, frescoes and icons from the island's churches.

If you go through Porta Maggiore, east of the square, you reach the ruined **kastro**, or fortress. The original Byzantine fort was considerably improved in the 14th century by the Genoese, and the Venetians added their bit later. Ramparts still protectively hug old buildings. Within the walls you can visit the small **Turkish cemetery**, the 15th-century **Giustiniani Palace** and the lovely 10th-century **St George's Church**, which was converted into a mosque in the 16th century. Inside are murals of the Ottoman period, while in the courtyard is a fountain formerly used for ritual ablutions.

Walk to Odos Aplotarias, the main shopping street of Chora, to the west, and turn left into Odos Argenti, where the **Koraïs Library** has a wonderful collection of old maps and 13,500 books bequeathed to the town by the Greek writer Adamantios Koraïs, son of an old Chiot family. In the same building—itself an interesting blend of different styles—is the **Argenti Folklore Museum**, which has a worthy display of costumes, painted porcelain and statuettes.

Mycenean vases, decorated red ceramics, marbles and terracotta figures from the 7th to 4th centuries BC are on display in the **Archaeological Museum**, south of the port near the university. You will also see a stone stela with an inscription by Alexander the Great.

Samos

In **Samos Town**, start your visit at its heart, **Pythagoras Square** where a marble lion listens impassively to the buzz of small talk rising from the café terraces. Every morning a boat leaves the nearby harbour for Kusadasi in Turkey, where you can take a bus for a day-trip to the ruins of Ephesus.

Walk along the sea front, lined by high weatherbeaten 19th-century mansions, to the municipal park and the two buildings forming the **Archaeological Museum**. The modern structure houses a remarkable collection of antiquities excavated from the ancient city of Samos and from the Sanctuary of Hera, or Heraion, on the south coast. Among the sculptures, see the giant marble *kouros* (male statue) from the 6th century BC, 5 m (16 ft) tall. The seated female statue is thought to represent Hera herself. A group of Archaic votive statues, also 6th century BC, probably represent members of the same family and were sculpted by the Samian Geneleos. They were discovered at the entrance of the Sacred Way. A neoclassical building on the other side of the courtyard displays finds from Mediterranean countries—carved objects in ivory and wood, vases, ceramics, statues, figurines, and a superb bas-relief depicting the messenger god Hermes.

Up on a hill behind the port, **Ano Vathi** is the old Turkish capital. Time stands still in its steep, narrow streets lined with exquisite Ottoman houses with red-tiled terraces.

The bay of **Mourtia**, about 6 km (4 miles) to the east, offers pleasant bathing away from the crowds. After your swim, visit the monasteries of **Ayia Zoni** (1695) and **Zoodokhos Pigi** (1756). The latter, perched on a hill, affords a splendid view of the bay and the Turkish coast. Both monasteries have architectural merit, especially the church interiors with resplendent icons adorning the screen separating the nave from the choir stalls.

Rhodes and the Dodecanese

Rhodes is the administrative capital of the Dodecanese archipelago, a long way from its government in Athens. Almost half the 120,000 population is concentrated in **Rhodes Town**. Rimini Square, between the Old and New Towns, is the hub of the capital.

There are several entrances through the walls. The closest to Rimini Square is **Pili Eleftherias** (Freedom Gate) which takes you directly into the Knights' Quarter. Pass beneath the archway over the street. To the left is the church of St Mary of the Castle, Panagia tou Kastrou, originally the Knights' cathedral, which the Turks turned into a mosque. It makes an imposing setting for the

The entrance to the Palace of the Grand Masters. | **Stone arches on Odos Omirou.**

Byzantine Museum, displaying 14th-century frescoes and 15th-century icons from all over the Dodecanese.

Fronting Museum Square is the **Knights' Hospital**, one of the most interesting buildings in the Old Town and the treasure house of Rhodes. Above the Gothic doorway, there's a bas-relief of two angels bearing the coat of arms of the Order of St John. On the first floor of the hospital, the **Archaeological Museum of Rhodes** is not to be missed. A superb collection of coins, vases, jewellery and sculpture tells the story of the island from the 9th century BC. One of the most intriguing exhibits is the life-size marble statue of Aphrodite, known as the Marine Venus.

Leaving the museum, stroll along Odos Ippoton, the **Street of the Knights**, meticulously restored by the Italians. The knights lived here in compounds called inns, according to language, under an appointed prior. You can look around the **Inn of France**, which now houses the Institut de France, and pause for reflection in the peaceful courtyard. This inn's façade is the most richly decorated of all.

The imposing **Palace of the Grand Masters**, at the top of the street, was seriously neglected during Turkish rule and severely damaged in 1856 when a forgotten store of gunpowder exploded. The Italians restored it under Mussolini's orders, and it became the holiday residence of Italian leaders. The best features of the lofty rooms—apart from the mosaics—are the windowseats permitting good views over the old town and harbour.

Several afternoons a week a section of the **ramparts** is open to the public, enabling you to walk along the top of the walls from Amboise Gate to Koskinou Gate and see into hidden gardens.

Next to the **Clock Tower** (now a café with a view), is the rusty-pink landmark of **Suleiman's Mosque**. Its pretty double-balconied minaret has been nicely restored.

If you want to do some souvenir shopping, now is the time to plunge into **Sokratous Street**, where the little boutiques are stashed to the ceiling with ceramics, icons, alabaster statues, T-shirts and leather sandals, all in a souk-like atmosphere. Halfway down, escape into the typical wood-fronted **Turkish café**, four centuries old. You could, alternatively, wander along **Ippodamou**, which has attractive, gallery-type boutiques and an old-fashioned wood-fired bakery.

At the bottom of Sokratous, just past Hippocrates Square is the **Castellania**, the medieval stock exchange downstairs, and courthouse upstairs. The building was finished in 1507.

Forge ahead to **Platia Evreon Martiron**, the square with the seahorse fountain. It is named for the 2,000 Jews who were assembled here in 1943 and deported to concentration camps. The streets east of Pithagora form the **Jewish Quarter**. Straight on from the seahorse square, you will come to the majestic ruins of the Gothic **Church of St Mary of the Bourg**. It dates from the early 14th century; the choir and two side naves have been restored.

In the New Town, across from Rimini Square and facing Mandraki Harbour, the **New Market** is a seven-sided, Oriental-looking building. It now has more souvenir shops, kebab stands and cafés than market stalls.

The Colossus of Rhodes was said to have stood astride the entrance to **Mandraki Harbour**, but today it is guarded by the statues of a stag and a doe. The three stone windmills were built in the Middle Ages to grind grain for departing cargo boats.

St Nicholas Fort, at the end of the pier, was built in the 15th century. It is now a lighthouse and contains a chapel dedicated to the Orthodox patron saint of sailors. The large **Church of St John** is the seat of the archbishop of the Dodecanese. Just beyond it, the **Governor's Palace** is a fanciful version of the Doge's Palace in Venice. Across the busy road near the tip of the island, look for the **Mosque of Murad Reis**, the chief admiral of the Sultan's fleet, and the **Turkish cemetery** where he is buried. The gravestones are beautifully incised in flowing Arabic script, entwined with leaves and flowers. Just after the mosque is the entrance to the beach.

After a 51-km (32-mile) drive along the east coast, the village of **Lindos**, dominated by its acropolis, suddenly appears before you. This was once one of the most

hemis.fr/Slatter

Lindos is regarded as one of the most beautiful sites in the Aegean.

important harbours and trading centres of antiquity, with far-flung colonies.

It's a steep climb to the **acropolis**, but donkeys are there to carry you if necessary. At the base of the staircase up to the fortress, you will see, hewn out of the rock, a huge 2nd-century BC **relief** of a Greek trireme warship. The fortress of the acropolis, with its characteristic swallowtail battlements, was built by the Knights of St John. It contains a Byzantine church and the Commander's Palace. The most splendid sight, however, is that of the wide Doric **portico**, with its dramatic monumental stairway leading to a higher terrace. From here you can see the surprisingly small **Temple of the Lindian Athena** across a forecourt. It's perched on the edge of a cliff that plunges 121 m (400 ft) into the sea below.

From the cliff you'll look down onto a small rocky harbour, **Agios Pavlos Limani** (St Paul's Bay). This is where the apostle is said to have landed during a storm in AD 51, on his way from Ephesus to Syria. The spot of his landfall is marked by a small white church.

Simi

Patrician houses overlooking the main harbour of Simi Town remind you of the island's past prosperity from shipyards and sponge-fishing, both activities dating back to earliest antiquity. The harbour, **Egialos**, forms the lower area (or *Kato Poli*) of the town. The neoclassical houses here, pale pastel yellow and white with deep red roofs, stem from the island's 19th-century heyday. This was proclaimed with one last flourish in 1881 by the lofty clocktower. The **Sea Sponge Centre** presents an audio-visual show on the skills and perils of the island's ancient sponge-fishing industry. **Ano Simi**, also known as Chorio, the upper town where most Simi-

ans live these days, is reached by the long and steep Kali Strata stairway starting out from Platiatis Skala opposite the clocktower. At the top, visit the old **apothecary shop**, Symotikon Pharmakeion. The **folklore museum** is also worth hunting down, both for its traditional musical instruments, costumes, furniture and Byzantine icons and for the handsome patrician house in which they are displayed. The **Knights' Castle** (1507), with the French Aubusson coat of arms on its gate, makes use of massive stone blocks from the ancient Greek acropolis.

At the southern end of the island, **Panormitis Monastery** is a popular stop-over for day-trippers. The church is dedicated to the Archangel Michael, celebrated with a silver icon of 1724.

Kos

At first glance, the Italian public buildings and knights' castle on the waterfront of **Kos Town** make a similar impression to Rhodes, on a smaller scale. But there is something more casual about the pleasant tree-shaded promenade. Beyond these historic monuments, the nearby vestiges of the ancient Greek city and the Turkish minaret looming behind, the town is resolutely modern. Its hotels, shops, cafés and restaurants are all built in the anonymous international style of the post-1960s and 70s tourist boom.

With characteristic swallowtail battlements, the **Knights' Castle**, built largely in the 15th century by Genoese and Venetian grand masters, has two sets of ramparts one inside the other. As can be seen by the frieze accompanying the knights' coats of arms over the gate, the castle has made abundant use of ancient Greek masonry from the Asclepium.

A venerable **plane tree** sprawling across Platia Platanou is named after Hippocrates, but like the Hippocratic Oath, the tree post-dates the death of the great doctor. Beneath the branches is a fountain fashioned from an ancient marble sarcophagus.

Remains of the ancient Greek and Roman city extend south of Platia Platanou on the **agora**. They were revealed by the earthquake that devastated the town in 1933. Columns of the shopping arcades and masonry from public buildings have been resurrected.

On Platia Eleftherias, the **town museum** exhibits sculpture from the Hellenistic period to late Roman times.

Behind the old hammam, now transformed into a restaurant, steps lead down to the **ruins** of an acropolis, a stadium and an old basilica. Ruts made by the wheels of chariots can be seen in the paved road.

The **Asclepion**, or health spa, the island's first mass tourist attraction back in the 4th century BC, lies on a hillside at the end of a charming avenue of cypress trees, 4 km (2.5 miles) out of town. The setting is entirely in keeping with the Asclepian therapy, which laid great stock by an attractive landscape for its patients. Patients combined their cure with games, theatre and other entertainment. The resort complex and sanctuary were laid out on three terraces. Remains of a Roman bathhouse (1st century) stand on the lower level. Visitors soothed their aches and ailments in the hot springs rich in iron and sulphur. A stairway leads to the middle terrace and two temples, the one on the left Roman (2nd or 3rd century), that on the right Greek, dedicated to Asclepios (3rd century BC). Since a major part of the Asclepian treatment was dream therapy, patients spent the night here and had the priests interpret their dreams the next morning.

A monumental stairway rises to the upper terrace and the sanctuary's principal temple, a Doric edifice. Originally it had six columns at each end and eleven down each side. From the terrace, there is a superb view across orchards and green fields to Kos Town, the harbour and across the sea to Bodrum on the Turkish mainland.

Arid and windswept, Patmos has preserved its charms.

hemis.fr/Guiziou

Patmos

The port for Patmos is **Skala**, a small, friendly town spread out around a bay which has provided ships with safe anchorage for five centuries. Once the site of Patmos's shipbuilding industry, it is now the tourist hub of the island, with a few shops and boutiques, hotels and restaurants, a handful of friendly cafés and tavernas and a tiny strip of beach. Taxis, island buses and tour coaches congregate by the harbour to shepherd visitors along the winding road up to Chora at the top of the hill.

If you want to walk up, follow the beautiful old cobbled path (1794), which will take you there in an hour or so.

Partway up the hillside, the **Monastery of the Apocalypse** is a cluster of high white constructions covering the cave where St John is said to have spend 18 months dictating the Revelation to his disciple Prochorus. To reach the **Holy Grotto of the Apocalypse,** you have to walk down several flower-bedecked staircases to the bottom of the monastery, which dates from the 16th century. Behind the Chapel of St Anne, in the dimly lit cave, you can see the hollow, set in silver, on which the saint is supposed to have laid his head, another, smaller hollow where he put his hand to pull himself up (he must have been at least 80), and the ledge of rock that Prochorus used as a desk.

Above the little town of Chora looms the **Monastery of St John the Theologian,** crenellated like a Crusaders' castle, a bastion of the Orthodox faith since its founding in 1088 by the Blessed Christodoulos. A document preserved in the archives shows that the Byzantine Emperor Alexis Comnenus granted him the island, a ship for the community, and freedom from taxes in perpetuity. The present monastery buildings date in the most part from the 15th century. Over the ages, they have been enlarged and reconstructed.

You have to climb a flight of stone stairs to the monastery's single entrance, flanked by well-fortified towers (over the door is a hole for pouring boiling oil and molten lead onto unwelcome visitors). Beyond is a series of pebble-paved courtyards, arcaded galleries, chapels and churches. In the forecourt, a series of golden frescoes illustrate the life of St John.

In the monastery **treasury** you can admire a splendid 11th-century mosaic and silver icon of St Nicholas, and amulets and gold medallions given to the monastery as a centre of Orthodox art and learning by Peter the Great and Catherine II of Russia, together with rich vestments for the clergy. There are 50 icons, the oldest of which date back to the 11th century. However, the most impressive exhibits come from the monastery's famous library, one of the most ancient in the world, containing thousands of priceless books and manuscripts, including 900 early Christian and Byzantine illuminated volumes.

Astipalaia

This remote little island is favoured because of its very remoteness, in particular by French and Italian romantics and Greek bohemians.

Chora is the island capital. Its wealthy visitors have done a fine job of renovating the white-washed houses that climb the hillside from Perigialo harbour and its pepperpot windmills. Above them is the 13th-century Venetian fortress. Inside the castle walls are two churches, St George, notable for its finely carved icon-screen, and the Annunciation.

The butterfly-shaped island's beaches are scattered among bays and coves along the deeply indented coastline, the best accessible only by boat and each for the most part a nameless secret to be kept by the individual visitor. On the southern butterfly wing, the pretty fishing village of **Livadia** is a popular exception, known both for its nudist beaches and its good tavernas. On the northern wing, **Vathi** is surrounded by several caves well worth exploring.

Karpathos

The mountainous island thrusts up its long narrow arm of land midway between Crete and Rhodes. Off the beaten track and so preserving its traditional village life, it measures 48 km (30 miles) from north to south and 11 km (7 miles) at its widest part. As a Venetian possession, it avoided the attentions of the Knights of St John and thus has no Crusader castle. The population of nearly 5,000 is largely concentrated in the southern region, fertile enough for terraced farmland, orchards and market gardens.

The capital, **Pigadia**, is architecturally a largely modern creation built with funds sent home by émigrés to the United States. Its principal attraction is the long crescent of sandy beach on **Vronti Bay** extending west of the harbour. There is a lively evening atmosphere among the harbour front tavernas. At the western end of **Afodi Beach** are the excavated marble remains of a 6th-century early Christian basilica, **Agia Fotini**.

At the northern end of the island, the fine old village of **Olimbos** is the island's main attraction, preserving its medieval charm. You can get there by car over a dirt road, or go by boat via the port of Diafani. The journey itself is a delight, sailing up the east coast from Pigadia past cliffs crowned by weirdly twisted stunted pines. From Diafani harbour, take a bus 9 km (5.5 miles) up to the village past ancient windmills on the slopes of Profitis Ilias.

The village's grand stone houses are built in a style that has not changed much since Byzantine days. Notice the balconies and friezes painted with birds and flowers, mermaids, the Venetian lion of St Mark and the Byzantine double-headed eagle.

Kastellorizo

Scarcely 5 km (3 miles) from the coast of Asia Minor, Kastellorizo is Greece's easternmost territory. Its prosperity as a warehouse for the timber trade with Turkey disappeared with the advent of steamships that bypassed the island. Today, emigration has reduced the population to barely 150. Some of the wooden balconies and windows of the houses around **Mandraki Harbour** show the strong Turkish influence of nearby Anatolia.

Officially known now, as in antiquity, as Megisti, the island derives its other name from the red-stone medieval **castle** built here by Juan Fernando Heredia, the Spanish Grand Master of the Knights of St John. Its ruin commands a hill on the eastern edge of the town.

Half the houses in the capital were destroyed in an ammunition explosion in 1943, but the tavernas around the main square are popular with the yachting fraternity. Just above the mosque, a folklore museum has been installed in a sturdy fortified medieval house.

The **Parasta Grotto**, famous for its blue waters and spectacular stalactites, is located on the south side of the island. This, like the rare coves for swimming along the craggy cliffs, is accessible only by boat.

PRACTICAL INFORMATION

Banks. Opening hours can fluctuate from place to place and season to season, with an afternoon siesta. Banks generally open Monday to Thursday 8 or 8.30 a.m.–2 p.m. and Fridays to 1.30 p.m. Some open for money exchange on Saturday mornings. Everywhere that cruise ships land, you can be sure of finding an automatic cash distributor.

Climate. Greece enjoys a typical Mediterranean climate, with relatively mild winters and hot, dry, sunny summers. It is the ideal season for sunbathers and swimmers.

Credit cards. An increasing number of hotels and shops accept credit cards in touristic areas, but some add a surtax of 3 to 5 per cent, sometimes without informing the client.

Currency. The Euro (€), divided into 100 *lepta*.

Electricity. The current is 230 V AC, 50 Hz; plugs are the standard European type with two round pins.

Emergencies. Most problems can be resolved at your hotel reception desk. Apart from 112 (the European emergency number), you can dial 100 for the police, 199 for the fire brigade. The Tourist Police can be reached 24 hours a day on 171.

Museums and archaeological sites. Generally closed Mondays and sometimes Tuesdays. Some, especially the smaller ones, close for winter, November to March. Hours are generally 8 or 8.30 a.m. to 3 p.m. off season, and to 5 or 7 p.m. in July and August. Last entry is usually half an hour before closing time.

Shops. Normally they open Monday, Wednesday and Saturday, from any time between 8.30 and 10 a.m. to 3 p.m, and again from 5 to 8 or 9 p.m. This rule does not apply to local grocery shops, which sometimes also open on Sundays.

Tipping. Service is included in the bill, but it is customary to leave a small extra tip to waiters and taxi drivers.

memorable excursions

SIGHTSEEING

coffee culture

mystical dancing

ancient civilizations

TURKEY

Nothing is straightforward in Turkey. Is it in Asia? Yes and no. In Europe? No and yes... What makes it so fascinating, is that nothing is quite what you might expect. It is a big country, with the sea on three sides. In the east, the waters of the Black Sea flow into the Bosphorus, then, south of Istanbul, pass into the Sea of Marmara. From there they roll towards the Aegean by the Dardanelles Strait in the west, before mingling with the waves of the Mediterranean, on the south coast.

Istanbul

The Galata Bridge leads from the modern district of Istanbul to the Old City, where Istanbul's most venerable sights lie.

Old Town

The district at the foot of the bridge is **Eminönü**, teeming with ferryboats heading off in all directions and craftsmen and vendors conducting their affairs in a labyrinth of narrow streets and often steeply sloping back alleys. Eminönü is noisy, aromatic and full of colour, a great place in which to forget your camera and just look, smell and listen.

The big, clumsy Yeni Mosque towering over the Golden Horn attracts more beggars than architectural buffs. But behind it is the wonderful **Spice Market** (*Mısır Çarsışı*), also known as the Egyptian Bazaar, since it collected customs duty on goods coming in from Cairo. Not only will you find every imaginable spice and herb, culinary, aphrodisiac or rejuvenating, but the best Turkish delight and hazelnut or pistachio-flavoured *helva* made from ground sesame seeds. Flowers, exotic love-birds and parrots grace the open section of the market.

The **Mosque of Suleiman the Magnificent**, or Süleymaniye Camii, is beautifully positioned above the Golden Horn. It was built between 1550 and 1557 on Suleiman's orders by the great Turkish architect, Mimar Sinan. Story has it that the builders dug to sea level to plant the foundations. The Süleymaniye is con-

More than 21,000 ceramic tiles cover the interior walls of the Blue Mosque.

sidered the finest of all the mosques in Istanbul for the harmony of its domes, cupolas and arcades. Sinan drew inspiration from St Sophia for his creation. The porphyry columns at the entrance to the sanctuary were brought here from the old Hippodrome.

The **Grand Bazaar** (*Kapali Çarşi*) looks like Ali Baba's cave and sounds like the trading-post for the Tower of Babel. This is the biggest bazaar in the world. It's more like a complete city, with a many-domed roof. There are quiet alleys, animated crossroads, and main streets. The shop windows sparkle with silver, gold, jewels, silk and carpets.

History comes alive in **St Sophia**, once one of the greatest churches in the world. It was Constantine the Great who built the first basilica here, in 325. Destroyed by fire, it was rebuilt from 532 to 537 by the Emperor Justinian, who dedicated it to the Holy Wisdom of God (in Greek, *Hagia Sophia*). Special light bricks, made in Rhodes, went into the enormous cupola, red porphyry columns were brought from Rome, silver and gold work from Ephesus, white marble from the islands of Marmara and yellow marble from Africa. Above the marble facing were brilliantly coloured mosaics. The whole was like a vast jewel, lit by silver candelabra.

When the Turks entered Constantinople, they converted the basilica into a mosque and added four minarets. St Sophia was restored in the 19th century, and finally Atatürk turned it into a museum in 1935, and such it has remained ever since.

The narthex (vestibule) contains fine mosaics. Nine doors open from here into the main basilica with its enormous cupola, 31 m (100 ft) in diameter and 55 m (180 ft) high.

The Mosque of Sultan Ahmet, better known as the **Blue Mosque**, is another of the world's most remarkable buildings. It was designed in the 17th century by the architect Sedefkar Mehmet Ağa. From the outside it is supremely graceful, with six slender minarets shooting skywards. Sultan Ahmet made a gift of a seventh minaret to the mosque at Mecca so that Istanbul should not outdo the Holy City.

Inside, everything seems to float in an azure haze, the result of the blue tiles which give the mosque its name. There are 21,403 of these ceramic tiles, where hyacinths, carnations, tulips and roses bloom in ageless, stylized splendour. Superb carpets are spread over the floor. Four fluted pillars support the cupola, somewhat smaller than that of St Sophia: 22.20 m (70 ft) in diameter and 43 m (142 ft) high. Behind the mosque is the **Mosaic Museum**, worth a visit if time permits.

The **Hippodrome**, next to the Blue Mosque, was inspired by the great Circus in Rome and was one of the most important places in the city. First built in 203, it was enlarged and improved by Constantine and, in its heyday, was decorated by statues transported from every corner of the Roman Empire. The famous horses in St Mark's Basilica in Venice were removed from here in the 13th century. The Hippodrome was destroyed during the Fourth Crusade and only three battered monuments have survived. The **Egyptian Obelisk**, dating from around 1500 BC, is of pink granite and was brought here by Theodosius in 390. Hieroglyphics tell the story of Thutmose III of Egypt and his "conquest of the entire world".

A second obelisk of indeterminate date is known as the **Column of Constantine Porphyrogenitus**. It must have been beautiful in its time when it was covered with gilded bronze plates. The Crusaders pulled them off and melted them down for coins.

The most interesting monument is what is left of a column brought here from Delphi. It is known as the **Serpentine Column**, since it was made of three bronze snakes, twisted together, supporting a gold vase. Originally, it celebrated the Greek victory over the Persians in 479 BC, and it is the oldest Greek monument left in Istanbul.

The **Museum of Turkish and Islamic Art** is housed in Ibrahim Paşa Sarayı, a palace on one side of the Hippodrome. The museum contains an impressive collection of Turkish carpets, embroidered garments, metal-work, jewellery and Islamic calligraphy. The exquisite miniatures are Turkish and Persian work from the 16th and 17th centuries.

The Seraglio Palace or **Topkapı**, the ancient residence of the Ottoman sultans, was built by Mehmet II, the conqueror of Istanbul, in 1462. No one but the sultan was allowed to pass on horseback through the second doorway into the courtyard which has, on the right, the old kitchens displaying collections of priceless Chinese and European porcelain and, on the left, an entrance to the famous **harem**. The sultans could have up to four official wives and innumerable concubines. They all lived in this dimly lit labyrinth of staircases and corridors, bedrooms and bathrooms, largely engaged in ambitious intrigues which centred around being the first to produce a male heir and then assuring his accession to the throne.

The **treasury** will leave you amazed at the incredible wealth of the Ottoman Empire. Here is the throne of Ismail, covered in gold and decorated with more than 2,500 precious stones. Here, too, are the emeralds made famous in the film, *Topkapi*: three enormous, flickering, greenish-blue stones set into the handle of a dagger. You will also see an 86-carat diamond, surrounded by 49 smaller diamonds and a huge, uncut emerald weighing more than 3 kg.

Other places of interest

Interesting, if time is available, is the **Archaeological Museum**, near the Topkapı. The most famous exhibit is the Alexander sarcophagus, so named because scenes from his life are sculpted into the marble (in fact, it was the sarcophagus of a Phoenician king). It dates from the end of the 4th century BC. The nearby **Museum of the Ancient Orient** not only has objects from the Hittite, Assyrian and Egyptian periods but also an enchanting garden with Byzantine sculpture. Be sure to stop at the **Çinili Köşkü**, an ancient pavilion in the courtyard converted into a Ceramics Museum—it's a treasure trove of faience and gorgeous tiles.

Out near the northern ramparts is the **Kariye Camii**, formerly the Church of St Saviour in Chora and now a museum. It contains some of the loveliest Byzantine mosaics and frescoes to be seen in Istanbul. The works devoted to the lives of Mary and Jesus were created in the 14th century, some 200 years after the church's foundation. The most celebrated of the frescoes, depicting the Resurrection, are in the parecclesion, or burial chapel, at the rear of the church.

Modern Istanbul

Back across the Galata Bridge in modern Istanbul, a sprawling latterday Versailles, **Dolmabahçe Palace** is the monumental last gasp of the Ottoman Empire. In the 1840s, feeling threatened by growing rumbles of revolt outside the walls of Topkapı palace, Sultan Abdülmecit I sought a safer home on the city outskirts. Atatürk turned the place into a public museum, and a high point for tourists is the modest apartment where the great leader died on November 10, 1938, at 9.05 a.m., the time at which all the palace clocks have been stopped. Atatürk is still greatly revered by the Turks today.

The main thoroughfare, **Istiklal Caddesi**, leads south from Taksim Square, sweeping past foreign consulates, the Europeans' churches and fashionable boutiques, cinemas and nightclubs. Apart from the tramway, the boulevard has been transformed into a pedestrian zone. The side streets are full of bars, cafés, colourful restaurants, some of the best-known being the old artists' haunts in the elegant covered arcade **Çiçek Pasaji** (Flower Passage).

Asian Shore

Reached by ferry from the Eminönü jetty, the blessedly peaceful district of **Üsküdar** on the Asian shore enjoys an intriguing coexistence between Islamic traditionalists and a growing colony of avant-garde artists and writers. After the noise of European Istanbul, it is a pleasure just to wander around the narrow winding lanes of old wooden balconied houses, cafés, studios and galleries.

Up on a terrace right by the ferry landing, **Mihrimah Mosque** is an early work of Mimar Sinan built in 1548 for the daughter of Suleiman the Magnificent. Across the broad Iskele Square is the 18th-century **Yeni Valide Mosque**, built by Ahmet III for his mother.

The **food market** is scattered in side streets leading off Iskele Square, with a remarkably rich variety of fruit and vegetables brought in from the Anatolian farms. South of the square, along Büyük Hamam Street, the Üsküdar flea market has a good array of jewellery, brassware, wood carving and other ornaments.

Üsküdar was known as Scutari to 19th-century Europeans, when it served as a British military base in the Crimean War. Florence Nightingale ran the army hospital, now part of the Selimiye Barracks on the southern edge of town. The small **Florence Nightingale Museum** displays the nurse's personal belongings and books; you need the permission of an army officer to enter. The nearby British War Cemetery contains graves from the Crimean and two world wars.

The Bosphorus

A trip by public ferry or private charter along the channel linking the Black Sea and Sea of Marmara is a highlight of any visit to Turkey. As the boat cruises along the Galata coast, you start with a whole new perspective on monuments you may have already visited on land—the Dolmabahçe Palace and, newly renovated as a luxury hotel since a devastating fire in 1910, the Çirağan Palace built by Sultan Abdülaziz in 1874. Between the two is a monument to Barbarossa, the 16th-century pirate extraordinary promoted to admiral of the Ottoman fleet.

You will pass a succession of wooden waterfront villas called *yalıs*, both grand and dilapidated, fishing villages, seafood restaurants, consulates and palaces. In the shadow of the first arching Bosphorus Bridge, on the European shore opposite Beylerbeyi Palace, is Ortaköy's delightful neo-baroque mosque.

Beyond the bridge, prosperous Istanbul families have residences in Arnavutköy, an old Albanian settlement, and Bebek.

Further up this European shore, **Rumeli Hisarı** is the fortress built by Mehmet in 1452 to prepare his assault on Constantinople. Across the straits are the remains of the Ottomans' earlier castle, **Anadolu Hisarı**.

The fishing villages most popular for their seafood restaurants are Tarabya, Sarıyer and Rumeli Kavağı on the European shore, and the cheaper Anadolu Kavağı over on the Asian side. This is the terminus for the public ferry. Climb up to the hilltop Byzantine castle ruin for a magnificent view over the Black Sea and back down the Bosphorus.

Princes' Islands

Of the nine islands out in the Sea of Marmara, four are inhabited as holiday resorts for the Istanbul bourgeoisie. After a pleasant ferry trip from Sirkeci Pier, you can tour the islands in horse-drawn carriages, on a donkey or on a rented bicycle. Surrounded by pine forests and gardens of bougainvillaea and wisteria, elegant old villas and cottages enjoy a tranquillity free of motor traffic. The princely name dates back to the time when the Byzantine emperors used the islands as gilded cages for their family enemies.

Büyükada, the biggest and now most popular island, was for four years the home of Bolshevik leader Leon Trotsky after he was expelled from Russia by Joseph Stalin in 1929. The old revolutionary took time off from writing bitter tracts denouncing his arch-enemy to fish for mackerel and lobster. The restaurants down by the ferry landing still offer some good, but expensive seafood. The monasteries on the island's two hills were founded in the Middle Ages and occasionally served as asylums for the insane. On **Heybeliada**, the lovely beaches attract water sports enthusiasts, while ramblers head for the pine woods. The smaller Burgaz and Kınalı islands are remoter retreats for hermits and artists.

Bursa

Inland from the Sea of Marmara's industrialized south coast, Bursa is attractively set in a fertile poplar-lined plain of fruit and nut orchards. Behind it, olive groves cover the lower slopes of Uludağ, the "great mountain" rising to 2,543 m (8,344 ft). The town prospers from its silk and textile industries and owes its animated atmosphere to an active university community. In the ancient citadel are the tombs of Osman Gazi, founder of the Ottoman dynasty, and his son Orhan, dating back to the 14th century when Bursa was the empire's first capital.

Heading east, you can stroll through the street market, its stalls piled high with the region's produce. The covered bazaar is popular for its locally manufactured silks and other fabrics.

Among the town's many notable mosques is the 14th-century 20-domed **Ulu Cami** (Great Mosque), with a pretty fountain protected by a cupola. The splendid 15th-century **Yeşil Cami** (Green Mosque) has a superb tiled interior; Mehmet I made it his headquarters and took up residence in a suite above the main entrence. He is buried behind the mosque, on the other side of the street, in the turquoise-tiled **Yeşil Turbe** (Green Mausoleum).

On the menu

Arnavut ciğeri – sheep's liver
Biber dolması – stuffed peppers
Cacık – yoghurt with garlic and cucumber
Çoban salatası – lettuce with tomato and cucumber
Kokoreç – mutton tripe
Kuru fasulye – white bean soup
Kuzu dolması – stuffed leg of lamb
Midye tavası – fried mussels
Patlıcan salatası – mashed aubergines with lemon
Şiş kebap – lamb, mutton or beef kebabs
Türlü sebze – stewed mixed vegetables

The **Museum of Turkish and Islamic Art** is attractively housed in the Green Mosque's old theology school. Around the Muradiye Mosque complex, look out for the Ottoman houses. In Koza Park, you may catch a Karagöz puppet show with its cheeky clowns, a genre which originated in Bursa.

Gallipoli

Commanding access from the Mediterranean to Marmara and the Black Sea beyond, the Dardanelles strait has been a bone of contention throughout history, from the time of Homer's Troy to Atatürk's Gallipoli (Gelibolu). The battlefields and Allied cemeteries of World War I are strung out along the picturesque pine-covered peninsula. With Turkey on the German side in 1915, this region became the target of a two-pronged attack by Anglo-French forces to the south and Australian-New Zealand (ANZAC) troops to the north. Pinned down by the Turks, the Allies found that what was planned as a lightning assault turned into disastrous trench-warfare costing both sides a total of over 100,000 dead. Casualties were particularly heavy for the Australians and New Zealanders. Cemeteries and assault beaches are eloquently signposted Shell Green, Shrapnel Valley and Anzac Cove. On Conkbayırı Hill is the New Zealanders' memorial obelisk and a Turkish monument celebrating the deeds and words of field commander Mustafa Kemal, the future Atatürk.

Troy

The setting of Homer's epic *Iliad* has been uncovered on an inland hill near the entrance to the Dardanelles. Any lover of history or legend will want to make the pilgrimage.

On the main highway 25 km (15 miles) south of the port city of Çanakkale, signposts point west to Troy (Truva). This is the place where Sparta's beautiful Queen Helen was kept in Priam's royal palace, where Odysseus sent in an armoured personnel carrier disguised as a wooden horse. Here are remains of the walls around which Achilles dragged the body of his heroic enemy, Hector. The legends are commonly regarded as a splendid embellishment of actual deeds of piracy and war carried out by Greek ships on the Anatolian coast in the 13th century BC.

Fact or myth, the stones first excavated by German amateur archaeologist Heinrich Schliemann are real enough: nine layers of different cities on the same site, from a Bronze Age settlement of about 3000 BC to the Greco-Roman metropolis that disappeared around AD 400. The scholars' date of 1250 BC would favour Troy VI as most likely scene for the Homeric events, though evidence shows this city was destroyed by earthquake. Others consider Troy VIIa, built on its ruins, to be the best candidate. In either case, apart from ramparts, a tower or two, a paved ramp and a fanciful model of the wooden horse, the remains demand some imagination to reconstitute the royal city coveted by the Greeks. But if you come as Alexander the Great did, with a copy of Homer in your hand, you will surely hear the echo of battle cries from Agamemnon's fleet across the Trojan plain.

Pergamum

Modern excavations have done much to reveal what, at its zenith, was one the grandest cities in the eastern Mediterranean. The two main sites—the ancient city centre of the Acropolis and the Asclepion health spa—stand north and south of the modern town of Bergama.

The Attalid dynasty of philosopher kings built their royal capital in the 4th century BC in a glorious setting of hillside terraces. Only the outline of the great Altar of Zeus remains since the German excavators carried off its monumental friezes to use as the centrepiece of their archaeological museum in Berlin. But the magnificent Theatre, seating 10,000 spectators on its 80 steeply raked rows, is ample consolation. Nearby are remains of the Temple of Athena and the Pergamene Library, which amassed in its heyday a collection of 200,000 books. The massive Roman Corinthian temple of Emperor Trajan is further up the hill.

Pergamum built its health spa to honour Asclepius, Greek god of healing. The processional colonnade led patients to the waters and baths in the hot springs, and to the temples for sleeping cures, complete with dream-interpretation by the priests. Like any modern spa, the Asclepion provided entertainment and relaxation at its own theatre and library. The town's great physician Galen (130–200) worked here, getting plenty of practice as official doctor to the gladiators.

Izmir

The uncompromisingly modern look of Turkey's second port city, known as Smyrna after its reconstruction by Alexander the Great, is a result of the fire of 1922 during the Greco-Turkish War. In two days, it destroyed three-quarters of the buildings. Gone are the Greek, Armenian, Italian, French and Jewish merchants who ran the town under the Ottomans, making way for a bustling new city of industry, commerce—and the air base for NATO's south-east Mediterranean command.

At the southern end of the palmtree-lined Kordon, now officially known as Atatürk Caddesi, is Izmir's landmark, the Saat Kulesi clocktower, built at the beginning of the 20th century. Konak Bazaar is located among the narrow streets east of the Kordon, and just beyond that are the excavations of the Roman Agora.

South of the clocktower, the **Archaeological Museum** displays a fine collection of Greek and Roman statuary, mosaics, ceramics, metalwork and jewellery in silver and gold. Next door, the **Ethnographical Museum** reconstitutes the decors and costumes of Smyrna's cosmopolitan heyday and the folklore and craftwork of the Anatolian hinterland.

Up on the hill southeast of the city centre, the Byzantine and Ottoman citadel **Kadifekale** encloses a pleasant pine-shaded park and family playground. It offers an outstanding panorama over the Bay of Izmir and is the best vantage point from which to view the columns of the Roman Agora. It's especially appealing at sunset.

Çeşme

At the tip of the peninsula west of Izmir, the lively resort of Çeşme is popular with Turkish families and much appreciated by serious windsurfers. Boat trips are organized up and down the coast, making halts at good swimming spots, and there's a ferry to the island of Chios.

The town is compact, with most sights and amenities grouped around the main square, **Cumhuriyet Meydanı**, and its statue of Atatürk. Dominating the centre is the **Kalesi**, a sturdy fortress built by the Genoese in the 14th century and expanded 200 years later by Sultan Beyazıt II. Inside you can see some archaeological finds and a collection of weapons. The view from the battlements is worthwhile. In front of the fortress is the statue of **Cezayrili Gazi Hasan Paşa** (1714–90) accompanied by a lion. This local hero became a Janissary when 25 and led a brilliant military, naval and political career. He participated in the famous battle in the Bay of Çeşme between the Ottoman and Russian fleets and became a very wealthy Grand Vizier.

South of the fortress, **Okuz Mehmet Paşa Kervansaray**, the former caravanserai, built in 1528, has been restored and converted into a luxuriously appointed boutique hotel. During Çeşme's golden age, it marked the end of the Silk Road for the camel caravans from Central Asia. Goods were unloaded here for export to Europe.

Wandering around the narrow streets north of Cumhuriyet Meydanı, you will come across the 19th-century Orthodox church of **Ayios Haralambos**, now restored and used as an art gallery.

Çeşme means "fountain", and the town has long been known for its hot springs. Even today you can relax in the thermal baths just outside the centre.

Wine has long been produced in and around Çeşme from *razaki* grapes, and the town hosts a Wine Festival in September, held in the Marina. Other local produce includes melons, artichokes, succulent date olives and *sakiz* (mastic), an essential ingredient of Turkish ice cream and other sweets.

Kuşadası

With its fine golden sands, good seafood and big marina, this boisterous beach resort concentrates strictly on hedonistic pleasures. For those moved by the higher claims of the spirit, the great archaeological sites of Ephesus, Priene, Miletus and Didyma are within easy reach. The best beaches are, north of town, **Tusan** and **Pamucak**, and to the south, the closer **Kadınlar Denizli**, for lovers of the mob scene. In the older Kale part of town, south of Sağlık Caddesi, attractive Ottoman houses have been transformed into bars and restaurants.

istockphoto.com/Creech

The towering remains of the Library of Celsus in Ephesus.

Ephesus

No site gives you a better sense of what an ancient Greco-Roman town actually looked like than magnificently preserved Ephesus (Efes). As a prosperous port and centre of the great Artemis cult, it became capital of the Romans' Asia province. It has since silted up and now, beginning at the car park, a vast green plain covers the old harbour. From it, the long Arcadian Way leads straight to the Great Theatre seating 20,000, reconstructed for modern music and arts festivals. South of the

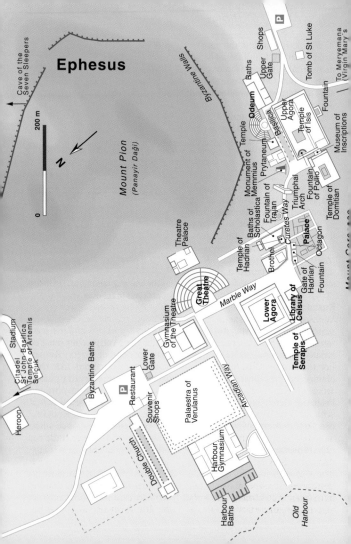

theatre, the Marble Street with its central gutter passes between the Lower Agora market square and the town brothel, whose mosaic decoration suggests it was a quite handsome establishment. Behind it are the municipal toilets.

On the far side of the junction of Marble and Curetes streets is the superb two-storey façade of the **Library of Celsus**, a memorial to the Roman proconsul Celsus built by his son around AD 135. Nearby are terraced houses from late imperial and early Byzantine times. The street of Curetes (priests) curves around between the temples of Hadrian and Domitian on its way to the Prytaneum town hall and the Upper Agora market square.

Set in the mountains east of the main site, the **Cave of the Seven Sleepers** evokes an early Christian legend of seven young men who were shut up there by a pagan emperor and awakened 200 years later to discover that Christianity had become the state religion.

Selçuk

The town closest to Ephesus has a first-class **Archaeological Museum**, noteworthy for its arresting multiple-bosomed Artemis sculptures. On the western outskirts of town, a solitary pillar and a few blocks of granite are all that remain of the **Sanctuary of Artemis**, one of the seven wonders of the ancient world to which worshippers flocked from all over the Mediterranean.

Another pilgrimage shrine, in a pretty mountain setting just outside Selçuk, is the so-called **Virgin Mary's House** (Meryemana). A small chapel is built on the foundations of a 1st-century dwelling presumed to be Mary's last resting place, such as it appeared to a devout German nun in a vision 1,800 years later. The pilgrims who come here believe Mary accompanied the evangelist St John to this area. His burial place is marked by remains of the 6th-century **Basilica of St John**.

Bodrum

Here, in this upmarket resort of dazzling white houses around a picturesque harbour, the nightlife is bouncing, the marina bristling with luxury yachts and the cafés full of the chatter of an elegant, cosmopolitan clientele. Ancient Halicarnassus, it was the birthplace of Greek historian Herodotus. King Mausolus had his burial shrine built here in 355 BC and bequeathed to the world the generic name of mausoleum. Today it is just a rubble-strewn open-air museum, nearly everything either destroyed by earthquake or carried off as masonry and ornament for the nearby castle or as archaeological booty for the British Museum in London.

High above the harbour, the **fortress** was built by the Knights of St John in the 15th century as a counterpart to their strongholds on the nearby islands of Kos and Rhodes. The towers were allotted to four nationalities—English, German, Italian and French, the latter serving as a dungeon with a torture chamber. But the pride of the castle is its museum of underwater archaeology and treasures salvaged from the region's shipwrecks and other sites. The hull of a two-masted ship which sank in 1025 has been reconstructed and put on display, along with jewellery and glassware recovered from a wreck in Serçe harbour south of Bodrum. Another hall is devoted to treasure found at a Bodrum construction site with the sarcophagus and skeleton of a Carian princess of the 4th century BC. Identified by scholars as Ada, stepmother to Alexander the Great, she was accompanied in death by three gold rings, two necklaces, two bracelets, a crown, and a mouse that got trapped in the sarcophagus.

Boat tours make a day trip, leaving Bodrum around 9 or 10 a.m., visiting marvellous beaches all the way to Karaincir, and returning at about 6 p.m. Or take a land trip, to Turgutreis, for example, with a small island offshore, famous worldwide for undersea exploration.

Marmaris

Only a few years ago, Marmaris was an insignificant, inaccessible fishing village. Today it is the "in" place for Turkey's rich and famous, and highly popular with affluent yachtsmen. Yet it remains unspoilt, for tourist development is restricted to a few luxurious holiday village enclaves.

It won't take you long to get to know Marmaris. The centre of activities is the harbour, where you'll find the shops, the restaurants, the market and the tourist office. Just behind the tourist office you can see a *menzilhane*—pony express station dating from Ottoman times. A plaque on the doorway states in Arabic that Sultan Suleiman built the *menzilhane* in 1545. Now you can buy your souvenirs in there; it is used as a shopping centre. That is about the only "sight" that Marmaris has to offer, unless you would like to walk along the waterfront to see the equestrian statue of Kemal Atatürk. Incidentally, if you shop for souvenirs in Marmaris, try to do it before or after the day-trippers from Rhodes are in town, when prices are higher. But you can always try out your haggling technique.

Around the market, the restaurant tables spill out into the street, shaded by bright awnings. The atmosphere is noisy and cheerful, and you're guaranteed a feast.

But most people come to Marmaris for the beaches, or to charter a yacht for cruises along the coast. The ancient site of **Knidos** at the tip of the Marmaris peninsula can be visited by boat on a day trip. This is also the best way to get out to more secluded beaches such as **Turunç** and **Kumlubük**. With more time and at more expense, you can arrange a cruise on the gulf of Gökova, between Marmaris and Bodrum. It really is a boatman's dream—uninhabited islands, plenty of fish, forested shorelines and sandy beaches.

Turquoise Coast

Ever a favourite with enterprising sailors, this romantically named region coincides roughly with the ancient kingdom of Lycia. Geography favoured its fiercely defended independence with the sheltering natural ramparts of jagged Baba, Ak and Bey peaks at the western end of the pine-clad Taurus mountains.

Fethiye, a busy market town, combines good beaches and other admirable tourist amenities with fascinating vestiges of its ancient past. It is built on the Lycian site of Telmessos. Its rock-cut tombs are immediately visible on the hillside behind the town, and stone sarcophagi dating from the 4th century BC lie scattered around. Fethiye was known by its Greek inhabitants as Makri until

they were replaced by Turks in the population exchange of 1923; along with the nearby ghost town of Kaya, it is the setting of Louis de Bernière's evocative novel *Birds without Wings*.

Earthquakes in 1856 and 1957 destroyed most of the town's historic buildings, but the bustling bazaar (Çarşi) area tucked away in the narrow streets behind Atatürk Boulevard has lost none of its traditional atmosphere. The Lycians buried their dead in tombs cut from the rock face on the hillside looming as backdrop to the bazaar. Some of the more modest are carved in the form of ancient Lycian dwellings with the stone imitating elements of the wooden structure such as doorposts and roof beams. Others, influenced by the progressive settlement of colonists from Greece, are miniature versions of Greek temples with Ionic-columned porticoes and pediments, all carved from the stone. The best known of these is the Amyntas Tomb, bearing the Greek inscription *Amyntou tou Ermagiou* (Amyntas, son of Hermagios), well worth the climb of 150 steps.

The municipality has assembled in the **Archaeological Museum** some interesting finds from nearby ancient sites. They include a gold leaf tiara from Pinara (3rd century BC) and, from the sanctuary of Letoön, a stone slab in-

Necropolis of Telmessos: a tomb carved out of the rock.

scribed in three languages. Just as the British Museum's trilingual Rosetta stone permitted the deciphering of Egyptian hieroglyphics, so the text here in Greek, Aramaean and Lycian has enabled scholars to begin unravelling the local language, one of the earliest known examples of Indo-European. The text pays tribute to Kaunos, divine king of Xanthos, the Lycian capital.

The ruins of the **Castle of the Knights of St John** are popularly traced back to a medieval fortress built by Crusaders, who had their main stronghold on the nearby island of Rhodes. Much of the masonry was clearly recycled from the city's Lycian and Greek era and later used, too, by Byzantine and Turkish forces before earthquakes rather than foreign invaders reduced it to its present state.

Some of the best examples of Lycian sarcophagi can be seen scattered along the harbour's quayside promenade. From here you can take cruises around the 12 islands in the bay, some of them including opportunities for swimming and picnics in quiet coves. The diving here is particularly good, with the chance of spotting dolphins, turtles and other marine creatures as well as underwater caves and even submerged Byzantine ruins—but don't disturb the antiquities.

Among the best are **Çaliş**, an extended crescent of sand and pebble beach, and **Günlükbaşı**, 5 km (3 miles) north of town. Both of these are accessible by road or boat.

Just 15 km (9 miles) south of Fethiye, and once known as Levissi, **Kaya** is now just a ghost town, a poignant legacy of age-old Greco-Turkish hostilities but also of an effort to salvage a modicum of mutual respect. Some 2,000 little houses stand abandoned on their hillside since 1923. That was when the Treaty of Lausanne ordered the departure of hundreds of thousands of Greeks whose families had lived for centuries in Istanbul, Izmir or other towns of Anatolia and simultaneously of Turks who had never known any home but Crete or Rhodes or Salonica. Elsewhere, Turkish "immigrants" occupied or rebuilt the Greek houses and transformed churches into mosques. Here, almost all the houses were left untouched. On what was once the main street, the dilapidated 19th-century Greek Orthodox church of Panayia Pirgiotissa preserves its marble altar screen and a mural of Christ and his apostles over the altar. Some of the houses have been restored as holiday villas. In the restaurant near the ruins there is a small private museum filled with household objects that would have been in use at the time of the population exchange.

The enormously popular resort of **Ölüdeniz** which features on all the tourist office posters is idyllically situated around a blue lagoon backed by a pine-forested hill. The sheltered waters, once a favoured haven for pirates, are delightfully warm from April to October. Indeed, Ölüdeniz owes its name, "Dead Sea", to the tranquillity of its lagoon.

You may also like to try a couple of good beaches outside the lagoon—**Kidrak** and **Butterfly Beach**.

The best buys

Amber or turquoise jewellery
Ceramics
Copper and brass samovars and
  coffee pots
Kilims
Leather goods
Rugs and carpets
Silk
Traditional instruments
Tins of *helva*
Turkish Delight
  (*loukoum*)

Huber/Huber

A half-hour drive from Dalaman airport, the westernmost of the Turquoise Coast beach resorts is famous as a nesting and hatching place for loggerhead turtles, from May to October. As a result, Istuzu beach, at the mouth of the Dalyan river, has become a bone of contention between conservationists and the tourist industry. The turtles are often confused by the night-time lighting of hotels and restaurants. After dark, the beach is off-limits to protect the baby turtles, threatened by birds of prey on their birthday race for the safety of the sea. The next day, you can see the tracks in the

The travel-poster beach of Ölü-deniz and its unruffled waters.

sand of the lucky ones, particularly in July and August.

From **Dalyan**, you can hire a boat for a cruise to the ruins of **Kaunos**, an important Carian city in 400 BC. It was on the border with Lycia, and the ruins reflect both cultures. The theatre is well preserved and you can also see remains of the acropolis, but most interesting are the Lycian tombs, carved high in the rock face. The trip to the ruins and back takes about three hours.

The coastal highway No. 400 runs inland east of Fethiye to the town of Kınık, 64 km (40 miles) away, from which it is a 20-minute walk to **Xanthos**, the ancient hilltop capital of Lycia. For its historic interest and the beauty of its position high above the lovely valley of the Eşen river, the archaeological site is one of the most impressive in southern Anatolia. Over the centuries, it suffered three disasters. Facing attack by the Persians in 546 BC and again by Brutus, Julius Caesar's assassin, in 42 BC, the citizens set fire to their homes and committed collective suicide rather than surrender. Nearly 19 centuries later, there was nobody left to stop the British traveller Charles Fellows from plundering the site of its antiquities and carrying them off to London's British Museum—a fate similar to that of the Elgin marbles from the Parthenon.

At the entrance, a **monumental gate** from the Hellenistic era is coupled with the 1st-century Arch of Vespasian. A uniquely Lycian structure in the Mediterranean world of classical antiquity is the remarkable series of **pillar-tombs**—vaulted sarcophagi mounted on columns—from the 4th century BC and earlier. Some of the reliefs from the temples and tombs are copies of those taken by Mr Fellows. On the Obelisk Tomb, an inscription in the Lycian language is still being deciphered. A Greek verse describes exploits of the deceased as warrior and wrestler.

The **theatre** is Roman. On the hill behind it, the Lycian **acropolis** includes a square structure believed to be the royal palace burned down during the Persian invasion.

Also known by its Turkish name of Gelemiş, the ancient port and modern beach resort of **Patara** due south of Xanthos is above all famous as the birthplace of Santa Claus. The 4th-century St Nicholas became Bishop of Myra, east along the coast at what is now Demre. When you squeeze them, some of the Santa Claus dolls in the souvenir shops say "Ho, ho, ho!" in Turkish. The ancient site has a stately triple-arched entrance (1st century) and equally well-preserved Roman theatre from the 2nd century, partially smothered in sand.

The amazing white sandy beach stretches either side of the river-mouth for a total length of 15 km (9 miles). Part of it is a turtle-nesting beach protected by conservationists, i.e. out of bounds to humans after dark. With high surf waves in July and August, the best family bathing may be in spring and autumn.

Kalkan, originally a Greek village named Kalamaki, is a rather chic resort that's a favourite both with yachtsmen using the marina and with ramblers, who go hiking in the splendid woodlands of the Taurus mountains. They all meet up in the harbourfront's first-class restaurants, bars and nightclubs. East of town at **Kaputaş** there is a small but popular pebble beach.

Morning is the time to enjoy the pristine tranquillity of the ancient port of **Kaş**, its gently curving bay set against dramatic cliffs, with sarcophagi half-concealed in the olive groves. Antiphellos of old, Andişi till 1923, the town has kept its old attractively balconied Greek houses. Kaş is now a boisterous resort with a colourful mixture of foreigners and Turkish bourgeoisie from Istanbul.

The shops, bars and restaurants of Uzunçarşı, the "Long Bazaar", stay open till very late. This is the prime place on the Turquoise Coast for purchasing gold and silver jewellery, ceramics, fine carpets and other craftware.

Remains of the ancient port city of **Antiphellos** are scattered around town. At the east end of the Uzunçarşı bazaar, the double-chambered Lycian Lion Tomb is a monumental affair with lions' heads on the vaulted lid of the sarcophagus. Up the hill on Yeni Yol you can see some rock-cut tombs.

On the west side of the city centre are the ruins of a Hellenistic temple and a theatre with 26 rows of seats, where the modern town sometimes stages wrestling matches.

The only alternatives to the hotels' swimming pools are the aptly named **Büyük Çakıl** (Large Gravelly) and **Küçük Çakıl** (Small Gravelly) beaches east of town, or the pebbles of **Kaputaş** to the west, shared with the neighbouring resort of Kalkan.

Some 30 km (18 miles) east of Kaş, the island of **Kekova** lies opposite the port of **Üçağiz**. On a boat trip around its shores and in the inlet separating it from the coast you can see some of Turkey's most enchantingly located ruins: stairways, street-paving, pillars, remains of house walls, stone sarcophagi of anonymous Lycian settlements, all submerged in the shallows. (If you are not staying in Üçağiz itself, cruises are available from Kaş or the port of Andriake, near Demre to the east.) For those excursions that give you time on Kekova itself, the island has a delightful sandy beach. And quite apart from the rare joy of seeing the ruins sunk beneath the waves, this stretch of creeks and coves along the Turquoise Coast is startlingly beautiful.

Demre, called Kale on the maps, is the modern Turkish town that has grown out of the venerable city of Myra of which Santa Claus, that is to say St Nicholas, was bishop in the 4th century. Besides visiting the bishop's church in the city centre, it is worth seeing the remains of the ancient Lycian site on the northern outskirts, and its nearby port of Andriake, a starting-point for sightseeing cruises to the sunken ruins off the island of Kekova.

The first church built on Müze Caddesi was an early Christian edifice of the 3rd century, preceding Nicholas's appointment as bishop. It was rebuilt in 1043 to shelter his tomb, and subsequent

Busy Santa. The image of St Nicholas as a gift-toting Father Christmas is a creation of the West. The Eastern Orthodox church honours him as a patron saint for bringing back to life three little boys chopped up and pickled in salt by a butcher during a terrible famine—among other miracles. The legend of his generosity tells how Nicholas secretly threw three bags of gold through the window of a poor man unable to provide a dowry for his three daughters, thus saving them from prostitution. A later version transformed the bags into three gold balls and Nicholas became the patron saint of pawnbrokers—as well as virgins, sailors, scholars, merchants and, of course, children.

miracles prompted his beatification and attracted hordes of pilgrims. The church has since undergone extensive renovation, notably by the bishop's namesake, Tsar Nicholas I, who erected a belfry and replaced the nave's cupola with a vaulted ceiling in 1862. Turkish architects added the more characteristic Byzantine domes over the narthex. Further restoration is underway, partially financed by the Ministry of Culture.

The mosaics inside the narthex depict Jesus with Mary and John the Baptist. A sarcophagus to the left of the church entrance is identified as the tomb of St Nicholas, despite its carving of a married couple. The grave was located beneath paving near the altar; Italian sailors and three priests stole the bones from it in 1087 and took them to Bari's Basilica San Nicola to cash in on the lucrative pilgrim business. Tradition relates Myra to the Greek word for myrrh, a fragrance said to have befuddled the robbers when they opened up the tomb. More authentic is the impressive 11th-century Byzantine bishop's throne standing in the apse.

A bronze statue of St Nicholas (2,000) by Russian sculptor Gregory Pototsky stands in a corner near the church; he originally occupied a high pedestal in the square, where he was replaced by

Hans Weber

Lycian tombs sculpted in the cliffs at Myra, in the 4th century BC.

a more controversial red-suited plastic model of Santa Claus by the town mayor in 2005.

The remains of the Lycian city of **Ancient Myra** are located on a rocky hillside just north of Demre. The centrepiece is a Greco-Roman theatre built against a cliff. Its huge orchestra is littered with stone carvings from the proscenium, including two theatre masks. In the cliffs is a remarkable series of rock-cut tombs. Carved reliefs in the burial chambers depict scenes of battle and funerary processions.

Andriake, Myra's ancient port, Çayağzi, is 5 km (3 miles) west of Demre. As a vital outlet for supplying corn to Rome and the empire, it stored the harvest in Hadrian's Granary, south of the Androkos river. The massive outer walls still stand as an enclosure for eight storage rooms, with stone busts of the emperor and his wife Sabina over the main gate. Andriake's major attraction is the charming beach of sand dunes running down from the cliffs. Local fishermen sometimes accept passengers.

Kemer is a fast-growing beach resort has well-equipped holiday villages and superb marina. It also serves as a good base for exploring nearby archaeological sites or rambles in the **Olympos Beydağları National Park**.

Combine a visit to the ancient site of **Termessos**, 34 km (21 miles) northwest of Antalya with a bracing walk around the rugged Mount Güllük national park.

The formidable citadel was built on a terrace-like plateau 1,050 m (3,450 ft) up the mountain. It distinguished itself in 333 BC by dissuading Alexander the Great's army, forcing him to make a diversion inland to join reinforcements in the north. From the Roman era, the Royal Road was the main highway into town, past massive defensive walls to solid greystone buildings—the gymnasium with bath houses for the athletes, the agora (market-place) and monumental mausoleum. The theatre shows off the drama of the city's mountain site, with seats for 4,200 spectators. On the other side of the agora, the odeon doubled as a smaller theatre and open-air parliament.

Of the nearby temples, four in all, the most impressive has six Corinthian columns still standing.

Antalya

Start at the rose-tinted fluted minaret, **Yivli Minare**, built in the 13th century by the Selçuk sultan Ala'eddin Keykubad. Its adjacent mosque and mausoleum, of a later date, stand on the foundations of a Byzantine church. The fluting is a characteristic feature of Selçuk architecture.

On the eastern edge of the old town, **Kaleiçi**, the monumental Hadrian's Gate has a triple-arched marble entrance flanked by massive square battlemented towers. It was erected for the emperor's entry into the town in AD 130. Remains of the harbour walls protecting the citadel are Hellenistic and Roman at their base, reinforced with medieval additions by the city's Byzantine, Selçuk and Crusader occupants. At the south end of the ramparts, **Hıdırlık Kulesi** watchtower is of Roman origin. It now looks down on the tea gardens of Karaali

Park, shaded by palm trees and other sub-tropical vegetation.

A few elegant if sometimes dilapidated—though progressively renovated—Ottoman houses line the narrow streets of the bazaar area running down to the harbour. Monuments here include **Kesik Minare**, the "Broken Minaret" of a mosque damaged by fire. The harbour itself is lined with popular cafés humming with life from early evening, as visitors and townspeople mingle for the daily promenade along the waterfront. The luxurious yachts are moored out on the modern marina along the jetty west of the old harbour.

At the western outskirts of town on the Konyaaltı highway to Kemer, the **Archaeological Museum** handsomely displays its treasures with clear, multilingual explanations. In the prehistoric section, Stone Age cooking utensils and other implements retrieved from the Karain caves north of Antalya are the earliest traces of human life in Turkey, over 10,000 years old. In the ongoing contest between Turkey and Italy for the genuine remains of Santa Claus, the museum displays a reliquary said to contain some bones of Saint Nicholas, Bishop of Myra.

The most popular beaches are gravel **Konyaaltı**, 3 km (2 miles) west of town, and fine-sand **Lara**,

Hans Weber

In **Termessos**, it is hard to see what is the work of nature and and what was made by man.

12 km (7 miles) east of Antalya. Near Lara, the Düden stream meets the Mediterranean at the **Düden Falls**.

Antalya to Alanya

Remains of **Perge**, an important Pamphylian trading centre are situated 18 km (11 miles) northeast of Antalya. Both Greek and Turkish scholars agree that Trojan war veterans may have settled the area, but the Greeks attribute the town's creation to other Greek colonists around 1000 BC, while

Turks suggest a settlement 500 years earlier by Hittites. Perge is an Indo-European Hittite word meaning "high place", referring to the acropolis of its original foundation on a hill at the north end of the excavated site.

The ancient sports and entertainment complex is on the southwest corner of the city, near the tour entrance. A splendid horseshoe-shaped stadium seated 12,000 spectators for its chariot and foot races. The biggest in Asia Minor, it measures 234 m (767 ft) by 34 m (111 ft). Between the arches and pillars of its grandstands, the ancients built shops, taverns and other concessions. Across the road is the theatre. Make your way to the top of the 14,000-seat auditorium—42 rows of seats—for a fine view over the ancient city.

The site reveals several layers of building—Seleucid Greek ramparts, Hellenistic and Roman city gates, Roman baths and Byzantine basilica. The main street stretches from the square agora, with a gutter running down the centre and what were colonnades of shops on either side.

Four unmissable archaeological sites. The remains of Anatolia's ancient cities benefit from magnificent natural settings. The Greco-Roman port city of **Phaselis** has three harbours on its green and pleasant promontory south of Kemer. Near Antalya, the horseshoe-shaped stadium at **Perge** and superb theatre at **Aspendos** are without their equal in Asia Minor. The distinctive quality of **Side** is the way its ancient monuments are integrated in the modern town.

Huber/Fantuz

Just 20 km (12 miles) east of Perge, the Pamphylian town of **Aspendos** boasts one of Anatolia's most superb ancient theatres, certainly the best preserved—thanks to its being used and renovated by Selçuk Turks as a medieval caravanserai. (Its turquoise ceramic tiling is displayed in the Antalya museum.) Built in AD 180 by the great Roman architect Zeno, the stage backdrop rises in two lofty storeys above the Köprü river valley. Rectangular doorways provided five stage entrances. The hemispheric auditorium for 15,000 spectators rises steeply in two tiers of 19 and then 20 rows of seating to an arcaded gallery at the top. It is used for modern arts festivals.

Take a look, too, at the acropolis on the hill above the theatre, with remains of a small temple, nyphaeum and basilica. Striding across the plain to the north is a series of two-tiered arches of the Roman aqueduct that once extended 15 km (9 miles) from the mountain streams to the city.

Unique among Pamphylia's archaeological sites, the old port city of **Side** is fully integrated into the 20th-century town. Its buildings, hotels, shops, banks, post office and government offices have been erected along streets previously used by the town's Greek, Roman and early Byzantine inhabitants. Sand has silted up the historic harbour, but it has also provided two fine beaches, on either side of the rocky peninsula on which the town is built— 74 km (46 miles) from Antalya.

The modern highway enters Side through the original main city gate, with a nearby nymphaeum fountain (2nd century) that was fed by the Roman aqueduct. The turreted ramparts were built in the Byzantine era. From the gate, two paved colonnaded streets lead into the ancient city, the shorter one due south to ruins of a Byzantine basilica and bishop's palace, half-hidden in the sand dunes. The other, longer main street runs southwest down the middle of the promontory to the square agora where the slave market was held. On the opposite side of the road are the Roman public baths, transformed to house a museum of Side's sculptures, notably of Hercules and Hermes, and sarcophagi with carved reliefs of Eros. Many of the statues were decapitated by early Christian iconoclasts.

Immediately to the south of the museum, Emperor Vespasian's triumphal arch and fountains (1st century) lead into the modern town—and the entrance to the great theatre. The biggest in Pamphylia, it enjoys a spectacular location overlooking the two bays on either side of the promontory. Unlike other theatres in the region, the free-standing edifice is built on an infrastructure of arches and vaults once sheltering shops and living quarters for gladiators and wild beasts.

Alanya

The town's landmark castle looms on the horizon of its rocky promontory, rising beyond long green banana plantations. The Byzantines called the promontory Kalonoros, "beautiful mountain". In 1221, its Selçuk conqueror Ala'eddin Keykubad renamed it after himself, Ala'iya, and Atatürk, as part of his reforms, replaced the glottal Arabic sound in the middle with a more European "n" — Alanya.

As a tourist centre, this is a true boomtown, with modern resort complexes mushrooming along the beaches that extend either side of the promontory. But the place also has a strong characteristic Turkish atmosphere, derived from both the citadel's Selçuk and Ottoman monuments and houses and the traditional restaurants and cafés. This, along with the mild winter, makes it particularly pleasant out of season, too, when the Turks recapture their town from the visitors.

The old Selçuk and Ottoman **harbour** is on the east side of the promontory, making a delightful promenade among the seafood restaurants and old monuments. It is dominated by the massive **Kızıl Kule** (Red Tower), 35 m (115 ft) high, built by Ala'eddin Keykubad in 1226 as kingpin of the harbour's defences against perennial attacks from pirates. Today housing a small folklore museum, the octagonal redbrick tower still seems to protect the old wooden houses hugging the slope above.

Further along the waterfront are the **Tersane**, the workshops of the Selçuk shipyard, and a smaller tower, **Tophane**, that served as an arsenal.

Sprawling across the "beautiful mountain", the ramparts of **Alanya Castle** enclose in a citadel what was the whole medieval and Ottoman town. Beyond the main gate, with its Persian inscription, is the self-contained village of **Ehmediye** with Ottoman houses, a derelict 16th-century mosque and an older Selçuk mausoleum.

Past a lighthouse (1720), the winding road ends at the castle proper, **Iç Kale** (inner fortress), with an abandoned Byzantine church opposite the old bazaar. The view from the highest point, 260 m (853 ft) above sea level, looks out west along the Mediterranean and inland to the Ak Dağ range in the Taurus mountains.

Across the street from the Tourist Information Office, in the modern part of town, is a collection of local archaeological finds. The **Alanya Museum** also presents a typical Ottoman domestic interior, with fine furnishings and carved wood ceiling and shutters. Take a look, too, at the pleasant garden, once an Ottoman graveyard.

One of Alanya's more delightful attractions is the chance to dine while dabbling your feet in the refreshing waters of the **Dim Çayı** river. Just 6 km (4 miles) east of the city centre, riverside restaurants set up their tables in the shallows—most enjoyable if you walk all the way.

Around Alanya

Sandy beaches stretch for miles along the coast on either side of the old town, many taken over by hotels and beach clubs. The crowds dwindle as you approach Incekum (Fine Sand) beach at **Avsallar**, to the west.

As its name gently understates, **Damlataş** (Cave of Dripping Stones) has some impressive stalagmites and stalactites. (It is signposted close to Alanya Museum.) **Cleopatra's Beach**—one of many attributed to the Egyptian queen along the Cilician coast—can be reached from here on foot. Other caves, among the rocks on the western end of the promontory,

Old and new live together harmoniously in Alanya. | Stalactites in the Cave of Dripping Stones (Damlataş).

Huber/Schmid

Allie Caulfield

are best visited on a boat cruise—**Aşıklar** (Lovers' Cave), **Fosforlu** (Phosphorescent Cave) and **Korsanlar** (Pirates' Cave).

The coast east of Alanya is appreciated mainly for its isolated beaches, secluded coves or the occasional stretch of fine sand, with a backdrop of dense pine forests for rambles into the interior. The unruffled little town of **Gazipaşa** has fresh seafood, a pleasant beach and the disparate ruins of ancient Selinus.

Anamur

The town offers a handsome castle, a charming little harbour (Iskele) for waterfront dining and good beach hotels. Some 6 km (4 miles) to the west is the ancient Roman site of **Anamurium** with remains of an impressive two-storey bath house, assembly hall, theatre and vaulted houses. Outside the walls are an aqueduct, necropolis and the empty shells of three Byzantine chapels.

Silifke

Founded in the 3rd century BC by Seleucus I Nicator, a general of Alexander the Great, this was one of many cities to be named after him, Seleucia. As antiquities, the sleepy modern town boasts only the remnant of a temple of Jupiter (2nd century), the Roman bridge over its Göksu Nehri (Blue Waters) river, and a hilltop Byzantine castle—worth the climb for the view. With the road approaching the Syrian border, the cuisine here has more Arabian spice to it.

Uzuncaburç

The 45-minute drive north from Silifke passes grandiose countryside through a rugged gorge in the Taurus mountains, with glimpses amid the olive trees of Roman temple-like tombs, single and double-storeyed. Uzuncaburç takes its name—High Tower—from the 22-m (72-ft) structure that was part of the fortifications for the excavated Greek city of Olba. Known to the Romans as Diocaesarea, it stands on the site of an earlier Hittite settlement, but all the remains are Greco-Roman. The theatre is Roman, as is the monumental five-columned gateway leading into the ancient city.

Built in the 3rd century BC, the Hellenistic **Temple of Zeus Olbios** was one of the first temples to use the florid Corinthian order for its capitals—four remain here on the 30 surviving columns. The Roman system of water supply still feeds the modern city of Uzuncaburç.

Kızkalesi

This agreeable little resort, 25 km (15 miles) east of Silifke, thrives on its seafood restaurants, good hotels, decent beach and fanciful legends surrounding its two castles. The name, meaning Maiden's Castle, refers to the 13th-century pile out on the island, a stone's throw from the shore. An Armenian king is said to have put his daughter out there to protect her from a prophesied lethal snakebite. But the snake turned up in any case, hidden in a basket of fruit sent by a well-meaning servant—and did its stuff. The castle on land is a more sturdy ruin, interesting mainly for its use of ancient masonry with Greek inscriptions on the main entrance and a complete Roman gate built into the west wall.

Mersin

The large modern port is a departure point for the ferries to Famagusta (Gazimagusa to the Turks), in Northern Cyprus. If you are there, take advantage of the good sea food, reputed as the best and cheapest of all Mediterranean Turkey.

Tarsus

Little remains to commemorate its ancient fame as place of the first meeting of Antony and Cleopatra, leading to their romantic and political alliance, and as birthplace of the apostle Paul. Signposts guide pilgrims to St Paul's Well, a water source still functioning in the garden of the

Allie Caulfield

The castle of Kızkalesi surrounded by blue sky and blue sea.

house where he is said to have been born. The 16th-century mosque, Ulu Cami, stands on the site of St Paul's cathedral. A Roman gate has been named Cleopatra's Gate—in Turkish, **Kancık Kapısı** (Gate of the Bitch). The Queen of Egypt sailed into town on the Tarsus—then Cydnus—river in 41 BC.

In those days, a lagoon, now silted up, made Tarsus one of Asia Minor's most important trading ports. Paul, born Saul, son of a tent-maker, was justly proud of the ancient city now buried beneath the modern town—"I am a Jew of Tarsus, a city in Cilicia, a citizen of no mean city."

Adana

With a population of more than 1.5 million, Turkey's fifth-largest town (after Istanbul, Ankara, Izmir and Bursa) is a resolutely modern place since it was rebuilt by a French colonial administration after World War I. It thrives on a textile industry that draws much of its raw material from surrounding cotton plantations. Across the Seyhan river, the 14-arch Roman bridge built by Emperor Hadrian is rare testimony to the city's ancient origins—it was a constant bone of contention between Persians and the Greeks and Romans.

The **Archaeological Museum** contains some fine prehistoric ceramics, a few Hittite artefacts and some Hellenistic and Roman sculpture. The Syrian-style white and black marble **Ulu Cami** was built in 1507 by Emir Halil Bey, whose tomb there is decorated with mosaics and ceramic tiles.

Antakya

The Mediterranean coast turns south at Dörtyol, close to the battlefield of Issus, where Alexander the Great won a decisive victory over Persia's king Darius III in 333 BC. Nearby **Iskenderun** is the nondescript industrial centre and port built over Alexandretta, the first of the Macedonian conqueror's many commemorative cities. The Hatay region, of which Antakya is capital, is an Arab enclave given to Syria after World War I. The French handed it over to Turkey in 1939 and it has been a frequent object of dispute.

The atmosphere of the town (often signposted as Hatay) is distinctly Arabic, in cuisine, architecture and the relaxed pace of life. A strong Christian minority reminds us that for the apostle Peter, ancient Antioch was the most important Christian community outside Jerusalem. As capital of Roman Syria, it rivalled Rome and Alexandria in luxury and sin. The **Archaeological Museum** illustrates the fact with a collection of startlingly well-preserved mosaics from Roman villas. They depict, beside the usual heroics of mythology, some eye-opening scenes of opulence and debauchery. In the more sedate and virtuous modern town, there is considerable colour in the bazaar around Kemal Pafla Caddesi north of the ancient Rana Köprüsü Bridge.

On the northern outskirts of town is St Peter's grotto church, **Sen Piyer Kilisesi**, where the apostle is believed to have preached around the year 50. The 12th-century façade was added by Crusaders.

PRACTICAL INFORMATION

Banks. Open 8.30–noon and 1.30–5.30 p.m. in touristic areas.

Climate. The weather is at its mildest in spring and autumn. Summers are hot and stuffy, winters cool and rainy. From April to August, the average temperature in Istanbul at noon is between 12 and 23 ºC, and in autumn around 20ºC.

Currency. The Turkish lira (*Türk Lirası* – TL) is divided into 100 *kuruş* (kr). Coins range from 1 to 50 kr and 1 TL, banknotes from 5 to 200 TL.

Electricity. All the plugs have two round prongs; the current is 220 V 50 Hz.

Emergencies. To call the police dial 155, the ambulance 112, the fire brigade 110. Your consulate will help you in case of a serious problem, such as losing your passport, but they cannot provide funds if your money is lost or stolen.

Museums and archaeological sites. Generally closed on Monday.

Post office. Main branches usually open 8.30 a.m.–12.30 p.m. and 1.30–5.30 p.m.

Safety. Leave anything of value in the hotel safe. Do not tempt fate by keeping your wallet in a back pocket or an open bag. Be wary of pickpockts in bazaars and street markets.

Shops. Open all day 8 or 8.30 a.m.–7 or 8 p.m., later in the bazaars. Sunday is closing day, but many shops stay open.

Time. Turkey follows UTC/GMT +2 from November to March, and UTC/GMT +3 from April to October.

Tipping. Service is included in hotel and restaurant bills, but you can always add a little extra.

Toilets. Many public toilets are the "hole in the ground" kind, but in hotels and restaurants they are generally the modern European sort. There might not be any toilet paper (or it may be distributed piece by piece in exchange for a tip) so keep some in your bag just in case. Leave it in the bin next to the toilet if one is provided (sometimes the pipes are too narrow to dispose of paper).

the sweet life

SIGHTSEEING

religious fervour

Aphrodite's island

seafood

CYPRUS

At the crossroads of Europe, Asia and Africa, Cyprus is the third-largest island of the Mediterranean after Sicily and Sardinia—the isle of Aphrodite, goddess of Beauty and Love. Little wonder that so many men have come under her spell. Cyprus will please you, whether you like exploring ancient ruins, dancing in clubs, admiring icons, spotting rare orchids or spouting poetry by the pool where Aphrodite bathed. This "perfumed isle" is certainly the place for an idyll. But beware—Aphrodite ensnares the hearts of all who come to stay.

Nicosia

It needed 10,000 Cypriots and three years to construct the thick wall that still encircles the heart of Nicosia (Lefkosia in Greek). Once inside the walls, make for **Eleftheria Square**, the hub of the city. Architect Zaha Hadid has planned a modern redesign of the square.

Close by is **Laiki Yitonia**, the "Popular Neighbourhood" revived in 1984 to recreate the atmosphere of old Nicosia—the first stage in a plan to renovate hundreds of 19th-century buildings. Some of the houses are restored, others specially constructed in the old style, with whitewashed walls and roofs of round red tiles; the little bou-tiques and artisans' galleries are a delight. You'll find an office of the Cyprus Tourism Organization here, too. The **Leventis Museum**, housed in a handsome neoclassical house on Hippocrates Street, illustrates Nicosian life from antiquity to the present day.

Join the throngs of shoppers and bargain-hunters in **Ledra Street**, leading northeast from the square—and don't be afraid to explore the fascinating network of alleys and narrow streets snaking off to both sides.

Ledra Street takes you to **Ayia Phaneromeni**, the largest of the city's surviving churches, built in 1872 with stones from an old castle and monastery. The arch-bishop and bishops killed by the

A sculpted pillar holding up the roof of the Ethnographic Museum.

Turks in 1821 are buried here. Nearby is a library with a display of icons.

In Arkhiepiskopos Kyprianos Square, the **Archbishop's Palace** is closed to visitors though you may admire its façade, a pretty pastel pastiche of Venetian architecture dating from 1956. Do not miss the **Byzantine Museum** in one of the palace wings, displaying a unique collection of icons salvaged from churches all over the island. The oldest icon, and perhaps the most moving, is the simple 9th-century painting of the Virgin Mary.

Next door is **St John's Cathedral**, built around 1660 in Late Gothic style on the site of a Benedictine Abbey. A series of frescoes inside depicts events of Cypriot religious history.

The adjacent monastery building has been transformed into the **Folk Art Museum**, where you can gain some insight on traditional designs of pottery, woodcarvings, painting, lace and embroidery, and admire the magnificent hand-woven and embroidered costumes for men and women.

Nearby is the **Museum of the National Struggle**, which documents, through weapons and photographs, the rebellion against the British rulers in the 1950s.

As you explore the maze of streets around the square, look particularly for the **House of Hadjigeorgakis Kornessios**, 18 Patriarch Gregorios Street, recognizable by its arched Gothic doorway and overhanging balcony in Turkish style.

For a close-up inspection of the ramparts, head for the Cultural Centre incorporated into **Famagusta Gate**, one of the three Venetian entrances into the city. Modern art exhibitions are held here, as well as concerts.

The city outside the walls, largely concrete and lacking in charm, nevertheless offers sophisticated shopping and dining opportunities.

Just south of Paphos Gate you'll find the **Cyprus Museum**, displaying archaeological finds from the Neolithic to Byzantine periods—tombs, gold objects, red-glazed pottery and beautiful archaic and classical statues. See especially the group of terracotta statues excavated from Ayia Irini in northwest Cyprus: only two female figurines were discovered among 2,000 warriors, minotaurs and charioteers.

South of town is the **Handicrafts Centre** on Athalassa Avenue. Founded in 1980, it was intended to provide refugees from northern Cyprus with a source of income. Here you'll find the best the island can offer in traditional embroidery, pottery, woodcarving, weaving and leatherwork.

The most popular border crossing to the **Turkish Quarter**, which the Turks call Lefkosa, is on Marcos Drakos Avenue, next to the former Ledra Palace Hotel. You can cross here on foot or on a bicycle. The crossing at Agios Dometios can be used by vehicles, pedestrians and cyclists. Upon presentation of your passport you'll be given a visa. You can take a hired car across but you will need to buy insurance at the crossing.

Selimiye Mosque, despite its name and soaring minarets, was originally a French Gothic cathedral, begun in 1209 under the first Latin archbishop and consecrated in 1326. The Lusignan princes were crowned kings of Cyprus here.

Next door is the **bedestan**, a now-disused covered market dating from the 12th–14th centuries when it was built as the church of St Nicholas of the English. See the carved Gothic doors, family crests and religious sculptures above the main portal.

Mevlevi Tekke, a many-domed 17th-century monastery once inhabited by whirling dervishes, was outlawed in 1925. It now houses a museum devoted to the Turkish Cypriot traditions of music and costume.

Along the Coast

Since the island was divided, the furthest you can travel along the east coast is the Cape Greco area, to the up-and-coming resort of **Paralimni**. The region is renowned for its luminosity, the beaches of Protaras and Fig Tree Bay, its charming rocky coves and tiny villages.

Not too long ago, **Ayia Napa** was a quiet little fishing village flanked by stretches of empty, golden sands. Since the partition of the island it has boomed as a holiday resort, modern hotels spreading ever further along the coast. The village is rapidly succumbing to an insidious encroachment of touristy tavernas

The cloisters of the Monastery of Ayia Napa.

Claude Hervé-Bazin

and noisy discotheques, pubs and clubs, souvenir shops and water parks.

The Venetians built the **Monastery of Ayia Napa** (Our Lady of the Forest)—still well preserved, though the conifers that originally surrounded it have gone. The Gothic cloister is a wonderful place for quiet meditation. Beneath a dome supported by four pillars is an octagonal marble fountain, its basin carved with garlands of vine leaves and human faces. The monastery church, hewn out of the rock, lies

partially underground. From the small chapel, go down the steps to ancient sycamores, said to be six centuries old, affording a spectacular view of the sea.

The **Marine Life Museum** consists essentially of the private natural history collection of George Tornaritis. In the basement of the modern town hall, it comprises a small display of shells, corals and stuffed animals. A highlight is the exhibit of marine fossils, up to 220 million years old, shown in a reconstruction of the sea bed.

Larnaca

This attractive holiday town, on the site of the ancient city-kingdom of Kition, is the oldest city on Cyprus, occupied as far back as the 2nd millennium BC and mentioned in the Old Testament. It grew in importance under the Lusignans and became a commercial and shipping centre.

Life in Larnaca revolves around the breezy **Palm Tree Boulevard** stretching from the modern marina along the sea front. Walk along as far as the **Turkish Fort**, built in 1625 and now used as a museum. More interesting is the view of the harbour from the upstairs terrace. Opposite the fort is the **Grand Mosque**, restored and open for prayer.

A few streets inland stands the **Church of St Lazarus**. After his resurrection, Lazarus is believed to have sailed to Larnaca, where he became a bishop. A tomb was discovered in 890 with the inscription *Lazarus, friend of Christ,* and the Byzantine emperor Leon VI had the church built over it—albeit removing the relics of Lazarus to Constantinople. With three Romanesque naves and three Byzantine domes, the church was restored in the 17th century. It contains a dazzling collection of icons portraying, among other subjects, the life of Lazarus.

Near the marina is the tourist office, and just around the corner you'll find the **Pierides Museum.** In the 19th century, the Swedish honorary consul Demetrios Pierides amassed this collection of thousands of archaeological artefacts from the Neolithic to Byzantine periods—sculpted pottery, terracotta figurines, ceramics and a fine selection of Roman glassware.

Towards the airport, just out of town, a **salt lake** glistens like snow in summer. It's the haunt of pink flamingos in autumn. The annual harvest of salt is carted away in baskets on donkey-back, for use in cheese-making and to preserve olives.

Surrounded by palms, cypress, eucalyptus and lemon trees, the sparkling white **Hala Sultan Tekke,** a revered Muslim shrine, overlooks the salt flats. It was built in 1816 by the Turks in honour of a pious lady, a friend of the Prophet Mohammed, Umm Haram, who came to Cyprus with a party of Arab invaders in AD 649, fell from her mule near the Salt Lake and broke her neck—exactly as had been revealed to the Prophet in a dream. She was buried on the spot. If you want to see inside the shrine, you must leave your shoes at the door.

Kiti, a few miles further west, is worth a visit for its famous church, Panayia Angeloktistos— "built by the angels" who lent a helping hand to the workmen during the night. The only remaining feature of the original 6th–7th century church (rebuilt in the 11th century) is the breathtaking mosaic of the Virgin Mary and child in the apse.

Limassol

Miles of sandy beach, high-rise hotels, bright lights and snack bars are the hallmarks of Limassol. A merry resort, even more so in September during the wine festival—for the city is also the island's main wine and spirits production and sales centre.

Most of the old city disappeared through earthquake and invasion. One of the rare survivors is the **castle** near the port, a 13th-century redoubt strengthened by the Lusignans and the Venetians. Inside is a medieval museum with a collection of tombstones and weapons. The modern **Limassol Museum** in Byron Street behind the public gardens has a more interesting array of archaeological treasures: ancient stone tools, relics of the Bronze and Iron ages, pottery and Greek and Roman coins and jewellery. And another Aphrodite—just her head, found in Kourion.

South of Limassol, the **Akrotiri Peninsula** has its own salt lake, also colonized by pink flamingos from October to March. Standing squarely on the west side of the peninsula, **Kolossi Castle** was built in the 15th century by the knights of St John. From here they governed vast estates of sugar cane and vineyards producing Commandaria, a red dessert wine.

Kourion (Curium)

Just outside Episkopi, on the main road to Paphos, lie the fascinating remains of an ancient city founded as far back perhaps as the 14th century BC. Excavations were begun here in 1876, revealing an unsuspected treasury of gold and silver jewellery, subsequently sold to the Metropolitan Museum of Art in New York, much to the displeasure of the Cypriots.

As you turn into the old city at the top of a 90-m (300-ft) cliff, take time to admire the fabulous view over the sea. There's much

On the menu
Barbounia – red mullet
Kleftiko – spit-roast lamb
Kotopoulo – roast chicken
Sheftalia – spicy meat balls
Sinagrida – red snapper
Souvlakia – spit-roast skewered cubes of meat served in a warm pitta pocket
Stifado – stew of tender beef or veal
Xifias – swordfish

of interest in Kourion (the Romans called it Curium) but you'll find it easier to appreciate if you collect a map of the site at the main entrance gate.

The first remains you come to are all that is left of the early Christian **basilica**, with a scattering of broken columns and capitals. Further along the road is the restored Roman **theatre**, spectacularly sited on the edge of the bluff. It seated 3,500 spectators for lion-and-tiger extravaganzas and still serves for occasional open-air shows.

Behind the theatre you'll see the remains of a Roman mansion of the early 5th century, the **Villa of Eustolios**, adorned with beautiful mosaic floors with bird and fish designs. Go back to the main road and drive half a mile to the U-shaped sports stadium, partly reconstructed. Further still, the

Sanctuary of Apollo Hylates (God of the Woodland) nestles in a pine grove. The buildings date from around the year 100. A processional avenue led pilgrims to the ceremonial stairway in front of the **Temple of Apollo**. Some of its columns and part of the pediment have been reconstructed to the way they must have been before the earthquake of 365 toppled them.

Leaving Kourion, take the winding cliffside road towards Paphos. Don't miss **Petra tou Romiou**, where a group of large rocks marks the spot where the islanders have always believed that the love-goddess Aphrodite rose from the depths.

Discreetly hidden away behind the curve of a hill is a tourist pavilion well stocked with refreshments.

Paphos

This small port is another favourite holiday resort, with the advantages of both scenery and antique sites.

Coming from Limassol, you'll first reach **Palea Paphos**, now Kouklia. Don't expect too much. There's little trace of Aphrodite here; her sanctuary has not been completely uncovered. Some minor finds are displayed in the museum housed in the nearby Château de Covocle; most of the objects are now in Nicosia.

Claude Hervé-Bazin

The Bay of Aphrodite, where the goddess appeared from the sea.

Two miles before Paphos, **Yeroskipos** served as a halting place for worshippers of Aphrodite on their way to her temple. The small five-domed basilica in the centre of town, **Ayia Paraskevi**, has a series of 15th-century murals. The **Museum of Folk Art** in a restored 18th-century stone house contains some unusual exhibits such as gourds that kept children afloat when they learned to swim.

In Paphos itself, the hilltop district of **Ktima** is an inviting, modern place with public buildings in neoclassical style, plenty of greenery and a good market. The **Paphos District Museum** displays finds from nearby excavations and sites such as the House of Dionysos. There's a lovely Greco-Roman Aphrodite, salvaged from the sea.

In Kato Paphos you'll see **St Paul's Pillar**, where St Paul was supposedly tied and lashed 39 times for preaching the Gospel—before he succeeded in converting the governor, Sergius Paulus, to Christianity. In fact the marble was imported 300 years later and used to make one of the columns that supported a 4th-century basilica, destroyed in AD 653.

More ancient remains lie to the west of Apostolos Pavlos Avenue. The owner of the **House of Dionysos**, a 3rd-century Roman villa of more than 20 rooms round an atrium, must have been fond of wine, for it's the main theme of the mosaic floors, together with landscapes and scenes of the hunt. The **House of Theseus**, southwest past the meteorological station, also has fine mosaics, including Theseus slaying the Minotaur. This once-palatial dwelling is thought to have been the residence of the Roman proconsuls. More to the north, the **Odeon** is a partial reconstruction of the original Roman theatre destroyed by earthquake. The **Old Fort**, at the elbow of the harbour jetty, offers a superb view.

The necropolis of the ancient city, known as the **Tombs of the Kings**, is located off the road to Coral Bay, a cliff-top holiday village where the sand is tinged with pink. Though no kings were buried here, the unpretentious chambers hewn from the rock below ground level are majestic in their simplicity.

The best buys
Brass candlesticks and trays
Copper pots, dishes and jugs
Embroidery from Lefkara
Jugs for wine or oil
Pottery
Terracotta figurines
Wooden objects

Claude Hervé-Bazin

PRACTICAL INFORMATION

Banks. Open 8.30 a.m.–12.30 p.m. for normal transactions and on Mondays also 3.15–4.45 p.m., but also often 4–6 p.m. for currency exchange.

Clothing. Light and loose-fitting cotton clothes are best for summer, with a sweater or jacket for the evenings, which can be cool. Women must cover their shoulders and knees for visiting churches and monasteries.

Currency. In the Republic of Cyprus the Euro(€), divided into 100 *lepta*. In the northern part, the Turkish *lira*.

Electricity. The current is 240 V AC, 50 Hz. Plugs are generally the British type, with three flat prongs. The big hotels are equipped with two-pin sockets with 220 and 110 volts for electric shavers.

Emergencies. Most problems can be resolved at the hotel reception desk. To call the police, ambulance or fire brigade dial 112. In case of serious problems, for instance if you lose your passport or travel tickets, contact your consulate.

Entry formalities. Residents of the EU can enter the Republic of Cyprus with an identity card (with photo) or a valid passport. To visit the Turkish Republic of Northern Cyprus you must have a valid passport, and you will be given a visa when you go through the checkpoint.

Language. Many people speak English, and road signs are usually bilingual. Spelling of Greek words transliterated into the Roman alphabet varies: you will see Agios and Ayios, Paphos and Pafos, Chora and Hora, for instance. But the pronunciation is the same.

Museums and archaeological sites. Opening times are variable; closing days are Sunday, sometimes also Saturday or Monday.

Shops. In touristic areas, shops generally open late in the evenings as well as on Sundays. Elsewhere, they close Monday, Tuesday, Thursday and Friday at 7.30 p.m. (from April to October at 8 p.m., on Wednesdays at 3 p.m and on Saturdays at 7 or 7.30 p.m., depending on the season. In summer, they close for the siesta from 2 to 5 p.m.

Tipping. Customs in this domain are more European than Middle-Eastern. Service is always included in restaurants and hotels, but you can add a little extra if you are satisfied.

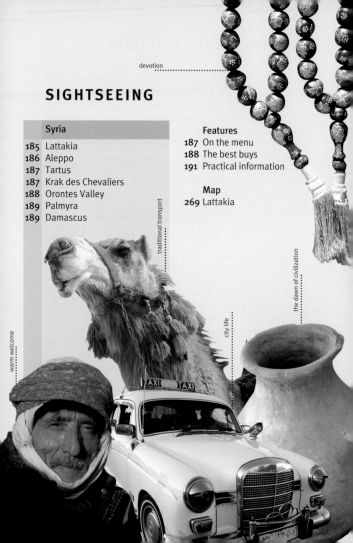

devotion

SIGHTSEEING

traditional transport

the dawn of civilization

city life

warm welcome

TAXI TAXI

SYRIA

Syria saw the discovery of the secrets of agriculture and of metallurgy, the invention of the first alphabet, and the birth of fabulous cities. In more recent times the country has continued to accomplish grand schemes, such as the great Euphrates dam, indispensable to its agriculture and industry. If they are undeniably proud of their achievements, Syrians never boast of them, tending to behave with dignity and reflection, occasionally unbending and allowing a tenuous smile to escape.

After the uprisings in Tunisia, Libya and Egypt in 2010–11, street protests by opponents of the Assad regime broke out in Syria. Rebellion spread to large parts of the country. While the conflict continues, it is not advisable to visit the country.

Lattakia

The activity at the port of Lattakia, one of the lungs of the country, reflects the effervescence of an expanding city (370,000 inhabitants). In 1920, the French detached Lebanon from historical Syria and reduced the Syrian coastline to a simple window onto the sea, thus depriving the new State of the ports of Beyrouth and Tripoli. Lattakia took over as the most dynamic port city of modern Syria.

A few vestiges dating from the Roman occupation are worth a detour. To the south, 500 m (550 yd) from the Moghrabi Mosque, four columns with Corinthian capitals survive from a **Roman colonnade**. A little further on, you will see a tetrapyle, a gateway with four bays, erected during the reign of Septimus Severus (193–211). It marked the crossing of two thoroughfares, *cardo maximus* and *decumanus*, which formed the skeleton of the Roman city.

However, the main attraction of Lattakia, at least for the tourist, resides in the beautiful beaches to the north. **Shatt al-Azraq**, a small Syrian "Riviera", is the most fashionable and well-maintained beach along the coast. From there, you can make a detour to see the cape of **Ras Shamra**, less for its innate interest—the ruins are fairly nebulous—than for the reminders of ancient Ugarit. This was one of the most prestigious of Phoenician cities, the place where the model for all alphabets was invented. (The best archaeological finds are displayed in the national museums at Aleppo and Damascus.)

Aleppo

This town is the metropolis of northern Syria, 340 km (212 miles) northwest of Palmyra by way of Homs. The ancient city, described in the Mari archives as the capital of a powerful state, lost its importance at the time of the Hittite invasions in the 17th century BC. Aleppo has suffered several major earthquakes, half the population perished in that of 1822. The **National Museum** houses finds from the sites of Ugarit, Mari (one of the oldest cities in the world) and Ebla. Its entrance is guarded by impressive basalt **statues** from the temple at Tell Halaf, a 9th-century BC settlement in the northeast of Syria.

The town's other curiosities are all to be found within the city walls, an area protected as a UNESCO World Heritage site. Your first priority has to be a visit to the famous covered **souks** (closed on Wednesdays), forming a true town within a town. Day-light enters only through openings in the vaulted ceilings which cover this amazing Ali Baba's cave where you could easily spend a whole day looking around. Inside are the old warehouses of the European merchants, the khans or caravanserais, including **Khan al-Wazir** (the Khan of the Minister) which has an interesting doorway. On the interior wall, the observant will pick out a detail which says much about the religious history of Aleppo: the window to the left of the porch is adorned with a cross, the work of a Christian artist, while that on the right is of Muslim design.

North of the souks, the **Great Mosque** (Jami'a Zakariyyeh, the Mosque of Zachariah) goes back to the beginnings of Islam. East of the souks is the mighty **citadel** surrounded by a moat. The throne room above the entrance has been restored but the rest is mostly in ruins.

The area around Aleppo has many sites, more or less well-preserved, known as the **Dead Towns**. Access is difficult and requires time. Try to see the **Basilica of Saint Simeon** (Qalaat Samaan), built in the 5th century and in particularly good condition. It marks the exact spot where stood the pillar on which St Simeon Stylites, the first pillar-hermit, spent thirty years of his life. People came from far and wide to hear the words of wisdom of this ascetic, who refused categorically ever to speak to a woman!

Tartus

To the south, there's another string of beaches along the 90 km (56 miles) between Lattakia and Tartus. Christianity was established early in this region, where pilgrims came to venerate an icon of the Virgin. The Crusaders took Tartus in 1102 and it became a virtually impregnable stronghold of the Knights Templar.

The Romano-Gothic **cathedral**, built at the end of the 12th and beginning of the 13th centuries, looks as though it could withstand quite an onslaught, like every other building constructed by the Franks. At the time of the Muslim reconquest it was inevitably transformed into a mosque, a practice that had the advantage of saving the building from destruction. Inside, one of the doors is thought to be that of the 4th-century Byzantine chapel which once held the famous icon of the Virgin: it was cut through the block of stone that lodges the base of the central pillar of the left colonnade. Today, the building is a museum of antiquities and ethnography.

The **Fortress of the Knights Templar**, in one corner of the surrounding wall, dates from the same era as the cathedral. Its remains are, however, swamped by modern urban buildings.

Krak des Chevaliers

the ultimate blueprint for childhood sand castles is to be seen 75 km (47 miles) southeast of Tartus. A UNESCO World Heritage Site, the **Krak des Chevaliers** (Qal'at al-Hosn) was completed in the 13th century and is regarded as a model of perfection in medieval fortification. Its name derives from the Syrian *karak*, "fortress". Like the castles at Moab and Montreal in Jordan,

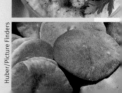

istockphoto/Angelafoto

Huber/Picture Finders

On the menu

Hummus – mashed chickpeas with sesame seed oil, lemon and garlic

Kebbeh – minced lamb meatballs with cracked wheat

Rikak bil djibne – fresh cheese pasty

Sambousik bil lahme – meat rissoles

this krak completed the northern part of the double line of defence of the Latin States of the East. Implanted high on the eastern slope of Jebel an-Nusayriyah, it allowed the surveillance of the Homs Gap, and could prevent Muslim access to the coast.

The best buys

Aleppo soap
Blown glass
Brocade
Copper trays with gold or silver inlay
Dried apricots
Embroidered tablecloths
Marquetry
Pottery

istockphoto.com/Housden

istockphoto.com/Ozarslan

Confided to the Knights Hospitaller in 1142, it finally fell to the Mameluk army of Sultan Al-Zaher Bibars in 1271.

Of the first stronghold built before 1170, the most striking feature is the gallery, 120 m (394 ft) long, which must have served to accommodate part of the garrison. The second and third surrounding walls, built between the end of the 12th century and 1271, encompass the **great hall**, where the knights assembled, and the three mighty towers of the redoubt, the central tower being the **keep**. The Arab additions, built after the victory of Bibars, include a **square tower** on the south side flanked by two semicircular buildings in the angles.

Lawrence of Arabia, who led the great Arab revolt in 1918, wrote a thesis on the Frankish fortresses, illustrated with sketches and photographs of the Krak and other castles.

Orontes Valley

The Arabs called it Nahr al-Aassi, the "rebel river", because it is the only river in Syria which flows in a northerly direction. From its source on Mount Lebanon, the Orontes flows into Syria by way of the ancient Qadesh (today Tell Nabi Mend), where in 1274 BC the Egyptian and Hittite armies clashed as they fought for control of the Syrian plain.

Hama, the biblical Hamath, is worth a detour, if only to see its famous norias. These gigantic waterwheels with wooden scoops were built to supply the town with water. There were about thirty during the Middle Ages, but now only 17 are left, some in the town centre, others about a kilometre (half a mile) away, above and below the town.

Palmyra

The proud ruins of Palmyra rise out of the sands some 240 km (150 miles) northeast of Damascus. Palmyra has been known by the Arabs as Tadmor ever since the 12th century BC. Clay tablets from the 19th century BC have been found mentioning the "city of palms". The oasis was an important stage for caravans travelling between the Persian Gulf and the Mediterranean. Palmyra reached its heyday in the 3rd century, during the reign of Queen Zenobia, a legendary personality who lost her kingdom by challenging the power of Rome. In 273, the Emperor Aurelian, in revenge for the massacre of 600 of his archers by the Palmyrenes, destroyed the city and put the population to the sword.

The **Temple of Bel**, the most ancient and the greatest of the temples in Palmyra, was dedicated to a Babylonian divinity (Bel or Baal). The sanctuary itself, the cella, has very characteristic sculptured ornamentation. Leading from the temple, the remarkably preserved great colonnade passes some of the most handsome buildings of the ancient city, such as the **Temple of Nebo** and a small theatre that has been restored and is used for performances during the Palmyra Festival.

Damascus

The Syrian capital has strong claims to be the oldest city in the world. It is mentioned among the cities conquered by the Pharoah Tuthmosis III in the 15th century BC, and in the Bible it is named as the capital of the Aramaeans, who dominated Assyria and Israel in the 9th century BC. Its situation at the edge of the fertile plain of Ghutah, irrigated by the waters of the Barada, has made it celebrated throughout the ages. Today, Damascus is a modern city of 3 million inhabitants.

The **old town**, a UNESCO World Heritage Site, contains most of the interesting monuments. The 13th-century **ramparts** that enclose it replaced a wall built by the Romans. Seven of the eight Roman gates remain today, more or less well preserved.

Begin your visit by skirting the **citadel** (al-Qalaa), built in the 13th century on the ancient Roman *castrum*. This will bring you to the nearby **Souk al-Hamidiyeh**, a covered market renovated in the 19th century.

From there, you will easily reach the **Omayyad Mosque**, or Great Mosque, standing on the site of an ancient temple dedicated to Jupiter. A thousand workmen laboured on the construction, which began in 705 and took 10 years to complete. The interior was restored after being almost entirely destroyed by fire in 1893. Despite this catastrophe, the building has retained some gold mosaics of the 8th century. In the depths of the prayer hall a domed shrine houses the head of St John the Baptist, known to Muslims as Yahia. The same head, in fact, that Herod offered to Salome after she had danced for him.

The mosque has three minarets; according to Muslim tradition, the minaret of Jesus will witness Christ coming to do battle with the Antichrist before the last judgement. On the north side of the building is the *Mausoleum of Salah ad-Din* (Saladin), constructed in 1193 and restored in the 19th century.

Immediately south, the **Azam Palace** is a jewel of 18th-century Damascene architecture. Its appointments and decoration are typical of the opulent residence of an Oriental dignitary. Some of the rooms display the collections of the Museum of Art and Popular Tradition.

Continuing south, you reach the Souk Midhat Pasha which follows **Via Recta**, the "street called Straight" mentioned in the Acts of the Apostles (*Acts* 9:11). It was here, in the house of Judas, that Saul of Tarsus—the future Saint Paul—blinded by the Lord, recovered his sight when Ananias laid on his hands. At the eastern end, **Bab Sharqui** (East Gate) has survived from the Roman period and has now been restored. Turn left before you reach the gate to see the **Chapel of Ananias**, an ancient cellar.

West of the old town, near the river Barada, the **National Museum of Syria** is rich in antiquities, from prehistory through the Greco-Roman and Byzantine periods to the Islamic era. A browse around this museum is a perfect introduction to the remainder of your itinerary.

The **Doura-Europos Synagogue**, removed from its original site beside the Euphrates, has been rebuilt in a wing of the museum. This place of worship, dating from AD 165, is chiefly of interest for the frescoes illustrating scenes from the Old Testament. As the Jews never decorated their places of prayer with human or animal effigies, such a feature may well be the result of pagan or Christian influence.

PRACTICAL INFORMATION

Banks. Open 8.30 a.m.–1 p.m., but some currency exchange offices stay open later, particularly at airports and in the big hotels.

Communications. The telephone system is being modernized and works well. Your mobile phone may work—check with your service provider. Internet access is available at major hotels and in Internet cafés, although some web sites are blocked. The postal service is adequate, as is the telephone—providing you can find a callbox in working order!

Currency. The currency is the Syrian pound or lira (£S or SYP). Coins range from £S1 to £S25, banknotes from £S5 to £S1000. It's worth taking a supply of US dollars, especially in the smaller denominations, and always carrying some. It may be hard to change $50 and $100 bills.

Electricity. The electricity supply (220 volts AC, 50 Hz) is variable, with cuts of several hours every day.

Language. Arabic is the official language. English and French are commonly spoken.

Opening hours. Shops have variable opening hours, generally 9.30 a.m. –2 p.m. and again 4.30 p.m.–8 or 9 p.m., mostly closing on Fridays. Government offices usually open 8 a.m.–2 p.m., except on Fridays.

Photography. Take care to avoid "sensitive" subjects—military or industrial installations—and also people in general, but particularly women.

Public holidays. There are several civil public holidays, such as Independence Day (April 17), to which must be added the Muslim and Christian religious holidays.

Safety. At the time of printing, because of current uprisings the situation in Syria is unsafe and visits are not advised.

Time. Syria operates on UTC/GMT + 2, and observes summer time.

Tipping. In hotels and restaurants it is usual to add 10 to 15% of the bill. Round up taxi fares. Chambermaids, porters and hairdressers expect a tip— a £S50 or £S100 bill is acceptable.

Water. Tap water is drinkable in towns, but you will find that bottled mineral water tastes better.

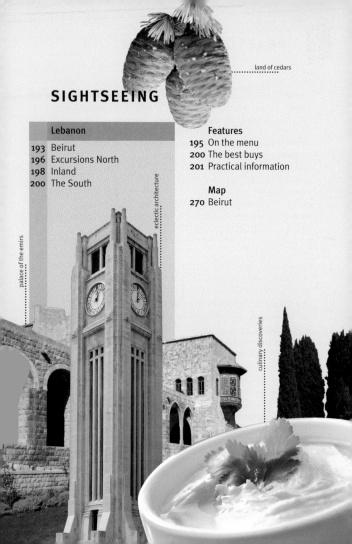

SIGHTSEEING

land of cedars

eclectic architecture

palace of the emirs

culinary discoveries

LEBANON

Lebanon packs an amazing variety of landscapes into a limited space—it's only 210 km (130 miles) long and 80 km (50 miles) across. The major historic sites and scenic areas are easily reached. Small though it is, the land is divided into a patchwork of pieces inhabited by different religious communities: some surviving from the earliest days of Christianity; Sunni and Shia Muslims; and Druzes, who broke away from the Shia in the 11th century.

Beirut

Set on a rocky peninsula with the Mediterranean on three sides, Lebanon's cosmopolitan capital may seem surprisingly large for such a small country, but it has always served as a port and centre of business, culture and education for a much wider region than Lebanon itself. After World War II and Lebanese independence, it grew rapidly into a westernized, liberal-minded and prosperous city and a fine example of communal coexistence. During the civil war (1975–91), the old city centre was reduced to rubble, and many high-rise buildings were gutted. The suburbs mushroomed haphazardly, with little thought for good design. Beirut had not been known for its historic monuments anyway, and with the war it lost many landmarks and places of interest, notably the Place des Canons (also called Place des Martyrs) and the souks, covered markets where all the classes and communities used to rub shoulders.

When the rubble was cleared, archaeologists had a unique opportunity to unearth the past. A Canaanite settlement was discovered, with burial jars and stone city gates 5,000 years old, a wall that defended Phoenician Beruta in the 7th century BC, and Roman streets and the foundations of many Roman buildings. The outline of the hippodrome had gone unnoticed for centuries—it had become the Jewish quarter—and now even some of its stone seating was revealed. Crusader fortifications emerged, and a great caravanserai (merchants' lodgings and warehouses).

The debris from the war was pushed into the sea to form a whole new **waterfront** with parks, promenades and a yacht marina. The worst-damaged buildings were demolished and replaced by modern constructions. The less damaged were repaired: the **Parliament** on Nejmeh Square (L'Etoile) and the **Grand Serail**, a former Turkish barracks which served as seat of government. The **Great Mosque**, which was in fact a converted Romanesque church, the cathedrals and churches of various Christian sects, and some typical buildings of the Turkish and French eras have been carefully restored using stone from the same quarries that supplied the material for their original construction.

Standing on the boundary between east and west Beirut, the **National Museum** (of art and archaeology) was built in neo-Egyptian style in the 1930s. Exhibits trace the history of Lebanon from prehistoric times and include some of the most eloquent relics of the Phoenician civilization. During the war, the museum staff put the smaller pieces in safe-keeping, while the unmovable sarcophagi and mosaics were buried beneath a protective shroud of concrete.

An interesting private museum is the former home of Henri **Pharaon**, at Zokak al-Blat near the Grand Serail. Born in 1898 (and murdered in his bedroom in 1993) he became the richest man in Lebanon (he also designed the national flag), and filled 25 rooms of his mansion with antiquities ranging from Phoenician and Greek sarcophagi to Mameluke ivory tables and Byzantine icons.

The best way to see this city is to pick up a street map (the big hotels have them) and explore on foot. In the western sector the main artery is the crowded **Rue Hamra**. Before the war, this area was considered the showcase of a prosperous country, resolutely focusing on Western-style expansion. Today it is a compendium of Middle Eastern society, banks and hotels, cafés and fast food outlets, bookshops, moneychangers and cinemas.

Rue Hamra leads directly to the seafront at **Ras Beirut**, already a fashionable place in the 19th century. The big attraction here, at the westernmost point, is Pigeon Rocks at Rawche, free-standing cliffs cut off from the mainland by the sea. A boat trip around the rocks takes about 10 minutes. Most of the tourist infrastructure is found at Rawche—hotels, holiday apartments and countless restaurants serving both local and foreign cuisine.

Follow the **Corniche** (coast road) northwards; strolling this seaside promenade is a favourite pastime of locals and visitors alike. You will pass the Manara (Lighthouse) district and, turning eastward, the gardens of the American University, arriving at a cluster of big hotels, including the celebrated Phoenicia, now restored to more than its former magnificence. Opposite is the so-called beach (in fact a swimming pool and small harbour) of the St George Hotel. There are several bathing spots here, but the yacht club at the St George is indisputably the trendiest; for years it was the rendezvous of the international press. The hotel itself is still a blackened shell, kept closed by legal disputes, but the club is as popular as ever with the Lebanese in-crowd.

The winding alleys of the old **Ain el-Mreisse** neighbourhood climb to Rue Bliss and the American University of Beirut, AUB, attended by thousands of students from many different countries. Its **Archaeological Museum** is one of the oldest in the Middle East,

founded in 1868, the same year as the university itself. The collections, mostly private donations, cover Middle Eastern cultures from prehistory to the recent past, containing more than 10,000 objects and as many coins. While you are here, stroll along the tree-lined avenues of the campus, a welcome change from the hectic city streets. The students make the area around AUB one of the liveliest in the city, with a wide choice of restaurants and clubs.

In east Beirut you might think you're in another city. The geographical division corresponds almost exactly to the religious difference between the Muslims in the west and the Christians in the east. The events of the past decades disrupted the old ways of life and patterns of behaviour, but the atmosphere still seems more sedate and less animated, in other words, less "oriental".

istockphoto/Cowan

On the menu
Babaghannouj – aubergine purée
Baklava – flaky pastry with chopped nuts and syrup
Batrakh – dried fish roe
Kebbeh – minced and seasoned veal or lamb served fried or grilled.
Khubz – flat bread
Labneh – fresh cheese
Tabouleh – parsley salad with tomatoes and cracked wheat

East of the old centre lies the residential Mar Nicolas neighbourhood, where the **Nicolas Sursock Museum** of art and sculpture is housed in the elegant 1914 mansion of a wealthy Lebanese who bequeathed it to the city in 1961. It has been expanded to become a veritable cultural centre. Especially beautiful is the lounge on the first floor; its walls and ceiling are covered with painted panelling of the 17th to 19th centuries, with floral patterns interspersed with small landscapes. Chinese plates and Islamic objets d'art are displayed in this room, including 12th and 13th century ceramics, Ottoman silverware, and a large jar dating back to Umayyad or Abbasid times (7th–9th centuries), decorated in a rope and garland design.

Here and scattered elsewhere throughout the city, look for surviving examples of traditional Lebanese architecture blending Arabic, Frankish and Ottoman influences: tall, handsome stone houses with ogival windows (usually three) and arches.

Inland from Mar Nicolas, the district of **Achrafieh** is the heart of Christian Beirut. Initially inhabited by adherents of the Greek Orthodox church, it developed at the end of the 19th century. There are no mosques, and the streets are embellished with little shrines depicting the lives of the saints.

The **Karantina** (Quarantine) district was originally the place where suspect merchandise arriving by sea was examined. It was later inhabited by impoverished families—émigrés from the countryside, Armenian and Kurdish refugees. Across the once-beautiful and tree-lined Beirut river, now like an open drain, the **Borj Hammoud** neighbourhood began as an Armenian refugee camp; memories of those times remain in the numerous tailors' and jewellers' signs.

Excursions North

The coastal highway north soon reaches the **Dog River** (Nahr al-Kalb), where invaders and conquerors from Ramses II and Nebuchadnezzar to Romans, Turks, British and French have carved inscriptions in the rock face. Up river, the **Jeita Grottoes** are limestone caverns with fantastic formations of stalactites and stalagmites. Further inland the road climbs through spectacular scenery to Lebanon's **ski resorts** at Faraya and Mzaar, 2400 m (8000 ft) up but less than an hour away.

Further up the coast, **Jounieh** was a pretty fishing village and beach resort until the civil war, when, vastly expanded, it became the port for the Christian-held zone, with high-rise apartments and nightclubs. A cable-car can take you up to the basilica of Our

Lady of Lebanon at Harissa for great views of the coast, mountains and Beirut. The Casino du Liban offers gambling and a Las Vegas style show.

The charming little town of Jbeil, 38 km (24 miles) north of Beirut, is the site of ancient **Byblos**. It counts among the oldest continuously inhabited sites in the world, and its ruins, dating back to early Phoenician times, have been admirably restored. The town was first called Gebal, but the Greeks gave it the name of Byblos from their word for papyrus, *bublos*, as the material was shipped from Egypt to Greece via Gebal. The inhabitants are mentioned in the Bible as able carpenters who carved the cedarwood beams for the Temple of Solomon.

Excavations begun in the 19th century brought to light remains dating from 7000 years ago, as well as a royal necropolis from the 2nd millennium BC. One of the sarcophagi unearthed, that of Ahiram, is inscribed with the oldest known form of the Phoenician alphabet. It is now in the National Museum.

Next to the archaeological site, the Crusaders' Castle is well preserved, especially the keep, built with large stones taken from nearby Roman temples. The Romanesque Church of St John the Baptist was also built by the

R. Holzbachová

The church of St John the Baptist at Byblos.

Crusaders. A narrow street takes you down to the little harbour.

North of Byblos, at Batroun, a road inland climbs to the **Qadicha Valley**, famed for its scenic beauty. This part of Mount Lebanon is the spiritual home and heartland of the Maronite Christians, who found refuge here around the middle of the 7th century when the Islamic expansion began. Fiercely independent by nature, the Maronites transformed the valley into a defensive enclave, with fortified villages and inaccessible monasteries.

The cedar forests have all but disappeared, but the noble "tree of God" remains the emblem of the country's independence.

Bcharré (altitude 1,400 m; 4,593 ft) is the birthplace of the poet Khalil Gibran (1883–1931), author of *The Prophet*. He lived here for only 11 years before emigrating to the USA, but he is buried in Mar Sarkis monastery, in a chapel hewn from the rock. A small museum displays some of his manuscripts, notebooks, drawings and paintings. Among other monasteries worth visiting in the region is Mar Licha (Saint Elysius), built inside an enor-mous grotto—a good hour's walk. Close by is the Qadicha Cave, where the river of the same name has its source.

Climbing higher into the mountains to about 2,000 m (6,600 ft), you will reach the **Cedars of Lebanon**. The Maronites called them the cedars of God (*arz er-Rab*). Don't expect a forest; there are only a dozen of the ancient trees left, although there are successful programmes to grow seedlings of *Cedrus libani* here and elsewhere in Lebanon, and abroad.

If you have time, continue up the coast to **Tripoli**, the Phoenicians' "triple town" 86 km (54 miles) north of Beirut. Its labyrinthine old city, dating from Mameluke times (14th and 15th centuries) grew up around the Crusaders' imposing St Gilles citadel. About 40 km (25 miles) northeast of Tripoli lie the rugged landscapes of the Akkar and then the Syrian border. Beyond it stands the greatest castle of them all, the formidable Krak des Chevaliers, reachable on a long day's excursion from Beirut.

Inland

The Lebanese emirs, semi-independent rulers under the Ottoman Turks, lived in palaces in the Chouf mountains, less than 50 km (30 miles) southeast of Beirut. If you only visit one of these magnificent dwellings, it should be **Beiteddine**, built by Beshir II and considered the best example of early 19th-century architectural style. The design is definitely oriental, though parts resemble Andalusia's Alhambra. In the rooms where business was discussed the tinkling of fountains was intended to cover the sound of any state secrets being exchanged.

Not far from Beiteddine, the sleepy town of **Deir el-Qamar** shows little sign of its past importance. The origin of its name—Convent of the Moon—is uncertain, but in the 16th and 17th centuries it was the residence of the Lebanese governors. It is almost an open-air museum, as the principal monuments, surrounding a central square *(midan)*, have been recently restored. The charming mosque with octagonal minaret dates from the 16th century; whereas the silk souk *(Kaissarie)* and several palaces were built between the 17th and 19th centuries.

A 90-km (58-mile) drive inland from Beirut takes you over the Lebanon mountains to the Bekaa Valley and the majestic site of **Baalbek**. The ruins date mainly from Roman times: in the 1st century BC, Emperor Augustus had a magnificent temple built to honour Jupiter. Centuries before, the Phoenicians had wor-

R. Holzbachová

Baalbek—a history book carved in stone.

shipped Baal Shamen on the same spot, and the Greeks had named it Heliopolis, the City of the Sun. The massive foundations and six columns, each 20 m (65 ft) high, remain of the Temple of Jupiter; together with the cedar tree they are familiar symbols of Lebanon.

The Temple of Bacchus, on a lower terrace, is wonderfully preserved. The portal is exquisitely decorated, and part of the coffered ceiling has survived: a rare feature in such ancient constructions.

Another of Baalbek's land-marks, the Palmyre Hotel, is said to be the first establishment of its kind in the Middle East. Numerous personalities have stayed here, from Emperor Wilhelm II to General de Gaulle.

While in the Bekaa, you may have time to see the impressive remains of the Umayyad city of **Aanjar** (8th century), near the road to Damascus. No one is sure of the purpose of this isolated settlement, built on a symmetrical plan within four fortified walls.

The South

Security in the southern part of the country is fragile; remain informed about the situation and ensure you have your identity papers at all times. The army has set up checkpoints on many of the roads.

About 40 km (25 miles) south of the capital, Saida is the present name for the ancient port of **Sidon**.

The old town is distinguished by its Sea Castle (Qalaat el-Bahr), a fortress built by the Crusaders on a small island linked to the main-land by a bridge, also fortified. Murex Hill, a reminder of Phoenician and Roman times, takes its name from a sea-snail used by the ancients as the source of an extremely valuable purple dye. The hill is said to consist entirely of discarded shells.

Further down the coast, 80 km (50 miles) from the capital, Sour is the former **Tyre**, a merchant city and great rival of Sidon. It was from here that the founders of Carthage set sail around 800 BC. In order to conquer Tyre, a rocky island, Alexander the Great built a causeway from the mainland; since then sand and silt has gathered to form a broad peninsula. The archaeological excavations, begun in 1948, extend over the city and outside the walls; they are the largest in Lebanon (more than 15 ha). Roman and Byzantine remains cover a wide area, crossed by a splendid monumental way, 175 m (190 yd) long, which ends at the ancient port. In the modern town, excavations of the necropolis have revealed a number of sarcophagi, some of which have been transferred to the National Museum. A Roman hippodrome was also unearthed, one of the biggest and best preserved of its kind.

PRACTICAL INFORMATION

Climate. Summers are hot and humid on the coast, cooler in the hills; the Bekaa Valley is hot and dry. Winters can be rainy, with snow in the mountains. Spring and autumn are generally sunny and warm.

Communications. International telephone code for Lebanon is 961. Internet access is available in hotels and cybercafés.

Currency. The Lebanese pound (LL or LBP), known as the *lira*, in notes from 1000 to 100,000, coins from 50 to 500. The US dollar and the Euro are accepted in Beirut. Credit cards are widely accepted. ATMs deliver local currency.

Driving. Drive on the right. Take special care at night and on twisting mountain roads. Respect military checkpoints (some zones are out of bounds, especially in the south).

Entry formalities. Most nationalities are required to have visas, but these are generally issued on arrival. Check with your airline or travel agent. Passports must not show evidence of a visit to Israel.

Language. Arabic. English and French are widely understood.

Public Holidays. Muslim and Christian holidays are observed. The national holiday, Independence Day, is celebrated on 22 November.

Safety. In some regions, especially in the south and around Tripoli, the Bekaa Valley and anywhere near the border with Syria, the political situation is fragile. Before going there, consult the competent authorities and keep well informed about events.

Taxis. As well as normal taxis, there are "service taxis" which follow preset routes with a fixed charge. You can get on or off anywhere along the route. If you pay for all the seats you can "charter" one as a normal taxi. All official taxis and service taxis have red number plates.

Time. GMT + 2, and GMT + 3 from April to October.

Tipping. Restaurant bills include a service charge, but extra tips are welcomed. Taxi drivers do not expect a tip.

Water and health. Tap water is best avoided, as are unpeeled fruit. Public beaches may be polluted; if you want to swim use private beaches or swimming pools.

fertile coast

SIGHTSEEING

emblem of the state

golden stones

fruit from the desert

ISRAEL

A link between three continents—Europe, Africa and Asia—Israel is a modern and flourishing democracy with a rich heritage of Biblical tradition. The Holy Land does not only possess a great diversity of customs, peoples and religions, but also wonderful landscapes. From the wooded hills of Galilee and the fertile soil of the Jordan Valley, to the Negev desert, Israel offers visitors a wealth of diversity to discover.

The Coast

Located just north of the modern city of Haifa is **Acre**, capital of the coastal region from Phoenician times until early in the 20th century. Acre, also known as Akko, has received prestigious visitors such as Caesar and Saladin, the Knights of St John, Richard the Lion-Heart and Napoleon Bonaparte, who laid siege to the town in 1799 but eventually had to retreat. You can still see much evidence from this romantic past within the medieval walls of the Old City. The Mosque of El Jezzar is one of the most impressive buildings in the country; it was built in 1781 by the ferocious Turkish governor, Jezzar Pasha. Next door, the Hammam el-Pasha, once the mosque's luxurious Turkish bath, is now furnished as the municipal museum.

Haifa is known for both its industry and scenic beauty. After many centuries of colourful history, which included Crusader conquest, the city was rebuilt as a defence outpost in the mid-18th century. Its rebirth as a modern city came about when European immigrants began to arrive a hundred years later and started to plan the new Haifa, which Theodor Herzl had predicted would be the "city of the future."

Board the Carmelit underground train which climbs the heights of **Mount Carmel**. At the end of the line, Rehov Yefe Nof (Panorama Road) affords a view overlooking the city and port. Just below Panorama Road are the monumental terraces of the Baha'i Gardens, which surround the domed Shrine of the Bab, resting-place of Mirza Ali Mu-

The waterfront of Tel Aviv, a lively, modern town.

hammad, the noted 19th-century visionary.

Further south along the coast, **Caesarea** was built in about 20 BC by Herod the Great. The Jewish uprising against the Romans was launched there in AD 66; in 1101 it was taken by the Crusaders, in 1187 by Saladin, and in 1191 by Richard the Lion-Heart. A century later it was destroyed by Mameluke invaders. The Crusader city is worth visiting. There are also remains of a 2nd-century Roman aqueduct and the well preserved ancient amphitheatre serves as the stage for modern musical performances.

Tel Aviv is the centre of Israel's commercial, industrial and cultural life. A sprawling high-rise city established on sand dunes in 1909, Tel Aviv offers its visitors a wealth of interesting sights, non-stop nightlife, a shopping paradise, and long stretches of seashore. The city's central section, with thousands of buildings built in the Bauhaus architectural style, was designated as a World Heritage Site by UNESCO. Popular tourist destinations include Independence Hall, where the State of Israel was officially declared in May 1948; the Yitzhak Rabin Memorial, at the place where Israel's late prime minister was assassinated; and Sheinkin Street with its Bohemian atmosphere.

Of particular interest among the city's several dozen museums is the Museum of the Jewish Diaspora, as well as the new Design Museum in the suburb of Holon.

The Biblical port of **Jaffa** is now completely engulfed by the modern city of Tel Aviv. Jaffa is a must-see destination for visitors to Tel Aviv; its cobblestone alleyways and twisting lanes are full of galleries, boutiques and cafés clustered around St Peter's Catholic Church and Monastery. Below the artists colony is the port itself.

Jerusalem

Jerusalem's **Old City** is large by medieval standards, but quite small by modern ones. Its streets are narrow, full of twisting lanes, oriental souks, steep stairways and dark, covered passageways. Nowhere else on earth are you likely to see such a variety of costumes. Hassidic Jews wear black fur hats and tailcoats, Arabs are clad in flowing robes and keffiyes (chequered headscarves). Nuns in their habits, tourists in Bermuda shorts, Israeli women in military uniforms, berobed Greek Orthodox priests and Bedouin women in richly embroidered dresses all vie for seats on the buses, wait at traffic lights and haggle over vegetables in the bazaars.

Jaffa Gate, a pair of massive towers, is a good place to set off on a visit to the Old City. Built by Suleiman the Magnificent in 1531–32, this entrance to the Old City and terminus of the 19th-century road linking Jerusalem with the port of Jaffa bears inscriptions in three varieties of Arabic script. Known to Arabs as Bab el-Khalil (Hebron Gate), it leads to a bridge over the remains of the dry moat of the **Citadel of David**. You can mount the stairs to the roof and battlements for views of the city and explore the ruins and excavations. Jerusalem's **Municipal Museum** is set up in the Citadel, with displays outlining the history of the city.

The **Church of the Holy Sepulchre** occupies the spot that Helena, mother of Constantine the Great, identified as the site of Golgotha in AD 326. Constantine had a magnificent basilica and rotunda built to house the tomb of Jesus. This, the grandest and richest of the succession of churches that stood here through the centuries, was destroyed in 614 by invading Persians. It was later rebuilt, but the form it takes today dates mostly from Crusader times.

The portal by which visitors enter the church was built in 1149, during Crusader times. Only the western door of the pair is open: the eastern door was bricked up a few years after the church's completion and has stayed that way ever since.

The last five Stations of the Cross are sheltered here. Of the Holy Sepulchre itself, all that remains today is the stone shelf on which Jesus' body lay, now covered in polished marble. Over the years each nook and cranny of the church has taken on some significance, and small chapels have been dedicated to the different people and events related to Jesus' crucifixion and resurrection.

The **Via Dolorosa**, or Way of the Cross, holds a fascination for visitors to Jerusalem no matter what their beliefs. Some of the events mentioned in the Gospels can still be matched with places along the Via Dolorosa. The 14 stations were mapped out in the 16th century by European Christians who had never set foot in Jerusalem, and by Franciscan monks actually living there, who used documentary and hearsay evidence—

which explains how the legendary stations crept in.

The **Temple Mount** (Mount Moriah), where Solomon built the First Temple and later generations the Second, is holy ground to all three of Jerusalem's great religions. So sacred are the confines of the Temple site that strictly observant Jews dare not even come here, and Muslims and Christians come with great reverence. The First Temple was destroyed in 560 BC by the Babylonians, and the Second by the Romans some 600 years later. Jews round the world pray fervently for the establishment of the Third Temple on this very spot.

Today the visit of the Temple Mount is reserved exclusively for Muslims or people with a special authorization. Opening hours are mornings from Saturday to Thursday, and a few hours in the early afternoon.

Muslims believe that the Prophet Mohammed stepped upon the rock on the Temple Mount during his Night Journey into Heaven while mounted upon El-Burak, a miraculous beast. Known to Muslims as El-Haram es-Sharif, the Mount is home to the El-Aqsa Mosque, the third holiest in Islam, and the more colourful Dome of the Rock, which is Jerusalem's most strikingly beautiful house of worship.

The **Dome of the Rock**, *Qubbet es-Sakhra,* was built on Temple Mount in 691 over the rock from which Mohammed is said to have made a night journey to pray in heaven with Abraham, Moses and Jesus. The belief derives from a verse in the Koran: "Praise be to Allah who brought his servant at night from the Holy Mosque to the Far Away Mosque, the precincts of which we have blessed." The great dome, brilliantly regilded by Jordan's King Hussein in 1993, has become the landmark symbol for the whole city. The decoration of the octagonal mosque's interior of marble and coloured tiles is an equally splendid blend of Koranic verses with arabesque and floral patterns.

El-Aqsa Mosque, the silver-domed shrine at the south end of Temple Mount was originally built in the 8th century, from which time only a mosaic floor survives. The "furthest spot" mentioned in its name is where Mohammed stopped on his ride from Medina to Jerusalem before his miraculous night journey. The largest mosque in Jerusalem, and the third-holiest shrine to Muslims after Mecca and Medina, it suffered the indignities of earthquake and transformation by the Crusaders into a residence and church before Saladin reclaimed it for Islam in 1187. King Abdullah of Jordan was assassinated in the mosque in 1951 by a Palestinian extremist. It has been restored with massive marble pillars and handsome Oriental carpets.

The **Western Wall** ("Wailing Wall"), just below the Temple Mount, is considered almost as sacred by Jews as the site where the Holy Temple once stood. The Wall itself is but a retaining wall of the Temple Mount complex, but it has become a symbol for the ancient house of worship. Since the time of the Second Temple's destruction and the exile of the Jews in AD 70, Jewish people have come here to pray and to weep at the Temple's loss, and to hope for the restitution of Jerusalem to the Jewish people. When the city was reunited in June 1967, the old buildings that crowded the Wall were demolished and a wide plaza was constructed to accommodate the hundreds of worshippers who arrived daily. Today the plaza forms the largest outdoors synagogue in the world. On weekday mornings you're bound to witness more than one Bar Mitzvah ceremony in progress. Whatever your beliefs, you'll feel a sense of awe when approaching the giant stone ashlars (blocks) which supported the foundations of the ancient Temple.

The large rectangular stones at the base of the Wall date from the

E. Mandelmann

The Dome of the Rock was built over the footprint of the Prophet Mohammed.

time of Herod the Great, with later constructions of smaller blocks higher up. This is only a small section of the Western Wall, which overall extends from one side of Temple Mount to the other and is sunk deeply in the rubble-filled earth. A treat is to visit the **Western Wall Tunnels**, which reveal the massive extent of Herod's original construction. They form a passage meeting up with a tunnel that runs north beyond the Temple Mount to emerge at the Via Dolorosa.

To visit the **Mount of Olives**, the historic hill overlooking Temple Mount, take a bus or taxi to the top and walk down—or ride a camel. From the observation point in front of the Seven Arches Hotel, there is a superb view of Old Jerusalem. The vista has never failed to stir the souls of the pilgrims who have made the long journey to the Holy Land. Below the hotel are the Tombs of the Prophets—tunnels of burial niches attributed, among others, to Haggai and Malachi. Gnarled olive trees still grow among the ancient tombs, most evocatively of all in the **Garden of Gethsemane** where Jesus spent his last hours before being arrested by the Romans. Among the modern churches on the lower slopes are the Russian Orthodox **Church of Mary Magdalene** with gilded onion-shaped domes, and the Greek Orthodox **Church of the Assumption**, built over a Crusader church housing Mary's rock-hewn sepulchre. The **All Nations Church**, or Basilica of the Agony, was built in this century on the site of Byzantine and Crusader ruins.

Just outside the walls of the Old City is historic **Mount Zion**, traditional site of King David's Tomb and the room where Jesus and his disciples ate the Last Supper. Its most prominent landmark is the modern Benedictine **Dormition Abbey** (1910), built over a crypt where Mary is believed to have begun her dying sleep.

To the south of the Old City is the **City of David**, a historical and archaeological treasure, offering insights into the Jebusite city pre-dating Jerusalem.

Jerusalem is also renowned for its many fascinating museums. A visit to **Yad Vashem** is a tribute to the memory of the 6 million Jews slaughtered in the Holocaust; no visitor will be unmoved by the pictures, written testimonies and artefacts from that period. In the **Holocaust History Museum**, ten exhibition halls include personal stories of victims and survivors; a special monument commemorates the million and a half children who were killed.

The **Israel Museum** has a stunning new archaeological wing, and displays the oldest-known copy of a biblical text. The Judaica wing focuses on the recent past, with an extraordinary collection of Jewish objects. One room displays the remains of an ancient synagogue, church and mosque, emphasizing the fact that the three monotheistic faiths were born in the region. A fascinating addition since 2006 is a scale model of the ancient city of Jerusalem as it was in the Second Temple period in the year AD 66.

Modern art is represented by the painting of Europe and the Americas and a sculpture garden that includes works by Rodin, Picasso and Henry Moore.

In the grounds you can see the Shrine of the Book, which houses the Dead Sea Scrolls, the 2,000-year-old manuscripts discovered in caves near Qumran.

The **Rockefeller Museum**, with a vast archaeological collection, opened in 1938. The signage was designed by the famous British font creator Eric Gill.

The Desert

Just minutes south of Jerusalem is the ancient town of **Bethlehem**. Its church towers and minarets spread dramatically along the skyline on the summits of the Judean hills. Manger Square is the centre of the town's tourist activity, and is located right in front of the Church of the Nativity. One of the oldest houses of worship in the world, it has seen many changes since Constantine had it built in AD 325. The church is situated above the Grotto of the Nativity, a chamber in which a silver star marks the place of Jesus' birth. A side chapel is said to be where the manger stood. Bethlehem is under control of the Palestinian Authority, and visits there must be coordinated with security officials.

The Tombs of the Patriarchs in the town of **Hebron** further south attest to its great age: here lie the remains of Abraham, Isaac and Jacob and their wives Sarah, Rebecca and Leah. The tombs are now covered by a mosque and decorated with some of the finest Islamic art in Israel.

About 4,000 years ago, Abraham dug a well in **Beer Sheva**, in the centre of the Negev Desert, and it can still be seen. Beer Sheva pulls in the crowds on Thursdays from 6 to 9 a.m. for the Bedouin market.

The Dead Sea

The road from Jerusalem to Jericho descends through a bleak, barren desert landscape where you may see a few Bedouin tents here and there but little else, save a lonely sign marking "Sea Level." The Dead Sea itself is the lowest spot on the face of the earth, 390 m (nearly 1,300 ft) below sea level, and so full of minerals nothing can live in it. At its northern tip is **Qumran**, where in 1947 two shepherd boys discovered eight clay jars containing the Dead Sea Scrolls. Experience the oily buoyancy of the water at **Ein Gedi**, a pleasant resort and nature reserve. Take a mud bath or a revitalizing dip in the thermal sulphur pools at the spa nearby.

Further south, you can ride a cable car or attempt the hike up to the remains of the fortress on **Masada**, the flat-topped mountain where the last group of Jewish Zealots held out in the rebellion against Rome for three years until AD 73. They escaped final defeat by committing mass suicide.

Galilee

The Galilee stretches from the Mediterranean coastline in the west to the foothills of the Golan Heights in the east. The historic town of **Tiberias** is located on the western shores of Lake Kinneret, the Sea of Galilee. After the destruction of Jerusalem in AD 70, Tiberias became a centre for Jewish learning. With many Jewish sages and rabbis buried in the area, the city is a popular stop on tours around the beautiful lake, which serves as Israel's major natural water reservoir.

Jesus chose his first disciples from among the fishermen of **Capernaum**, and the foundations of a house said to be that of Simon Peter can be seen. Next door are the ruins of an important synagogue with richly carved pillars, built soon after the destruction of Jerusalem. Overlooking a nearby road is the **Mount of Beatitudes**, where Jesus pronounced his famous Sermon on the Mount.

In the mountains west of Tiberias is **Safed** (Tzfat), one of the four Jewish holy cities. It was a centre of Jewish mysticism, Kabbalah, and philosophy and is home to many 17th century synagogues.

Nazareth, also in Galilee, is where Jesus grew up. The Church of the Annunciation is a tremendous modern monument, built for the Franciscans in the 1960s. It is constructed over the grotto where Mary received the news that she would bear a son and should call him Jesus.

PRACTICAL INFORMATION

Banks. Open generally Sunday to Thursday 8.30 a.m.–noon, also Sunday, Tuesday and Thursday 4 p.m.–6.30 p.m. ATMs, located outside banks and near major shopping centres, allow NIS withdrawals against foreign credit cards.

Clothing. Women should avoid short skirts or shorts and sleeveless tops, and men should wear long trousers in holy places and religious districts. Men usually wear a skullcap in synagogues, and before entering a mosque you must remove your shoes.

Credit cards. Shops and restaurants welcome credit cards. Payment of hotel bills, organized tours, and car rentals in any foreign currency, by credit card or travellers cheque, exempts you from VAT.

Currency. The *shekel* (plural *shekalim*), officially NIS (New Israeli Shekel), divided into 100 *agorot*. Coins range from 10 agorot to 10 NIS; banknotes from 20 to 200 NIS. US dollars are still a favourite secondary currency.

Electricity. 220/240 V (50 Hz); plugs are the British type with three flat pins.

Entry formalities. In most cases, a passport valid for at least 6 months is sufficient; however, before leaving home check with your travel agent or the Israeli embassy in your country. If you intend to visit another Arab country, ask for the stamp to be placed on a separate sheet, as many countries will not admit visitors with an Israeli stamp in their passports.

Photography. In most museums, you can take photos as long as you ask for permission first. Avoid taking pictures of people praying. On the Sabbath, photography is not allowed in places such as Mea She'arim. Also avoid photos in sensitive areas such as airports, naval bases and border checkpoints.

Post office. Main post offices open Sunday to Thursday 8 a.m.–6 p.m., closing Friday at noon.

Shops. Usually open weekdays to 7 p.m. and Fridays to 1 p.m.; shops managed by Muslims close on Fridays, those run by Christians on Sundays.

Tipping. Restaurant bills are presented to dines clearly marked "Service not included", and it is customary to tip 15 per cent. Tipping taxi drivers is not compulsory. In hotels, the choice is up to the guest.

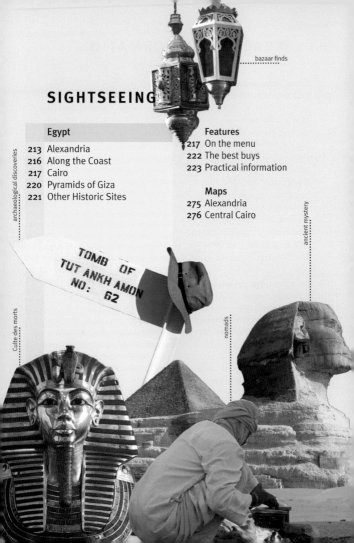

bazaar finds

SIGHTSEEING

archaeological discoveries

ancient mystery

Culte des morts

nomads

TOMB OF
TUT ANKH AMON
NO: 62

EGYPT

At various times in its history, Alexandria has shone out like a cultural and scientific beacon. It was founded by Alexander the Great and is today a charming resort. Cairo, founded around 969, seems almost modern by comparison. The Cairenes have made their city the cultural capital of the Arab civilization, considered by the Muslims as the guardian of the treasures of Islamic art, architecture and knowledge. And close to the city, in the suburbs, no visitor can fail to be awed by the sight of the majestic pyramids of the pharaohs at Giza.

Alexandria

Around **Midan Saad Zaghloul**, the bustling seafront square, colonial-style buildings recall the city centre's cosmopolitan atmosphere that so enchanted novelists such as E.M. Forster and Lawrence Durrell and the poet Constantine Cavafy. The French, Greek, Jewish, Italian and British expats have now gone, and a statue has been erected to Saad Zaghloul, one of the early Egyptian heroes of the independence movement, who prompted them to leave. But the 1929 Moorish-style **Hotel Cecil** and its bar are still there, refurbished, near the tourist office and not far from favourite cafés such as the Pastroudis, Délices and Trianon.

Running south past the tourist office, **Sharia Nabi Daniel** is lined with buildings bearing witness to the city's multicultural past. The **Nabi Daniel Mosque**, along the street, is believed to be built over the tomb either of the prophet Daniel or Alexander the Great. Across the street further south, the **French Cultural Centre** stages first-rate exhibitions.

At Kom el-Dikka, east of the Nabi Daniel Mosque, is a garden with well-preserved remains of a grey and white marble **Roman Theatre** (2nd century), the only one found in Egypt and brought to light in the 1950s. Its 13 rows of seating, where 800 spectators could cheer on gladiators, and later chariot races in Byzantine times, were built of white marble imported from Europe, with columns of red granite from Aswan and green granite from Asia Minor. In the 5th century it was used as a place of Christian worship. The theatre was built in what had been a wealthy residential neighbourhood. Ongoing excavations nearby have uncovered the Roman **Villa of Birds**, so-called because of the birds in its floor mosaics—in addition to a panther. Probably completed under Emperor Hadrian (AD 117–138), the villa had a bathroom, several bed chambers and a dining room built around a spacious courtyard.

The fascinating collections of the **National Museum of Alexandria**, expanded in 2003, include objects from the times of the pharaohs, and the Greco-Roman, Coptic, Islamic and modern eras.

On Sharia Ahmed esh-Shawari southwest of the city centre, the imposing **Pompey's Pillar**, 26 m (85 ft) high and approximately 2 m (6.5 ft) thick, was made out of one piece of polished rose granite from Aswan. Originally part of what had once been a grandiose temple to Serapis, the column was erected in honour of Diocletian and, in fact, has no connection with Pompey, the Roman general.

The **Catacombs of Kom el-Shugafa** ("Mound of Shards" just south of Pompey's Pillar) show how the Greeks and Romans were in thrall to Egyptian cultural influence. These were the most important burial grounds in Alexandria, probably dating from the 2nd century. The dead were lowered some 35 m (115 ft) through a shaft into the catacombs; modern visitors take a spiral staircase. The chambers are three storeys high and unique in their combination of Pharaonic and Greco-Roman styles of design and decoration. Typically, the spacious Chamber of Caracalla has niches, each originally bearing the name of the family buried there. In the Triclinium (dining room), the family would hold a banquet in honour of the deceased. A major feature is the Central Burial Chamber in which muscular statues of the jackal-headed Anubis and crocodile god Sobek have been clad in Roman armour.

Along the Waterfront

Alexandria's ancient **Eastern Harbour**, known to the Romans as Portus Magnus, is today traced by a coastal highway curving around from Fort Qaitbey on the site of the ancient Pharos lighthouse west to the Bibliotheca Alexandrina, the great new Library of Alexandria. Known since the quasi-colonial days of the 19th century as the Corniche—half French Riviera, half English seaside promenade—the highway now bears an official name that eloquently tells the tale of Egypt's "change of management": July 26th Street. That was the date in 1956 when President Gamal Abdel Nasser announced in Alexandria that his government was about to nationalize the hitherto Anglo-French-operated Suez Canal.

A veritable landmark out on a narrow promontory of the old harbour, **Fort Qaitbey** stands on the site of Alexandria's Pharos lighthouse. One of the ancient world's Seven Wonders, this has excited renewed interest since underwater excavations in the harbour in the 1990s began to bring up what many scholars believe are parts of the original structure. Other lighthouse masonry is thought to have been recycled by Sultan al-Ashraf Qaitbey when building his fort in the 1480s, such as red-granite pillars incorporated in the enclosure walls. He also used the same local white stone that hardened in contact with water. The Fort was subsequently reinforced by Mohammed Ali in the 19th century.

Besides a mosque in its interior (minus the minaret destroyed by British artillery in 1882), the Fort now houses a **Naval Museum**. It includes among its memorabilia, mostly from the Roman and Napoleonic eras, ammunition,

hemis.fr/Torrione

Most of the world's known alphabets are engraved on the walls of the Bibliotheca Alexandrina.

weapons and coins from the shipwrecked French frigate *L'Orient*, sunk by Anglo-Turkish forces at the Battle of Aboukir in 1801. From the fort's **ramparts**, there is a magnificent view along the Mediterranean coast and back over the city.

The gleaming disc of the **Bibliotheca Alexandrina**, the city's proud new library, emerges like a rising sun from the east end of the Eastern Harbour. Linking ancient past to the present and future, it emulates the Ptolemies' Great Library

In Alexandria, the architecture is a mixture of Oriental and Mediterranean influences.

hemis.fr/Orteo

accessible to the whole planet. The Ptolemies' library had catalogued 532,800 manuscripts by the 1st century BC; the new institution is collecting between 4 and 8 million real and virtual manuscripts in every language from Polynesian dialects to Mandarin Chinese. Reflecting this universality, the walls of unpolished granite are inscribed with characters from most of the world's known alphabets. Open daily to the public, the library is also adorned with mosaics, statues and other ancient Egyptian, Greek and Roman works of art recently salvaged from the harbour. The great reading rooms have eight terraces and there are also art galleries, three museums and a planetarium.

Along the Coast

The **Corniche** coastal highway leads east and west of the city to beach resorts popular with Alexandrians and holiday-makers from Cairo seeking fine seafood restaurants and the summer respite of the sea. In the eastern residential suburb of Zizinia is the **Royal Jewellery Museum**, housed in the opulent 1920s villa of Princess Fatma Al-Zahraa, a member of the Egyptian Royal family. The cool sea breezes that attracted Egypt's latterday monarchs to **Montazah Palace**, 16 km (10 miles) east of Alexandria.

built 2,300 years ago and destroyed by the city's invaders. The Bibliotheca Alexandrina's Norwegian architects, directed by Austrian-born Christoph Kapeller, developed an 11-storey circular design that is reminiscent of the Egyptian hieroglyph for the sun but also suggestive of a giant microchip. Just as the ancient library was a beacon of scholarship throughout the Mediterranean world, so the Bibliotheca will use modern technology to make its sources of knowledge

Built in 1892, the last home of King Farouk, who abdicated in 1952, is an extravagant stylistic combination of Italian Gothic and Turkish Ottoman. It is surrounded by 150 ha of beautiful parks and gardens of orange trees and umbrella pines.

Now a popular resort and fishing port, **Aboukir** was the site of Admiral Nelson's first victory over Napoleon Bonaparte's fleet in 1798.

World War II buffs may want to make the 90-minute drive from Alexandria out to **El Alamein**. Now a pleasant beach resort, it was the site of the decisive desert battle in 1942 between Marshal Montgomery's victorious British and Allied forces and Rommel's German and Italian armies. It is commemorated by a museum with tanks and armoured vehicles in its grounds and poignant cemeteries for the war dead of both sides. Do not venture off the highway into the desert where the battle actually took place, as there are still hundreds of unexploded mines beneath the sands with no safe route among them, whatever local guides may claim.

Cairo

With a population of more than 20 million, Cairo is the largest city in Africa and the Middle East. It was founded at the spot where the Nile valley widens into a fertile delta. The main part of the modern metropolis lies on the east bank and extends onto two islands, Gezira and Roda.

Tahrir Square is the town centre, a truly nightmarish place where you take your life into your hands every time you cross the street. Just north of the square is the **Egyptian Museum**. It was built in the mid-19th century to house the wealth of objects that came to light as a result of the French military and cultural invasion. No one could, or would want to, see everything on one visit. The section you *must* see is that devoted to King Tutankhamun's treasures. The young pharaoh who died at about 19 has become a

On the menu
Ful – mashed beans
Kanafa – shredded pastry
Makhallal – vegetables macerated in vinegar
Megdra – rice and lentils
Mezzeh – selection of appetizers
Molokhia – green vegetable soup with rice and chicken
Taamiah – bean and herb patties

hemis.fr/Orteo

legend for the variety and beauty of his funerary furnishings. As a ruler, he was insignificant, but he is now immortalized as the only pharaoh whose tomb escaped the attentions of grave-robbers. It was discovered intact in 1922 by the British archaeologist, Howard Carter. The priceless objects are displayed in galleries on the first floor. The famous gold mask is only one of 1,703 items so perfect in their workmanship that their modern monetary value means nothing at all. The *Guide to the Egyptian Museum* (on sale at the entrance) describes some of the remarkable objects in detail.

The **Coptic Museum** will help you understand this branch of the Christian church. Copt originally meant "Egyptian". St Mark preached in Alexandria in AD 42, and Christianity flourished for about six centuries until it was largely replaced by Islam. The **Museum of Islamic Art**, just off Place Ahmed Mahar, has neither guides nor catalogue but offers a remarkable display of prayer mats, stained glass, inlaid stonework, mosque lamps, illuminated manuscripts and weapons.

View of the University and El-Azhar mosque. | Fishawi Café in Khan el-Khalili. | The citadel and mosque of Mohammad Ali. | Muslim women in El-Azhar mosque.

Afterwards, you'll be ready for the **Islamic District** with its many mosques. Entering the area you'll see Bab Zuweila, the imposing remains of a medieval city gate. **El-Azhar Mosque and University**, on the south side of Shari El-Azhar, has been Islam's most prestigious place of learning for ten centuries. Begun in 970, it still accommodates 400,000 students who come from all over the world to study law, medicine and religion.

Across the road is Cairo's renowned handicrafts bazaar, **Khan el-Khalili**, where you can mingle with Cairenes and visitors alike in hunting down bargains. To appreciate the genuine effort that goes into many of these articles, ask a merchant if you can tour his workshops. The nearby **Kalawun Mosque** complex was finished in 1293. The façade incorporates Corinthian pillars, the result of Crusader influence. Its beautiful mausoleum, down a very uninviting passageway, has a carved and gilded ceiling.

Sultan Hassan Mosque (1362) and modern Rifai Mosque (1912) mark the approach to the **Citadel**. Sultan Saladin had this fortress built in 1176—by Crusader prisoners captured in Palestine. Its massive ramparts never had to resist foreign attack but were frequently subjected to the cannonballs of rival factions contesting the sultan's throne. Today, its silhouette is dominated by the domes and minarets of the Turkish-style **mosque of Mohammed Ali**, completed in 1857.

The entrance to Old Cairo lies between two Roman towers. Inside the walls are Coptic churches dating back to the time when Egypt was a Christian country. **El-Moallaqah** claims to be the oldest church in Egypt; evidence suggests that there was a church here in the 4th century. But **Abu Serga Church** puts out a similar claim—tradition has it that Mary, Joseph and the baby Jesus took shelter on this spot during their flight to Egypt. Next door is the 9th-century **Ben Ezra Synagogue**, where a caretaker comments on the Sephardic architecture and shows visitors a treasured collection of scrolls, including a Torah on gazelle parchment dating back 2,500 years. This is said to be the place where the Pharaoh's daughter found Moses in the bulrushes. Tradition claims that Moses prayed here before leading his people out of Egypt.

Before leaving Cairo, try to find time to visit the **Cairo Tower** (El Borg), 187 m (600 ft) high, which affords an excellent view of Gezira Island, and the **Papyrus Institute** on a houseboat near the Sheraton Hotel where the whole story of papyrus is told.

Barbara Ender

Bernard Joliat

Pyramids of Giza

Of the Seven Wonders of the ancient world, the pyramids of Giza are the only one to survive. So perfectly shaped from a distance, the smooth geometric shapes yield the secrets of their construction as you approach. Each one is made from millions of massive stone blocks, like giant staircases.

Visitors used to climb to the top of the **Great Pyramid of Kheops**, highest of the three at 139 m (450 ft), but this is now forbidden as too dangerous. Only the athletic and non-claustrophobic should follow the guide through the passage into the central funerary chamber—where the sole reward is a battered, empty sarcophagus.

The **Pyramid of Khephren** is a foot or two lower than the Great Pyramid, but as it's built on higher ground it looks taller from a distance. The remains of the original smooth covering of polished stone, a feature of almost all the pyramids, can be seen near the top.

The **Pyramid of Mycerinus**, 62 m (204 ft) high, was the last of the three Giza pyramids to be built. Temples and tombs called

The sphinx surveys the desert in front of Kephren's pyramid. | Modern papyrus painted with motifs inspired by the walls of ancient tombs.

mastabas surround the big three, erected here so that family, friends and noble servants could lie near their dead sovereign. All this building was accomplished during the Old Kingdom's 4th dynasty, about 2600 BC. Scores of earlier and later pyramids line the Nile, but those at Giza are the finest.

The **Sphinx**—Abu el-Houl or "Father of Fear" in Arabic—was sculpted in the image of Pharaoh Khephren to guard his tomb. For a thousand years, the desert sands drifted over it, obliterating it from sight. Then Thutmose IV (1425–08 BC) had the sand cleared away and restored the great beast, after a dream that promised he would only become pharaoh if he did so. Some 3,000 years later the Sphinx's nose was shattered by Mameluke Turks, using the monument for target practice and simultaneously honouring the Islamic proscription against graven images.

The **Grand Egyptian Museum**, under construction at Giza, is due to open in 2015.

Other Historic Sites

The pharaoh Menes founded **Memphis**, 28 km (17 miles) south of Giza, around 3000 BC. He is thought to have erected the temple of Ptah, while his son built the royal palace and made Memphis the first capital of Egypt.

Memphis also had religious significance, with the country's biggest temples, and pharaohs were crowned here. During the New Kingdom (from around 1550 BC), Thebes took over as the centre of power. When Al-Fustat (Cairo) was built in the Middle Ages, Memphis was abandoned and its stones were used as building materials for Cairo houses.

You can see a giant statue of Ramses II (1279–1213 BC), now reclining beneath a shelter. It stood 13 m (43 ft) tall, probably in front of the temple of Ptah. The red granite statue of Ramses II moved from Cairo to Giza in 2006 also came from Memphis. An alabaster sphinx, in fairly good condition and with an inscrutable smile, was discovered in 1912. It weighs 80 tonnes and measures 8 m (26 ft) in length and over 4 m (13 ft) in height.

The necropolis of pyramids of **Saqqara**, surrounded by smaller tombs of nobles stands on a desert plateau west of the vanished royal capital of Memphis—the west, where the sun sets, being the Land of the Dead. Many of the pyramids have been reduced by time and the elements to little more than piles of rubble, but the most important, serving as mausoleum for King Djoser, still stands proudly intact. Djoser's is not only the first of the pyramids (around 2670 BC) but the world's

The best buys
Amber
Bedouin crafts
Carpets
Cartouches with your name in
    hieroglyphics
Carved wood
Copies of antique statues
Egyptian cotton clothing
Jewellery
Leatherware
Papyrus
Water pipes

earliest known monument to be built of stone rather than brick. It won for its designer, the high priest Imhotep, world renown as the father of architecture.

To get to the **Step Pyramid**, you pass through a stone-walled precinct that was perhaps a replica in miniature of the king's palace at Memphis. In the corridor and side chambers, stone is used to imitate wooden beams and bundles of reeds lashed together to form columns. At the end of a broad courtyard, the pyramid rises in six tiers. The pharaoh's burial chamber (off-limits to all but professional archaeologists) lies at the bottom of a shaft cut into the bedrock beneath the pyramid, with other chambers for his family further down.

Not far from the Step Pyramid, courtiers were buried in tombs known as *mastaba,* an Arab word for their bench-like shape. Inside are delightful carved friezes of everyday life in ancient Egypt—harvest, hunting, boat-building—the netherworld being conceived as continuing business as usual. You have many tombs to choose from, but two of the best belonged to Mereruka, a royal chamberlain, and Princess Idut.

Eleven pyramids were built near the village of **Dahshur**, 15 km (9 miles) south of Saqqara, during the Old and Middle kingdoms. Until 1996, the area around the site was a military zone and inaccessible to tourists.

The most interesting structure is the Bent Pyramid, built under pharaoh Snoferu, father of Kheops. About halfway up, the angle changes from 55 to 43 degrees: maybe the architect changed his plans in order to speed up the work or save on building materials. It is the first real unstepped pyramid.

Further north, the Red Pyramid also dates from Snoferu's time. It is over 100 m (328 ft) high, with a base 220 m (722 ft) square. Its core was cased in Tura limestone; inscriptions were found on the backs of many pieces, including Snoferu's cartouche and the names of work gangs left for posterity in red paint. Snoferu was probably entombed in the funerary chamber.

PRACTICAL INFORMATION

Banks. In general they open Sunday to Thursday 8.30 a.m.–2 p.m. Banking desks at the airports and in the larger hotels have special hours for the convenience of tourists.

Clothing. When visiting mosques, women should wear skirts of modest length, cover their arms and wear a headscarf. Shorts (for men or women) are frowned upon. Comfortable footwear is essential for sightseeing.

Credit cards. Increasingly, shops and restaurants accept credit cards and often prefer them. Travellers cheques are best cashed at the bank or hotel.

Currency. The Egyptian pound (E£ or EGP) is divided into 100 piastres (pt). Coins range from 5 pt to E£1; notes from 5 to 50 pt and E£1 to £200. Foreign currency can be exchanged only at a bank or other authorized establishment.

Health. In the hot months, sunburn, sunstroke and dehydration are constant dangers. Keep insect repellent handy and wear a sun hat. The waters of the Nile are infested with the deadly bilharzia parasite. Do not drink unpurified Nile water, swim in the river or walk barefoot near it. Avoid ice cubes and stick to bottled mineral water for drinking.

Language. After Arabic, English is the language most commonly spoken; many signs are printed in English.

Post office. Generally open daily except Friday 7 a.m.–6 p.m. The postal service in Egypt is unpredictable. For faster service with postcards, mail them as letters inside an envelope.

Safety. Since the Arab Spring the political situation is unstable, and visitors should keep well away from popular demonstrations. Leave anything of value in the hotel safe.

Shops. In Cairo, most shops open 10 a.m.–7 p.m. in winter, to 8 p.m. in summer, interrupted by a siesta of two or three hours. Shops close one hour later on Mondays and Thursdays all year round.

Time. UTC/GMT+2, all year round.

Tipping. A service charge is usually added to your hotel or restaurant bills, although you may leave an additional small tip. Taxi drivers will appreciate a pound or two. Have a few small notes handy also for caretakers at mosques and temples.

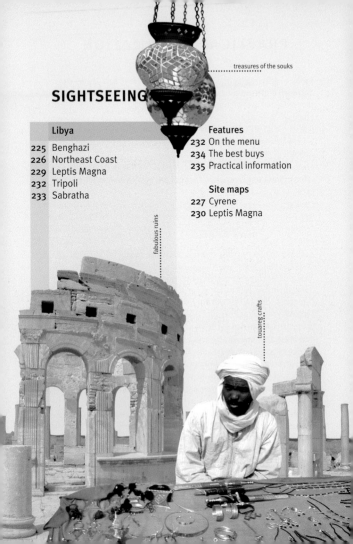

treasures of the souks

SIGHTSEEING

fabulous ruins

touareg crafts

LIBYA

Libya is vast, unique, and extraordinary. The profusion of Greek temples and theatres along the Mediterranean shore will enchant those who love ancient ruins. The most interesting sites are on the coast and in the hills. The Libyan people are now attempting to bring democracy to the country since the uprising against Colonel Gadaffi and his regime in 2011, resulting in his death.

Benghazi

Libya's second-largest city, Benghazi, east of the Gulf of Sirt, has been fought over and rebuilt so often that little remains of its Greek and Roman origins. After the Arab conquest it was by-passed by inland routes further south, but revived as a Turkish fortress and then as centre of operations for the Italian invasion. In World War II it was bombed by both sides, but quite a lot of the old city still stands next to the harbour. More recently, in February 2011, the city was taken by opponents to Gadaffi, and it became the site of the turning point of the civil war. There is at present a movement in favour of semi-autonomous status.

An Italian-built, arcaded street runs from the main post office to the central square, faced by a 17th-century mosque and the former Turkish governor's palace. A tra-ditional covered souk at the north-ern tip of the old quarter is notably clean and surprisingly quiet.

Cut off by a bridge from the harbour, the 23rd July Lake is the focus of modern Benghazi, with high-rise buildings and an impressive sports complex. From here, a semi-circle of suburbs and industrial zones spreads 10 km (6 miles) inland.

A low, dusty hill on the north-ern edge of Benghazi was the site of Euhesperides, one of the first Greek settlements in North Africa, dating from the 7th cen-tury BC. Later, its harbour silted up and it was abandoned in the 2nd century BC. To the south, streets formed a grid pattern, but the main interest centres on the Sidi Abed hill with traces of defensive walls built around 600 BC, and the cisterns and cellars of houses. The ground is littered with pot sherds, including fragments of black slip ware with finely detailed designs in red, characterstic of work from Attica in Greece.

As Euhesperides declined, Berenice along the coast to the west took over. It stands on the hill now called **Sidi Khraibish**, marked by a great square Ottoman lighthouse. Traces can be seen of the old city, dated to the 2nd century BC. The Romans added defences in the 2nd century AD to counter pirate raids and tribal incursions. The most prominent ruins are of a 6th-century Byzantine church with areas of mosaic floor.

Northeast Coast

On the coast 70 km (44 miles) northeast of Benghazi, **Tocra** is the present name for Teucheira, one of the cities of the ancient Greek Pentapolis. It remained important under the Romans, and historians wrote that it was the last stronghold of the Byzantines. Large parts of its walls survive, enclosing an area roughly 700 m (800 yd) square. The entrance is through the restored East Gate, near the Ottoman fort, leading to tombs, extensive walls and the foundations and mosaic floors of two Byzantine churches.

Probably founded in the 4th century BC, **Ptolemais** (now Tolmeita) stands on the coast north of Al-Marj. Inland from the present-day village, extensive remains of the Roman and Byzantine city cover a wide area of the coastal plain. A long **colonnaded street** runs roughly east-west, lined by what must have been palatial houses, perhaps built by merchants who had grown rich on trade between Africa and Rome. On a parallel east-west street is the so-called **Fortress-Church** of the 5th century, with a barrel-vaulted ceiling and an apse at the east end. The **Palace of Columns** to the east of the church is built on the grand scale, its halls rich with mosaics, and with large baths and pools. Water was evidently a worry in Ptolemais. Massive underground **cisterns** take up most of the area beneath the forum. Arcades with columns 3 m (10 feet) tall were built, roofed and paved over to create the open space above.

The **Odeon**, a small theatre beside the street leading to the West Gate, shows unusual alterations designed to allow the "orchestra pit" to be flooded, presumably for special waterborne effects.

At **Qasr Libya** (*Qasr al-Lebia*), excavations in 1956 of a 6th century church on a hilltop revealed 50 marvellously preserved mosaic panels. One shows the Pharos of Alexandria, and on its neighbour two sailors gaze at the lighthouse in an allegory of Faith. The panels are displayed on the walls of a museum at the site, with a larger mosaic on the floor.

Cyrene was founded in about 631 BC by refugees from Santorini (Thera) fleeing the earthquakes, droughts and volcanic activity afflicting the island. At first they settled on the coast, but soon found more fertile soil and a better climate in the hills just inland. They must have felt quite at home—it looks just like parts of Greece—and a natural spring in a cave decided the exact spot.

The first Greek colony in Africa, Cyrene expanded quickly, building its port of Apollonia and other cities in the region. Under the Ptolemies of Egypt it became a famous centre of learning. The Romans took over in the 1st century BC, and rebuilt the city on a grander scale. A revolt by the large Jewish community in AD 115–16 caused immense destruction, partly repaired on the orders of the emperor Hadrian (117–38) after a visit. By the 4th century, Rome's power was waning and tribal raids increased, threatening agriculture and trade. Cyrene went into a long decline, in spite of Byzantine efforts to revive its fortunes. The Arab village of Shahat grew up among the ruins; in recent years most of its people have moved into new houses further away.

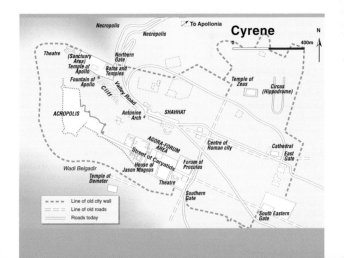

The water of the fountain of Apollo was considered to have healing powers. You can still see the pipes that carried it to the temple baths.

Bernard Joliat

The complex site comprises five main areas: the Temple of Zeus; the Roman city centre; the Greek agora and Roman forum; the Acropolis; and the Fountain and Sanctuary of Apollo.

At 70 m (230 ft) long, the **Temple of Zeus** is bigger than the Parthenon. Originally built in about 550 BC, it was radically altered by the Romans after being wrecked in the Jewish revolt, but they kept the original Doric style. As recently as 1950 only one of the great columns was still standing; an Italian team has worked a miracle in reassembling the fallen pieces.

The main street of the **Roman city** crosses the centre of the site, roughly east-west from the East Gate along a valley to the Antonine Arch. The village of Shahat lies along the western part of the street, which then curves to the right, downhill to the Sanctuary of Apollo (see below).

Civic buildings and temples clustered round the **Greek agora** (later the Roman forum).

Apollonia, the port which served Cyrene, is 20 km (12 miles) away to the northeast, next to the small modern town of Susa and its little-used harbour. A **museum** near the entrance has some statues and mosaics from the ancient site which spreads along the shore to the east. Parts of it have been submerged; some buildings stand at very edge of the sea, and traces of others can be seen by scuba divers or from the air.

Massive city walls, originally built around 250 BC, were strengthened in the 1st or 2nd centuries, and again in the 4th century, when most of the gates were blocked up to improve the defences. Inside the walls, most of the buildings date from the Byzantine period: houses with vaulted cisterns; three churches with lovely marble columns; and, next to the ramparts, the so-called **Palace of the Dux**, possibly the Byzantine governor's residence. Most striking of all is the **Theatre**, backing on to the outside of the city wall at its eastern end. The seating is partly carved out of the rocky hillside, facing the sea.

At the seaward end of a wadi, where enough water flows after rains to form the Chellal waterfall, **Derna** (or Darnah) was settled by Greeks soon after Cyrene. Renowned in the 19th century for its gardens and olive groves, it came to the world's attention in 1805 when the US Navy made it a base for their campaign to suppress piracy. The Italians turned it into a seaside resort in the 1930s. It changed hands several times during World War II and was badly damaged. When the German Afrika Korps under Rommel took the town, they cut off and captured a British force and its commander, General O'Connor. Derna today is less interesting than its history, but makes a convenient stopover between Benghazi and the Egyptian border.

You can visit the 17th-century Al-Aatik mosque, one of the biggest in the country, with 42 white domes. Beside it is a small covered souk. The Archaeological Museum displays mainly ancient Libyan statuary.

Now a modern port, **Tobruk** was famous during World War II, when British and Commonwealth forces defending it withstood a three months' siege. After it changed hands twice more in 1942, there was little left standing. Today, travellers heading for the Egyptian border 100 km (75 miles) away pass through it, and others come specially to visit the Commonwealth, German and Italian war cemeteries south of the town.

Leptis Magna

The largest city of ancient Tripolis, Leptis Magna was built on fertile land near a natural harbour, and became a major trade centre linking the African interior with the Mediterranean. The ruins are among the most impressive in the entire Roman world, for the huge scale of the monuments, the beauty of the stone and the dramatic location beside the sea.

Probably founded by Phoenicians from Tyre around 700 BC, Leptis was under Carthaginian rule from the 4th century BC until the end of the Second Punic War in 202 BC, when it became part of the Numidian kingdom ruled by Masinissa. It broke away in 111 BC to become an ally of Rome, and was peacefully absorbed into the empire in 46 BC. Gathering great wealth from exports of olive oil and the caravan trade with the central Africa, it prospered and expanded rapidly. The population at its peak is estimated at about 75,000. Most of them continued to speak Punic: many bilingual Latin and Punic inscriptions have been found. Trajan, emperor from AD 98–117, gave it full citizenship rights, but Leptis Magna really came into its own under Septimius Severus (193–211).

Leptis began to decline as the port gradually silted up and earthquakes caused extensive damage in the 4th century. Increasing insecurity culminated in the 5th century Vandal occupation. The Byzantines brought a revival of activity, although the defensive wall they built only protected the immediate harbour area.

After the Arab conquest, the city seems to have been gradually abandoned. At some point the dam the Romans had built across the Wadi Labdah broke, and in the centuries that followed, flash floods washed rocks and soil down the valley and over the site, permanently blocking the harbour. Such floods can still be a problem; huge blocks of stone are still strewn beside the Severan street after the floods of 1987–88.

The entrance to the site is off the old coast road, and past the museum. Inside the gate, you'll see steep steps leading down to the first landmark, the four-way triumphal **Arch of Septimius Severus**. Built to commemorate the visit of

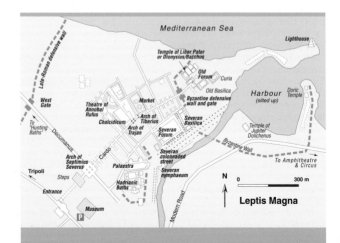

Severus and his sons Caracalla and Geta in 203, this marks the intersection of the Cardo and the Decumanus, the two main streets. To the right are the **Hadrianic Baths**, the largest in Roman Africa, and perfectly symmetrical. Imagine them covered in marble and mosaics, and decorated with polychrome statues.

The city's main artery, the Cardo, heads northeast beneath the arches of Tiberius and Trajan. To the left is the beautiful circular **Market** building dating from just before the Christian era, and the **Theatre of Annobal Rufus** (1st century). The Cardo then reaches the plain **Byzantine Gate**, in the solid wall round that small area of the city the Byzantines chose to defend. Passing through it, you come to the **Old Forum**, surrounded by the remains of temples, the Old Basilica and Curia. .

The ambitious development ordered by Septimius Severus involved creating a new axis for the city, parallel to the old cardo. Running from the Hadrianic Baths to the harbour, this **colonnaded street** is 410 m (450 yd) long and 20 m (22 yd) wide. On its left is the **Severan Forum**, with magnificent stone carving and majestic colonnades, sadly flattened by the great earthquake of 365. Adjoining it is the **Basilica**, with three aisles and an apse end, 70 m (230 ft) long and over 30 m

Bernard Joliat

An intricately sculpted column of the Severan basilica.

(100 ft) high. The basilica was later adapted to become a church: note the pulpit put together from various bits and pieces — and then incorporated into the Byzantine wall as a strong point.

Continue along the Severan street to the **Harbour**, where you can see the original paved quaysides, and the marks where ships' cables wore grooves in the stone.

Near the site entrance, the **museum** is a fine modern building housing some of the best finds from Leptis Magna, as well as a display of Libyan prehistory —

flints and rock art. From the Punic era, tombs found under the theatre bear the strange image of the Carthaginian goddess Tanit, symbolized as a triangle with round head and raised arms.

East of the main site, a short distance away, the amphitheatre and Circus date from the 1st and 2nd centuries. They are reached by road, and then by a rough track which climbs to a hilltop overlooking the sea. The **amphitheatre** is dramatically revealed when you suddenly find yourself on its upper rim, gazing down as if into a volcanic crater lined by stone seating, partly restored but mainly original. Deep tunnels lead directly into the arena to allow the entry of participants, human and animal — exotic beasts were brought from far and wide to take part in the spectacles.

Tripoli

The capital and main port of Libya is a sprawling modern city with a population of over a million. At its heart, next to the harbour, is the old quarter or *medina*, on a site continuously occupied since the arrival of Phoenician traders. As capital of Roman Tripolis, "Three Cities", it took the name Tripoli as the other two declined into obscurity.

The modern city spreads far out to the east, south and west. Old and new meet below the castle walls at the eastern end of the medina, in the wide open space of **Martyrs' Square**, the former Green Square. Southeast from there runs the former waterfront **corniche**, now left inland by landfill schemes covered in concrete and highway overpasses. Next to it stand the Al-Kabir Hotel, Gazelle Fountain and the tall Mehari Hotel. Inland from Gazelle Fountain, the Italian-built cathedral is now a mosque, and the former royal palace has been labelled the People's Palace.

To the west of the harbour, the **medina** is a maze of narrow alleys and covered markets; a guide is almost essential if you want to see the sights.

At the eastern corner, the **Castle** (*Assarai al-Hamra*) stands on much earlier foundations: excavations have revealed Punic

---

On the menu
Asida – a soft pastry with fig syrup, eaten with the fingers
Batata mubatana – potatoes stuffed with mincemeat, covered with beaten egg and breadcrumbs
Bazin – porridge of wheat, salt and water
Chorba – minestrone spiced with red pepper

(Carthaginian) tombs and Roman baths. The walls are mainly 16th century work, and the buildings inside date from the 17–18th centuries, when a moat still surrounded the citadel.

Facing the castle across Souk al-Mushir, the **Ahmed Pasha Karamanli Mosque**, 1738, is the city's largest. Not far away is the **An-Naqua Mosque**, a little gem from the 8th–10th centuries with a variety of classical columns supporting the roof of its prayer hall.

The **Bab Draghut** gate in the medina's north wall leads to the most prominent Roman relic in Tripoli, the four-way **Arch of Marcus Aurelius** (AD 165). Close by is the **Gurgi Mosque**, with its tall minaret, 16-dome prayer hall and fine marble courtyard. Mustafa Gurgi was the son-in-law of the last Karamanli Pasha, a Georgian by birth and probably a convert to Islam, who demonstrated his faith by paying for this lavishly decorated building, completed in 1834.

The **Jamahiriya Museum** is set into Tripoli Castle, its entrance facing Martyr's Square. The ground level has sections on prehistory, notably the rock art of the southern Sahara, and the Phoenician and Carthaginian era. But the main glories are the Roman galleries, with magnificent mosaics showing fishing, farming and ships in fine detail—the mosaic artists of the 1st and 2nd centuries used such tiny *tesserae* pieces that the effect is like a painting. Giant statues, busts and heads have been brought here from all the major sites; an upstairs gallery has some of the finest from Leptis Magna. The two top floors cover the Islamic period up to modern times.

Sabratha

On the coast 70 km (44 miles) west of Tripoli, Sabratha flourished under the Romans from the 1st century BC to the 4th century. It never fully recovered from a devastating earthquake in 365. After the Arabs swept through North Africa, it declined into obscurity and was partly buried by sand until the Italians started major excavations before World War II.

At the entrance, your eyes are drawn to the imposing theatre, but that is probably best left as the climax of your tour. Inside, you are faced by the main gate in the wall built by the Byzantines in the 6th century. Reflecting their shortage of manpower and correspondingly reduced ambitions, it only enclosed the older part of the city, about one-third of the area.

To the left, outside the wall, is the **Mausoleum of Bes**, a strange Punic monument of the 2nd century BC, reassembled from fragments. The three-sided pinnacle

hemis.fr/Guiziou

The best buys

Basketwork

Burnous (the robes worn by men
during the cold season)

Beduin jewellery

Carpets and rugs made of
sheep's wool or camelhair

Leather bags and chests
decorated with silk
embroidery

Leather slippers

Old postcards

Terracotta pottery

ities. To the west is the Capitoleum where the great head of Jupiter, now in the museum, was found.

Beyond the forum are the **Basilica of Justinian** and the **Seaward Baths**, with beautiful mosaics and a hexagonal, marble-lined latrine, in such good condition it could be used today. East of the wall you'll see more temples and churches and the *Baths of Oceanus*, next to the encroaching sea, luxuriously surfaced with marble and mosaics.

Across the old Roman road, the 2nd-century **Theatre** with its imposing three-tiered, 108-column backdrop to the stage, is largely the result of an ambitious Italian restoration project in the 1930s. The carved frieze on the curved recesses at the front of the stage is beautifully preserved, depicting groups of players and theatrical masks.

Built in the style of a Roman villa, the main **museum** near the entrance houses mosaics from the 6th-century Basilica of Justinian, a huge grapevine design on the floor and mosaics from the church's aisles on the walls. Other rooms display wall paintings and marble statuary including a colossal head of Jupiter from the Capiteoleum.

A small **Punic Museum** displays relics from the pre-Roman period.

with its concave faces plays beautiful tricks with light and shade.

Inside the **Byzantine Gate**, the main street leading to the *Forum* passes, on the left, the South Forum Temple and the Basilica of Apollonius, a 5th-century church. On the right are the Antonine Temple and, facing the forum, the Temple of Liber Pater, or Dionysius. On the north (seaward) side, the Curia was the meeting place for the city author-

PRACTICAL INFORMATION

Banks. In summer, generally open Saturday to Wednesday 8 a.m.–1 p.m.; in winter they also open Wednesdays and Saturdays 4–5 p.m., as well as Thursday morning.

Climate. The Mediterranean coast is dry and warm in summer, though partly refreshed by sea breezes. Winters are colder than you might imagine, especially in the east. Summers are hot in the desert, winters dry and sunny with very cold nights, especially in high regions. The best season is from October to April.

Currency. The Libyan dinar (LYD or LD) is divided into 1000 dirhams. It is illegal to change money outside banks and official bureaux de change. There are some cash distributors, but credit cards are generally only accepted in big hotels. Travellers cheques are difficult to change. It's best to take a cash supply of US dollars or euros.

Entry formalities. To visit Libya you need a valid passport and a visa. If your passport bears an Israeli stamp you will not be allowed into the country. It can take several weeks to obtain a visa. The entry formalities are subject to frequent change and it is best to consult your travel agent or the Libyan embassy in your country before you think of visiting.

Language. Arabic is the official language, used for all documents and signs, making it practically impossible to find your way around without a guide. However, in more recent times a few signs in Roman letters have appeared.

Safety. The continued existence of various armed militias after the fall of Gadaffi makes for a precarious peace, and at present visits are not advised.

Time. UTC/GMT +2 all year round.

Tipping. Service is generally included in restaurant and hotel bills. If you take a taxi, settle on the fare in advance, and you will not need to tip the driver.

Traditions. Pork and alcohol are prohibited.

Water. Stick to bottled mineral water for drinking purposes.

devout people

SIGHTSEEING

diving expeditions

culture and traditions

7000 years of history

British influence

MALTA

Sprawling in the sun of the southern Mediterranean, Malta has a history as crucial as its location. Mystery, tragedy and heroism pepper its past; its fate, more than once, has changed the story of Europe. Conquerors and liberators have been passing through since the Stone Age; there are more archaeological sites than beaches. Buffeted by the stream of invaders, the Maltese character, language and culture are unique.

Valletta

A UNESCO World Heritage site, the golden city of the knights has something for all interests: ingenious fortifications, baroque stone palaces, churches, museums, sea views, shopping and a relaxed way of life anchored in open-air cafés. Named after Grand Master Jean Parisot de la Valette, it was built after Malta's triumph over the Turks in the terrible siege of 1565. The city's grid plan was sketched out by Francesco Laparelli, the Pope's own architect.

Enter the peninsular city across a deep moat and through the City Gate. Just ahead, on the left, is a 19th-century *palazzo* with striking details in Venetian Renaissance style. Opposite are the ruins of the Opera House, built in 1866 and destroyed by German bombs in 1942.

The **Auberge of Castille and Leon** is the most majestic of the inns where the knights lived, segregated according to their origin. Spanish and Portuguese knights were quartered here. The elegant baroque details were added in the 18th century. **Sacred Island**, at Dar l-Emigrant on Castille Place, is an audio-visual show focusing on Malta's cultural heritage from the time of the Fertility Goddess to the visit of Pope John Paul II in 2001.

The **Upper Barracca Gardens** offer a tremendous view of the Grand Harbour and the historic Three Cities beyond. Among the attractions of this small 18th-century park perched on the edge, literally, of town, are the greenery, statues and calm.

Valletta's main street, seething with pedestrians most of the day,

Bernard Joliat

Statue of the Mother Goddess of Fertility. | **The Prime Minister has his offices in the imposing Inn of Castille and Leon.**

is called **Republic Street**. Straight as a spear, it goes all the way down the slope to Fort St Elmo at the tip of the peninsula. Turn off into the narrow side streets where washing flaps overhead, drying in the sun.

The **National Archaeology Museum** occupies the 16th-century Auberge de Provence, the most influential of the French inns of knightly Valletta. Here you'll find all you need to know about Malta's megalithic monuments, and more. The prehistoric gallery displays ten fertility goddesses from the Ħaġar Qim temple, all headless; the plump "sleeping woman" from the Hypogeum; and from Tarxien (2200 BC), a standing statue with head, looking a bit like an old-fashioned schoolmarm's bobbed hairstyle, though it's probably a skirted man. There are examples of Stone Age pottery of all sizes and uses.

The **National Museum of Fine Arts** is housed in a stately palace that was erected in the days of the knights, but rebuilt in the 18th century. From 1821 until independence, it was Admiralty House, the official residence of the Commander-in-Chief of the British Mediterranean Fleet; Lord Mountbatten of Burma lived here. On display are worthwhile works of art by European and local artists from the 14th to the 20th century.

St John's Co-Cathedral is figuratively built on the bones of the Knights of Malta. Hundreds of knights are buried in the floor under slabs of marble. Even if your Latin is rusty the illustrations—of coats of arms, trophies, skeletons and angels—tell the story. Although the exterior, designed by Girolamo Cassar, seems drab, the baroque interior of the Co-Cathedral is a revelation of dazzling art and decoration. It's worth the price of admission to the oratory and museum to see the Caravaggio painting, *The Beheading of St John,* a landmark of 17th-century art. Elsewhere in the museum are displayed tapestries of great value, and vestments donated to the church by the knights.

Take a coffee break in **Republic Square**, with its concentration of outdoor cafés. A curiosity here— a **statue** of Queen Victoria which outlived independence—presides over a forest of café umbrellas. Behind her, the National Library contains all the knightly documents over nearly seven centuries. An interactive show, The Great Siege of Malta 1565 and the Knights of St John, helps you relive the island's history (tours last 45 minutes).

By Malta's standards the **Grand Master's Palace** is an enormous building, filling an entire city block. Only a small part is open to the public; the rest belongs to the parliament. But you can penetrate two peaceful courtyards and admire the sculpture, the fountain and the 18th-century clock. The main part of the palace that's open is the transplanted **Armoury** of the knights. Nineteen dummies in armour show off full regalia with swords and pikes. Apart from historic suits of armour, you can see Turkish shields and swords, trophies from the great siege.

In 1731, Grand Master Antonio Manoel de Vilhena, from Portugal, built the **Manoel Theatre** to offer the people of Malta some "honest" recreation. A small museum next door displays costumes and old photographs.

As Valletta first took shape, the Knights Hospitallers of St John, who began tending the sick in the 11th century, built the **Sacra Infermeria**, or Holy Infirmary, a vast hospital near the end of the peninsula. The main ward was 155 m (more than 500 ft) long, and as wide as it was high—11 m (36 ft). At the time it was the longest

---

On the menu

Bragjoli – beef olives in wine sauce
Cerna – hake
Dentici – sea bream
Fenek – rabbit
Lampuki – the national fish, a kind of dorado
Minestra – thick vegetable and pasta soup
Pixxispada – swordfish
Timpana – macaroni and mincemeat bake

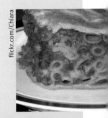
flickr.com/Chiara

hall in Europe. The knights took in anyone of any faith who was ill and treated the sick as *seigneurs malades* (sick lords) with respect and humility. The standard of medical treatment was high and the patients were given good food served on silver dishes. Now the Holy Infirmary has been transformed into the Mediterranean Conference Centre. Here, too, is the **Malta Experience**, a patriotic audio-visual 7000-year history of the island, with commentary on headphones in many languages.

During the great siege of 1565 **Fort St Elmo**, at the very tip of the peninsula, held out for a whole month before it fell to the Turks, who lost five times as many soldiers as the defenders. At the start of Malta's struggle in the World War II, the star-shaped fort was one of the first targets; on the first day of the war six Maltese artillerymen died on the ramparts. Now the fort is the home of the police academy. You can assess its size and powerful bulwarks during the historical re-enactments in period costume, held throughout the year except in peak summer periods.

A separate entrance to the fort leads to the **National War Museum**, an old-fashioned museum detailing daily life in the siege of the 1940s. A replica of an air-raid shelter has authentic furnishings. A jeep called *Husky*, used on Malta by President Roosevelt and General Eisenhower, looks ready to roll, and a restored Sea Gladiator fighter would fly if it hadn't lost its wings.

Vittoriosa

When the homeless Order of St John first arrived on Malta, the knights settled across the harbour from what later became Valletta. The centre of their world was Birgu, where they built fortifications, churches, palaces and a hospital. Most of the grand project was wiped out in the great siege of 1565, after which Birgu's name was changed to Vittoriosa. A parallel peninsula, L'Isla, was renamed Senglea. And Bormla became Cospicua. In the 17th century elaborate fortifications—the Margherita Lines and the Cottonera Lines—were laid out to protect the Three Cities. They are still impressive.

Vittoriosa has been defended for more than a thousand years by a fort at the extremity of the peninsula. **Fort St Angelo** never surrendered in the darkest days of the Turkish assault, and in World War II it was again the military headquarters for the siege, and again victorious.

Overlooking the harbour, the **Collegiate Church of St Lawrence** traces its history back to the 11th century. It claims to have been Malta's first parish church. The

The best buys
Blown glass from Mdina
Figurines of knights in armour
Honey
Lace
Liqueurs and wines
Jewellery and small objects in
   silver and gold
Knitwear
Olive oil
Pottery
Scale models of ships
Replicas of old statues

dome, bombed out in World War II, has been rebuilt bigger and better than ever.

St Joseph's Chapel, built in the 18th century, has become a museum of Malta memorabilia. Here are the robes and seals of office of the Inquisitors, who kept the knights on their moral toes.

The Royal Navy has gone away, so Malta has converted its 19th-century harbourside bakery—at one time it fed the whole Mediterranean fleet—into the **Maritime Museum**. The exhibits run from ancient Roman anchors to plates from the British officers' mess, vintage 1938.

Prehistoric Sites

Malta's prehistoric sites boggle the minds of archaeologists. The most detached layman must be awed at the sheer age of the Neolithic temples, their advanced architecture, their mysteries.

In the middle of Valletta's modern suburb of Paola are two neighbouring sites. The best maintained are the **Tarxien** temples, whose three main temples date from 3000–2500 BC. The site came to light just before World War I, and Malta's great archaeologist, Sir Themistocles Zammit, led the excavations. Among the astonishments of Tarxien are the precision with which giant stone slabs were cut and aligned and the wealth of sculpture and pottery discovered inside the temples. The inner walls reveal bas-relief carvings (the originals are in the National Museum of Archaeology) of animals of the kinds that were ritually sacrificed here: cows, sheep, goats and pigs.

The nearby **Hypogeum** was discovered by well-diggers in 1902. They had stumbled upon the site of a burial ground dating back to about 3000 BC. Thousands of people were buried in this elaborate subterranean sanctuary along with jewellery and pottery. To protect against damage caused by exhalations of carbon dioxide, entry to the Hypogeum is restricted; tickets are on sale in all the Heritage Malta museums or on the internet site:

booking.heritagemalta.org
Book at least two months in advance.

St Paul's Cathedral in Mdina is the architectural heart of the old fortified city.

hemis.fr/Wysocki

Mdina

Hunched on a high ridge, the bulwarks and domes of Mdina rule the horizon. Its history is said to go back 4000 years. Its supremacy dates to Roman times when the city became the island's capital. When the Order of St John took over the island, the knights chose to make their capital on the harbour of what later became Valletta. Thus the inland city became a backwater of history, happily well preserved. Today it is known as the "silent city", inhabited but secretive, noble and reserved. The entire walled city is a pedestrian zone.

The façade of **St Paul's Cathedral** introduces Malta's most majestic church. According to legend, this is the spot where St Paul himself converted the Roman governor, Publius, to Christianity. Invisible from the plaza, the great **dome**, seen from inside the cathedral, is

the most uplifting design, with light streaming in. Don't miss the sacristy door of carved Irish oak, a silver tabernacle by Benvenuto Cellini, and a bejewelled icon of the Madonna in the chapel of the Blessed Sacrament. The **Cathedral Museum** is strong on art works by Dürer. The archives of the Inquisition are held here, along with vestments decorated with ancient Maltese lace.

Rabat

Beyond the ramparts, Rabat has kept its Arabic name. Outside the gardens abutting the Mdina moat, a **Roman villa** was unearthed towards the end of the 19th century. Built in the 1st century BC, the house presumably belonged to a Roman official or rich merchant. In the atrium are some very interesting **mosaics** with three-dimensional effects. A museum of Roman antiquities has been built around the villa.

Legend says St Paul spent his three months in Malta underground in what is now called **St Paul's Grotto** in Rabat. The site has been adorned with tributes, from a statue of the saint to a silver galley donated by the knights.

Malta's early Christians buried their dead in **catacombs** carved out of the bedrock. These underground cemeteries are honeycombed beneath Rabat on many levels. Not for the claustrophobic.

PRACTICAL INFORMATION

Banks. Monday to Thursday 8.30 a.m.–1.30 or 2 p.m., Friday 8.30 a.m.–3.30 or 4.30 p.m., Saturay 8.30 a.m.–12.30 p.m.

Climate. From mid-June to mid-September the average maximum temperatures go into the 30s °C (the upper 80s °F), but sea breezes relieve the swelter. The rainiest months are October through January.

Credit cards and travellers cheques. The major cards are widely accepted. Travellers cheques can be cashed in banks and bureaux de change.

Currency. The Euro, divided into 100 cents.

Electricity. The current is 220 V AC, 50 Hz. Most plugs are the British kind, with three flat pins. Hotels are often equipped with outlets for European-type plugs with two round pins.

Emergencies. The emergency phone number is 112.

Language. The official languages are Maltese and English.

Museums and Sites. Many are managed by Heritage Malta, a state organization in charge of the national heritage. Most museums open daily 9 a.m.–4.30 p.m., except some pubic holidays. Private museums tend to keep shorter hours on weekends.

Post offices. The main post office on Castille Place in Valletta is open Monday to Friday 8.15 a.m.–4.30 p.m., Saturday 8.15 a.m.–12.30 p.m.

Shops. Open Monday to Saturday, 9 a.m.–1 p.m. and 4–7 p.m.

Taxis. All the taxis are metered but the meters don't always work. When in doubt, ask the driver beforehand what the fare will be.

Tipping. Taxi drivers are usually tipped 10 per cent of the fare. Waiters will expect a small tip of 5 to 10 per cent. And don't forget a few coins for the porter and the public toilet attendant.

Toilets. Malta's public facilities are prominently signposted and well maintained, but paper tissues might come in handy.

Transport. The bus network is well organized; buses are the most economical way of travelling to outlying villages and the main sights. The central bus station is next to the Triton Fountain in front of the City Gate in Valletta. You need small change to pay for tickets.

Venice

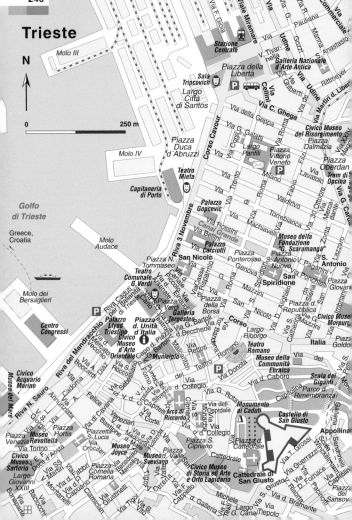

Trieste

N

0 — 250 m

Molo III

Viale Miramare

Via F. Gioia

Via G. R.

Via Pauliana

Commerciale

Via Anastasio

Stazione Centrale

Piazza della Libertà

Sala Tripcovich

Largo Città di Santos

Piazza Duca d'Abruzzi

Molo IV

Teatro Miela

Capitaneria di Porto

Golfo di Trieste

Greece, Croatia

Molo Audace

Molo dei Bersaglieri

Centro Congressi

Civico Acquario Marino

Museo del Mare

Riva N. Sauro

Piazza N. Tommaseo

Teatro Comunale G. Verdi

Palazzo Lloyd Triestine

Civico Museo d'Arte Orientale

Piazza d. Unità d'Italia

Riva del Mandracchio

Galleria Nazionale d'Arte Antica

Via Tivar-nella

Via Cellini

Via C. Ghega

Via della Geppa

Corso Cavour

Piazza Panfili

Piazza Vittorio Veneto

Civico Museo del Risorgimento

Piazza Dalmazia

Piazza Oberdan

Tram di Opcina

Palazzo Gopcevic

Canal Grande

Palazzo Carciotti

San Nicolò

Via Rossini

Via Bellini

Torrebianca

Museo della Fondazione "G. Scaramangà"

Piazza Ponterosso

S. Antonio Nuovo

S. Antonio

San Spiridione

Piazza della Borsa

Corso

Galleria Tergesteo

Piazza della Repubblica

Civico Museo Morpurgo

Largo Riborgo

Teatro Romano

Museo della Comunità Ebraica

Italia

Scala dei Giganti

Parco di Rimembranza

Municipio

Arco di Riccardo

Monumento ai Caduti

Castello di San Giusto

Appollina

Piazza Venezia

Museo Revoltella

Civico Museo Sartorio

Largo Giovanni XXIII

Piazza Hortis

Museo Joyce

Museo Sveviano

Piazza S. Cipriano

Civico Museo di Storia ed Arte e Orto Lapidario

Cattedrale di San Giusto

Piazza del Sansov

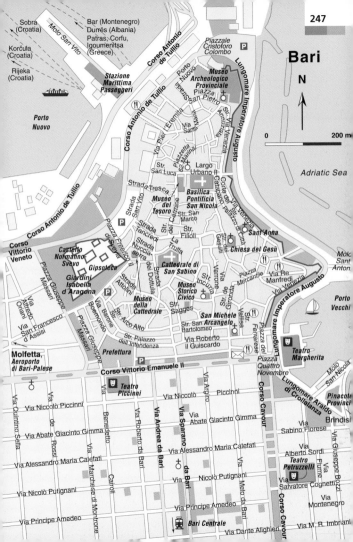

Koper

Adriatic Sea

Koprski zaliv

Marina

N

200 m

Samostan in cerkev sv. Ane

Destradijev trg

Volkovo nabrežje

Brkinska ulica

Mirenska ulica

Gasilska ulica

Leta ulica

Samostan in cerkev sv. Marte

Goriška ulica

Kumarjeva ulica

Kmečka ulica

Kreljeva ulica

Volkovo nabrežje

Samostan in cerkev sv. Frančiška

Sv. Justa

Cerkvica

Vrna sv. Tomaža

Ferraska ulica

Pekarniška ulica

Palača de Belli

Dijaška ulica

Cankarjeva ulica

Petronijeva ulica

Fontico

Martincev

Pobegova ulica

Gimnazijski trg

Benečanska gotska hiša

Obzidna ulica

Kamnita ulica

Kosovelov trg

Izolska vrata

Vergerjev trg

Sv. Blaža

Rotunda Janeza Krstnika

Palača Brutti

Stolnica Marijinega vnebovzetja

Sv. Jakoba

Trg Brolo

Ulica osvobodine fronte

Palača Barbabianca Küppelwieser

Sabinijeva ulica

Soška ulica

Porta della Muda

Sv. Bassa

Kopališko nabrežje

Belvederski trg

Verdijeva ulica

Patrijanov stolp

Luža

Tilov trg

Pretorska palača

Palača Totto Gravisi

Palača Orlandini

Cevljarska ulica

Palača Gravisi-Buttorai

Da Ponte vodnjak

Prešernov trg

Herijev trg

Sv. Bassa

Mladinska ulica

Kidričeva ulica

Garibaldijeva ulica

Palača Almerigogna

Goltakov

Pristaniška ulica

P

Muzejski trg

Pokrajinski muzej Koper

Kraljeva ulica

Župančičeva ulica

Valvasorijeva ulica

Belveder

Ressiova ulica

Carpacciov trg

Tavena

Steber sv. Justine

Kolaričeva hiša

Carpacciova ulica

Kolaričeva

Planiška ulica

cesta

Cesta Zore Perello-godina

P

Ukmarjev trg

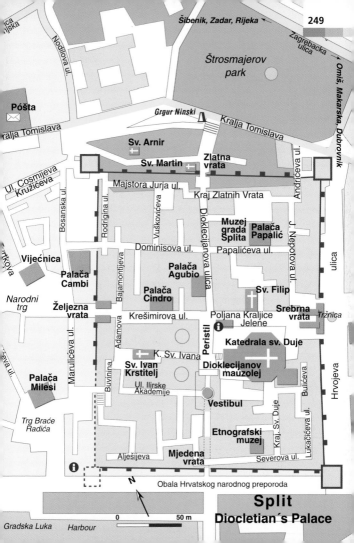

Split
Diocletian´s Palace

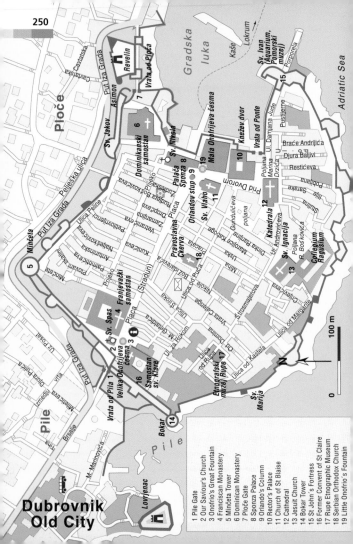

Dubrovnik Old City

1 Pile Gate
2 Our Saviour's Church
3 Onofrio's Great Fountain
4 Franciscan Monastery
5 Minčeta Tower
6 Dominican Monastery
7 Ploče Gate
8 Sponza Palace
9 Orlando's Column
10 Rector's Palace
11 Church of St Blaise
12 Cathedral
13 Jesuit Church
14 Bokar Tower
15 St John's Fortress
16 Former Convent of St Claire
17 Rupe Etnographic Museum
18 Serbian Orthodox Church
19 Little Onofrio's Fountain

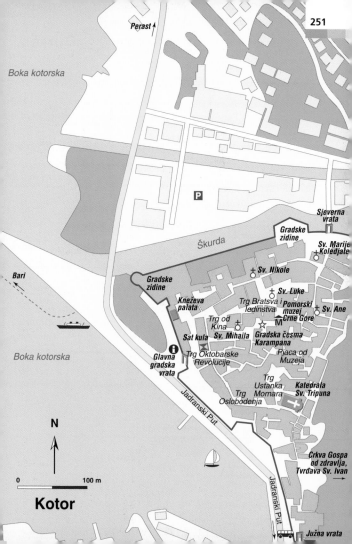

Perast ↑

Boka kotorska

P

Škurda

Sjeverna
vrata

Gradske
zidine

Sv. Marije
+ Koledjale

Gradske
zidine

Knezeva
palata

+ Sv. Nikole

+ Sv. Luke

Trg Bratsva i
Jedinstva

Pomorski
muzej

M

+ Sv. Ane

Bari

Trg od
Kina

☆

Crne Gore

Sat kula

Sv. Mihaila

Gradska česma
Karampana

Boka kotorska

ℹ

Glavna
gradska
vrata

Trg Oktobarske
Revolucije

Pjaca od
Muzeja

Trg
Ustanka
Mornara

Katedrala
Sv. Tripuna

Trg
Oslobodenja

Jadranski Put

N

↑

0   100 m

Crkva Gospa
od zdravlja,
Tvrdava Sv. Ivan →

Kotor

Jadranski Put

Južna vrata

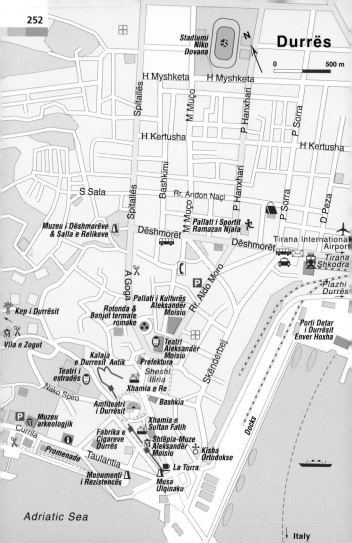

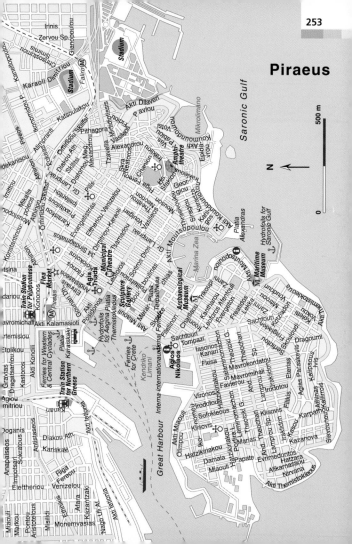

Piraeus

Saronic Gulf

500 m

N

0

Irinis
Zervou Sp.
Giaropoulou
Chrisostomou
Smirnis
Kanellopoulou
Faliro M
Stadium
Karaoli Dimitriou
Stadium M
Akti Dilaveri
P. Paviou
Vas. Pavlou
Koumoundourou
Mikrolimano
Katsoulakou
Alipranti
Omiridou Skilitsi
Pithagora
Skilitsi
Gr. Lampraki
Dianou Ath.
Alexandrou
Notara
Ipsilantou
Akti Koumoundourou
Epidavrou
Amphi-Theatre
dekanisou
Iroon Polytechniou
Mikras Asias
Ikoniou
Konstantinou
Karaoli D.
Omiridou Skilitsi
Afthitou
Tzavella
Vasileos
Pilis
Nestoros
Klanthi
Diakou Ath.
Vas. Georgiou
Geor.
tsina
Elefteriou Venizelou
Elefteriou-Karaoli
Vasil. Pavlou
Vas. Konstandinou
Iroon Polytechniou
Vongari
Santaroza
Akti Moutsopoulou
Platia Alexandras
Hydrofoils for Saronic Gulf
dariou
Karaiskou
Elefteriou
34 Sinadakou
Agia Triada
Municipal Theatre
Leoforos
Sotiros Dios
Filonos
Marina Zea
Akti Themistokleous
Ir. Polytehniou
Artemisiou
Konstandinou Kononos
Flea Market
Train Station for Peloponnese
M Piraeus
Akti Poseidonos
Gounari
Bouboulinas
Akti Miaouli
Akti Moutsopoulou
Zanni
Mouson
Nirvana
Maritime Museum
Vodurou
Etolikou
avromichali
Kastoras
Akti Kondili
Akti Kalamasioti
Sculpture Gallery
Filellinon
Ferres-Platia Terpsitheas
Archaeological Museum
Charilaou Trikoupi
Kantharou
Leoforos Afentouli
Ferres-Platia Terpsitheas
Evangelistrias
Freatidos
Sachtouri
Mitrou
Sotiros Dios
Kolokotroni
Drosopoulou
Androutsou
Dragoumi
Gravias
Anastasaos
Despotopoulou
Agiou Dimitriou
Train Station for Northern Greece
Platia Karaiskaki
Hydrofoils for Aegina
Platia Themistokleous
Ferres for Crete
Agios Nikolaos
Sachtouri
Tompazi
Iasonos
Kanari
Flesa
Satamaninaki
Theokriti G.
Theodori
Mavrokordatou
Philonos
Notara
Sachtouri
Evangelistrias
Gortu
Vironos
Karpathou
Athinas
Slavonbou Kallirrois
Doganis
Diakou Ath.
Kariskaki
Akti Tzelepi
Antistaseos
Riga
Fereou
Venizelou
Miaouli
Olimpou
Iko
Irodotou
Iakou
Kyriakou
Favierou
Irodotou
Sofokleous
Mavromihali
Irodotou
Theodori G.
Filikis
Iraklidon
Etenas
Agias Paraskevis
Iris
Kalipsous
Athinas
Internationauxima international Ferres
Kendriko Limani
Great Harbour
Ferres for Western & Central Cyclades
Ferres for Northern Greece
Eleftheriou
Pontou
Aristotelous
Misilidi
Naage Uli Al
Akti Tzelema
Klisovis
Hatzikiriakou
Damala
Papate
Hadji...
Popfira
Leoniou
Marias
Klisovis
Evrimedontos
Afikarnassou
Akti Themistokleous
Miaouli
Lampru Sp.
Lampru Sp.
Irakliton
Kazanova
Filika
Ellas
Miaouli
Markou
Affara
Kazantzaki
Monemvasias
Evterpi
Eleutheriou
Venizelou

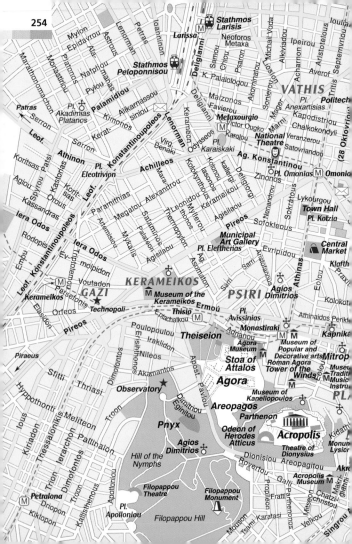

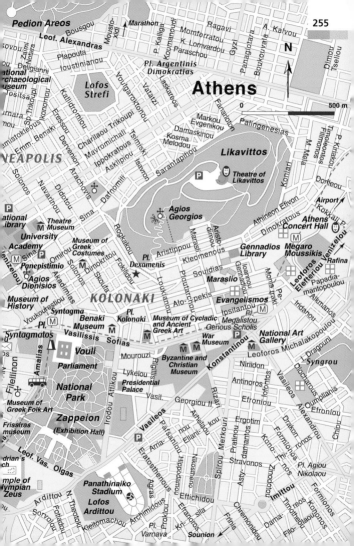

Pedion Areos

Bousgou

Marathon

Ragavi

A. Kalvou

Leof. Alexandras

Moustoxidi

Kalligra

Momferratou

Gyzi

Panagiotara

Plapouta

Ioustinianou

K. Lomvardou

Paraschou

Boukouvala

Dimou Tseliou

Deligianni

Notara

Ioustinianou

Pl. Argentinis

Dimokratias

P. Kinafou

Filimonos

national archaeological useum

Tositsa

Lofos Strefi

Voulgaroktonou

Laskareos

Vatatzi

Athens

Fanariton

Palingenesias

0   500 m

Markou

Evgenikou

Damaskinou

Kosma

Melodou

M. Meli

Charilaou Trikoupi

Mavromichali

Tsimiski

Ippokratous

Asklipiou

Isavron

Sarantapihou

Likavittos

Koniari

Theatre of Likavittos

Dorileou

Airport

NEAPOLIS

Solonos

Navarinou

Didotou

Sina

Arachovis

Dafnomili

Rogakriou

Fokilidou

P. Aristippou

Agios Georgios

Athineon Efivon

Aristo...

dinou

Kleomenous

Marasli

Dinokratous

Athens Concert Hall

national ibrary

Theatre Museum

University

Academy

Omirou

Sina

Akadimias

Dimokritou

Skoufa

Pl. Dexamenis

Loukianou

Ploutarchou

Souidias

Marasli

Gennadios Library

Megaro Moussikis

Leoforos Eleftheriou Venizelou

Rafina

Panepistimio

Agios Dionisios

Voukourestiou

Kanari

Koumbari

Pl. Kolonaki

Alo...pekis

Marasio

Ipsilantou

Ioannou Gennadiou

Evangelismos

Monis-traki

Papadia-mantopoulou

Alkmanos

Indanou

Museum of History

KOLONAKI

Benaki Museum

Museum of Cycladic and Ancient Greek Art

Megalistou

Genous Scholis

War Museum

National Art Gallery

Pl. Syntagmatos

Syntagma

Vasilissis   Sofias

Mourouzi

Byzantine and Christian Museum

Konstantinou

Niriidon

Leoforos Michalakopoulou

Dragouni

Syngrou

Amalias

Vouli

Parliament

Lykeiou

Attikou

Presidential Palace

Vasil.

Rizari

Antinoros

Iofontos

Vasileos Alexandrou

Efroniou

Oumplianis

Efroniou

Filellinon

National Park

Irodou

Georgiou I

Vasileos

Paisanou

Arneaiou

Ergotim...

Pratinou

idamanios

Drakon

Kono-Thr...ronos

Formionos

Chiou

Museum of Greek Folk Art

Zappeion

(Exhibition Hall)

Vasileos

Eftichidou

Ellani-kou

Merkouri

Astv...

Stravonos

Konol...

Pl. Agiou Nikolaou

Frissiras museum

rian's ch

Eratosthenous

Arria...

nou

Hippodamou

Nikostheno...

Spirou

Imittou

Formionos

mple of ympian Zeus

Leof. Vas. Olgas

Ardittou

Fotiadou

Sorvolou

Panathinaiko Stadium

Lofos Ardittou

Kleitomachou

Archimidou

Eftanos

silla

Pl.

Varvara

Sounion

Chremonidou

Darna...

Timotheos Kanonos

Filo-...gadoou

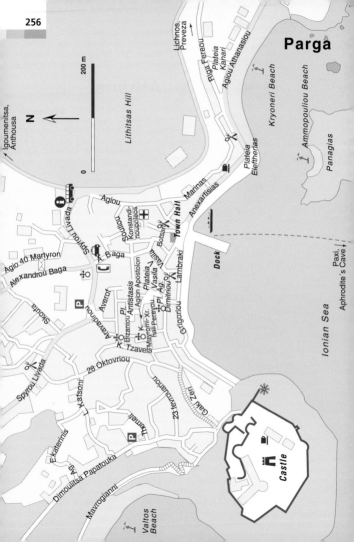

Parga

Lichnos, Preveza

Riga Fereou
Plateia Kanari
Agiou Athanasiou

Kryoneri Beach

Ammopouliou Beach

Panagias

Lithitsas Hill

Igoumenitsa, Anthousa

200 m

N

0

Plateia Eleftherias

Agiou

Marinas

Anexartisias

Town Hall

Konstandinoupoleos

Spyrou Livada

Botsari

Baga

Agiou Apostolon

Plateia Vasila

Lambraki

Dock

Paxi, Aphrodite's Cave

Agio 40 Martyron

Alexandrou Baga

Averof

Pl. Ag. Vasila

Pl. Dimitriou

Grigoriou

Ionian Sea

Skouta

Alexandrou

Pl. Bizaniou

Antistasis

Mavromichali

Pl. Pergou

K. Tzavela

Gaki Zeri

23 Oktovriou

28 Oktovriou

Katsoni

Ekaterinis

Tzameli

Castle

Spyrou Livada

Dimoulitsa Papatouka

Av.

Mavrogianni

Valtos Beach

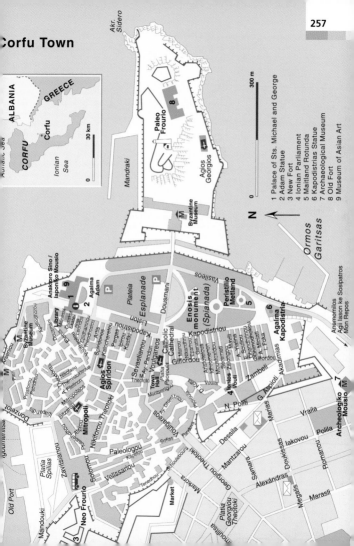

Corfu Town

1 Palace of Sts. Michael and George
2 Adam Statue
3 New Fort
4 Ionian Parliament
5 Maitland Rotunda
6 Kapodistrias Statue
7 Archaeological Museum
8 Old Fort
9 Museum of Asian Art

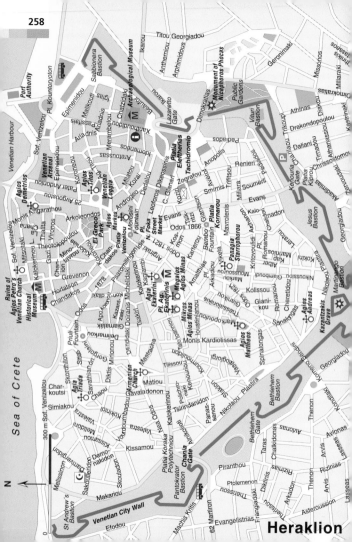

258

Heraklion

Sea of Crete

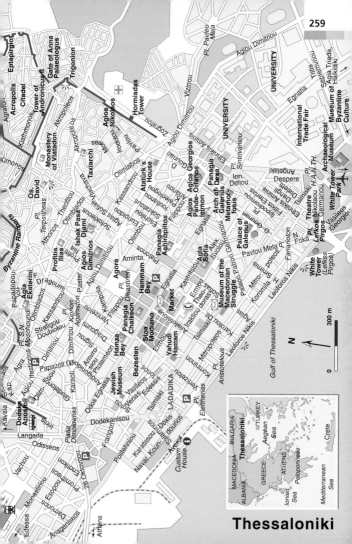

Thessaloniki

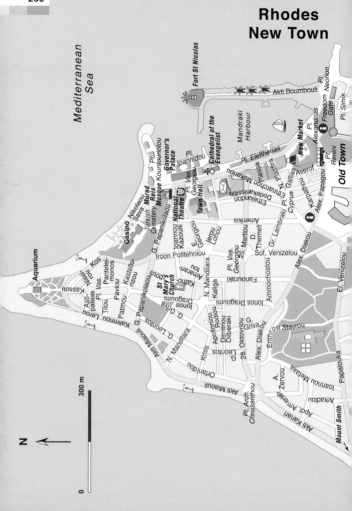

Rhodes
New Town

Mediterranean
Sea

Fort St Nicolas

Akti Boumbouli

Mandraki
Harbour

Pl. Neohon
Pl. Simis

Pl.
Ioannidou

Cathedral of the
Evangelist

Governor's
Palace

Pl. Eleftherias

Freedom
Gate

Old Town

New Market

Pl.
Alexandrias

Pl.
Rimini

Pl. Vas.
Georgiou

Etheridon
Dodekanission

Pl. Vas.
Georgiou

Town Hall

Plastira

Averof

Alex. Papagou

Kyprou

Cyrprou Gallias

Karpathou

Nikolaou

Casino

Turkish
Murad
Reis
Mosque

Sara
Reis
Cemetery

G. Papanikolaou

Kountourotiou

National
Theatre

Ioannou
Kazouli

Pl. Vas.
Georgiou

Eftherion
Einardronton Makarion

Odessa

Amerikis

Aquarium

Kos
Nisiri
Tilou
Patmou
Kassou

Pavlou
monos
Pantelei-
rizou

Kastellori

Iroon Politehniou

Ieleriou
Lofou

Gr. Lambraki Pl.

Alex. Diakou

25 Martiou

Sof. Venizelou

El. Venizelou

Astii-
paleas

G. Papanikolaou

Kalto-
Aharan-
tiou

Pl. Vas.
Georgiou

D.
Themelii

Ammohostou

St Mary's
Church

G. Griva

Ionos Dragoumi

N. Mandilara

Fanouraki

Leriou

Kallimnon

Ortholou

N. Mandilara

G. Leontos

Krits

Leontos

Apollonou

28. Oktovriou

Dimitriou
Diberaki

Alex. Diakou

G. Griva

Enthrou Stavrou

Ioannou Metaxa

Akti Miaouli

Pl. Arch.
Chrissanthou

A.
Zervou

Apol. Artemis

Arkadiou

Papalouka

Akti Kanari

Mount Smith

N ←

300 m

0

Rhodes: Old Town

Akti Sachtouri

Acandia Gate

Kisthiniou

Eolou

Diosios

Bastion of Carretto

St Catherine's Gate

Pindarou

Theseos

Achladei

Gavala

Eketonos

Triptolemou

Vironos

Gate of the Virgin

Akti Sachtouri

St Mary of the Bourg

Dossiadou

Episopat Palace

Platia Mariron

Evreon

Perikleous

Dimosthenous

JEWISH QUARTER

Leonidou

Praxitelou

Castellania

Mosque of Ibrahim Pasha

Pithagora

Ethimiou

Embrio

Marine Gate

Ermou

Platia Ippokratous

Aristotelous

Evripidou

Sofokleous

Arsenal Gate

Akti Sachtouri

Byzantine Museum

Platia Simis

Platia Agirokastrou

Platonos

Eschilou

Omirou

Koskinou Gate (St John's Gate)

Municipal Art Gallery

Museum of Decorative Arts

Archaeological Museum

Ippoton

Lachitos

Thoukididou

Aristonanos

Redjep Pasha Mosque

St Athanasius Gate

Knights'Hospital

Sokratous

Governor's Mosque (Aga Cami)

Menekleous

Agiou Fanouriou

Irodotou

Theofiliskou

Omirou

KNIGHTS' QUARTER

Palace of the Grand Masters

Ippodamou

Archelaou

Platia Ariolos Zinonos

Sultan Mustapha Mosque

Andoniou

TURKISH QUARTER

Antifanous

Ippodamou

Platia Kleovoulou

Panetiou

Turkish Library

Hamman

N

Apollonion

Mosque of Suleiman

Orfeos

Timokreondos

Ippodamou

Alexandridou

Spanish Tower

St Mary's Tower

Dimokratias

Antoise Gate

St george's Bastion

0

100 m

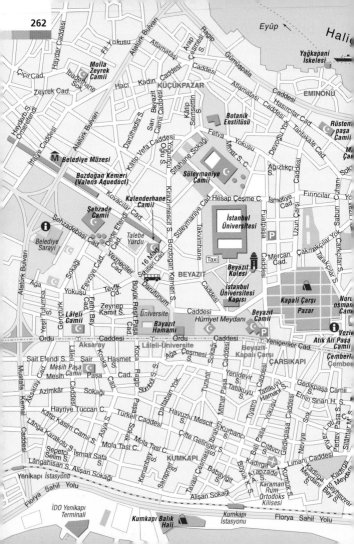

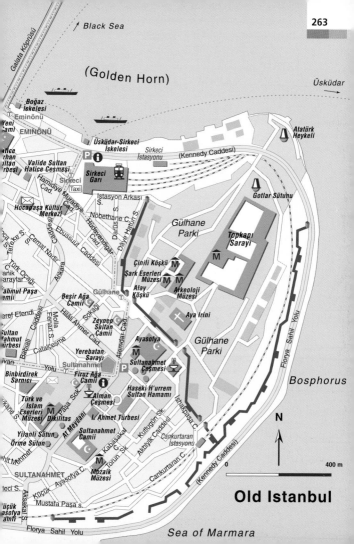

Old Istanbul

Black Sea

(Golden Horn)

Üsküdar

Galata Köprüsü

Boğaz
İskelesi
Eminönü
Yeni
Cami
EMINÖNÜ
Üsküdar-Sirkeci
İskelesi
Sirkeci
İstasyonu
(Kennedy Caddesi)
Atatürk
Heykeli

atice
rhan
ultan
rbesi
Valide Sultan
Hatice Çeşmesi
Hamidiye Muradiye Cad.
Sirkeci
Taxi
Sirkeci
Garı
İstasyon Arkası
S.
Gotlar Sütunu

Hocapaşa Kültür
Merkezi
Ebussuut Caddesi
Cemal Nadir
Nöbethane C.
Hüdavendigar
Dr. Hafız Cemal Loka
Dârüs Hatun S.
Daye Hatun C.
Gülhane
Parkı
Topkapı
Sarayı
M
M

ark S.
Türk Ocağı
anik
sarayı
Ankara
Çinili Köşkü
Şark Eserleri
Müzesi
M
M
M

ahmut Paşa
amii
Beşir Ağa
Camii
Gülhane
Alay
Köşkü
Arkeoloji
Müzesi

eref Etendi
Hilali Ahmer Cad.
Molla Fenari S.
Zeynep
Sultan
Camii
T
Aya İrini

ultan
ahmut
rbesi
Babıali Caddesi
Çatalçeşme
Hamdar Cad.
Yerebatan
Sarayı
Ayasofya
C

ivan
Yolu
Sultanahmet
Firuz Ağa
Camii
Sultanahmet
Çeşmesi
Gülhane
Parkı

Binbirdirek
Sarnıcı
P
Alman
Çeşmesi
Haseki H'urrem
Sultan Hamamı
Bosphorus

Türk ve
İslam
Eserleri
Müzesi
Dikilitaş
Paşa Sok.
At Meydanı
I. Ahmet Türbesi
İshakpaşa C.

Yılanlı Sütun
Örme Sütun
SULTANAHMET
Sultanahmet
Camii
Kabasakal C.
Kutlugün Sk.
Akbıyık Caddesi
Çankurtaran
İstasyonu
Çankurtaran C.
N

hit Mehmet
M
Mozaik
Müzesi
Torun Sk.
(Kennedy Caddesi)
0   400 m

eci S.
Küçük Ayasofya C.
Aksakal S.

üçük
asofya
S.
Mustafa Paşa s.

Florya Sahil Yolu
Sea of Marmara

Izmir

N

0 ————— 500 m

Gulf of Izmir

Karşıyaka → İstanbul

Feribot iskelesi

Altay Lokali
S. Yaşar Müzesi

Saint J. Koleji
Karakol
Ssk Has.
Bergam İstanb
Limar Şehitler C

ALSANCAK
1472 S
1469 S
Alsancak İstasyonu
Atatürk C
Cumhuriyet Bul.
Şehitler C
İlkögr. Ok.
İngiliz Kilisesi
Atatürk Ka Sport Salo.

Vahap Özaltay

Alsancak İskelesi

Park
Atatürk Müzesi M
Zübeyde Hanım Anıtı (Caravanserai)

1448 S
Mahmut Esat Bozkurt C
Ali
Talat Paşa Bul.
Eşref B.
Gökalp Bul.

Alsancak Camii
Çetinkaya
Gazi İlkögr. Ok.
Sarı
Alsancak İlkögr. Ok.
Ziya
Namık Kemal Lisesi
Dr. Mustafa Ender C
Mimar Sinan özel Saglık Hastanesi
1401 S
Mimar Sinan

İzmir Palas
Akademi
Vasıf Çınar B
Kızılay C
Pilevne C
1393 S 1382 S 1381 S
1390 S
1398 S

Cumhuriyet Meydanı
Equestrian Statue of Atatürk
Pasaport İskelesi

Nevresbey Ticaret Lisesi
Amerikan Kültür Derneği
Lozan Meydanı
Evlendirme Dairesi
Tenis Kulübü
Kültürpark Alanı
Beledi Meclis Salon

Akdeniz C
Gazi Osman Paşa Bul.
Şehit Nevres
Büyük Efes Oteli
Montrö Meydanı
Parasüt Kulesi
Havvanat Bahçesi
Gül Bahçesi

Church of St Polycarp
Kazım Paşa B
Halit Ziya
1337
Şair Eşref B.
1373 S
Fuar
Luna Park
Zabita Müd.

Borsa Saray
M. K. Emalettin B.
Gazi Bulvari
1369 S
Konak Belediye Bşk. Meydanı
9 Eylül Meydanı
H. Şakir Ecz.
Mürsel Paşa Bul.
Orta Ök
1260 S
1205 S

27 Mayıs Meydanı
Belediye (Town Hall)
Fevzi
Paşa
Basmane İstasyonu
Gaziler
Basmane Camii
1294 S
1275 S
1250

Karşıyaka

Konak İskelesi

Hisar Camii
902 S
1313 S
1310 S
İ. Fet. İlkögr. Ok.
Hasan Hoca Camii
Fettah Camii
1298 S
V. K. Dirik İlkögr. Ok.

Saat Kulesi (Clock Tower)
Konak Meydanı
Konak Camii

Çobanoğlu Zeki Bey
Kızlarağası Hanı
Kemeraltı Camii
864 S
Anafartalar Bul.
BASMANE
Hacı Ali

BAZAR
Gazi Osman Paşa Bul.
NAMAZGAH
Agora
920 S
816 S
Hürriyet Lisesi
1023 S

Kaym. Nihat Bey C
Nihat Bey C
850 S
856 S
842 S
Kestelli C
842 S
Kemeraltı C
846 S

Yaya Alanı Polisevi Ördüevi
Çeşme
Milli Kütüphane (İzmir State Opera)
KONAK
Adam C
Gazi Osman Paşa Bul.
827 S
746 S
1000 S
Hacı Elendi C
1014 S

Arkeoloji Müzesi M
Denizli, Efes
427 S
723 S
744 S
825 S
827 S
833 S
806 S
5250 S
KADİFEKALE
Kadifekale

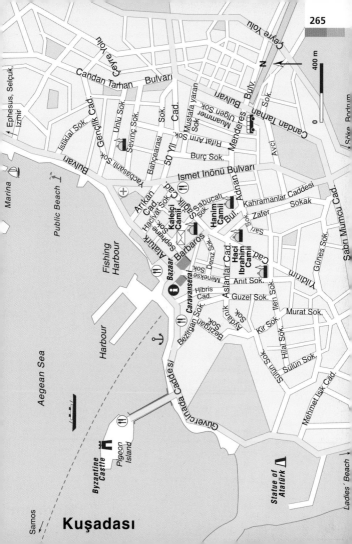

Kuşadası

Aegean Sea

Samos

Marina

Public Beach

Fishing Harbour

Harbour

Byzantine Castle

Pigeon Island

Statue of Atatürk

Ladies' Beach

→ Ephesus, Selçuk, İzmir

Çevre Yolu

Candan Tarhan Bulvarı

Söke, Bodrum →

N

400 m

0

İstiklal Sok.

Gençlik Cad.

Unlu Sok.

Sevinç Sok.

Bahçearası

50 YIL Cad.

Sok.

Cad.

Mustafa Yatan Sok.

Muammer Ügen Sok.

Menderes

Candan Tarhan Bulvarı

Bulv.

Sok.

Rıfat Arın Sok.

Burç Sok.

İsmet İnönü Bulvarı

Yeşbaşını Sok.

Bulvarı

Arıkan Cad.

Atatürk Bulvarı

Hacıyar Sok.

Sephane

Kaleiçi Camii

Sevgilik Cad.

Barbaros Cad.

Sabucalı Sok.

Hanım Camii

Bul.

Kahramanlar Caddesi

Sarı Zafer Sok.

Adnan

Sabri Mumcu Cad.

Avcı

Sokak

Deniz Sok.

Menkşe Sok.

Hibris Cad.

Aslanlar Cad.

Hacı İbrahim Camii

Cad.

Güzel Sok.

Anıt Sok.

İleri Sok.

Güneş Sok.

Yıldırım

Murat Sok.

Bazaar

Caravanserai

Bezirgan Sok.

Aydınlık Sok.

Kır Sok.

Hilal Sok.

Sülün Sok.

Sülün Sok.

Mehmet Işık Cad.

Güvercinada Caddesi

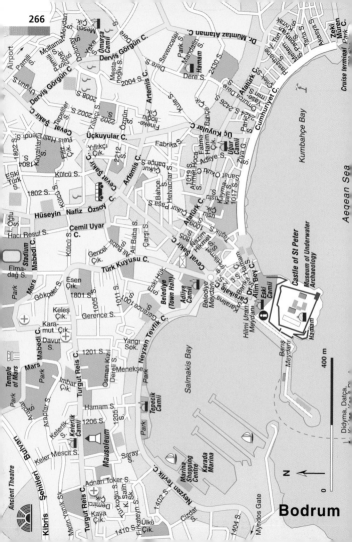

Bodrum

Düden Başı

Bazaar

Atatürk Caddesi

Alanya, Perge,
Aspendos, Side
Kurşulu-Şelalesi

Clock Tower

Cumhuriyet Caddesi

Antalya Müzesi

Cumhuriyet
Meydanı

Mevlevihane

Paşa Camii

Atatürk
Monumenti

Yivli
Minare

İskele Caddesi

Alaeddin
Camii

Tabakhane

Tuzcular

Aydoğdu S.

Karadayı S.

Mektep

Selçuk

Uzunçarşı S.

Afendi S.

Karanlık S.

Karatay-
Camii

Paşacamı S.

Mescit S.

Hanımeleni S.

Civelek S.

Hadrian's
Gate

İmaret S.

Kandiller

Musalla S.

Uzunçarşı S.

Kalfazanı S.

Barbaros

Kocatepe S.

Hesapçı S.

Kandiller Geçidi

Kandiller S.

Kocatepe S.

Marina

İskele
Camii

Mermerli

Aralık S.

Kaleiçi

Akarçeşme

Müze

Zafer

Kandiller Çıkmazı

Mediterranean
Sea

Mermerli Banyo S.

Kaledibi S.

Kılıçarslan

Hıdırlık S.

Hıdırlık S.

Yeşilminare

Hıdırlık S. Camii Sk.

Kurtuluş Sokak

Hesapçı S.

Sakarya

Kesik Minare

Zeytin Çıkmazı

Zeytin
Çeğdil Sk.

Zeytin S.

Fırın

2. Sakarya S.

Sakarya S.

Yeni Kapı

Haşam S.

Haşimişcan

Hesapçı Sk.

Tabakhane
Çeğdil

Kadıpaşa S.

Kadıpaşa S.

Fevzi Çıkmak Caddesi

Hıdırlık Kulesi

N

Sakarya

Park S.

0   150 m

Atatürk Caddesi

Antalya

K a r a a l i o ğ l u   P a r k ı

Limassol

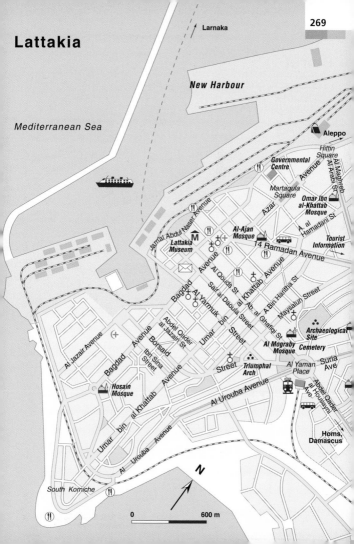

Lattakia

Mediterranean Sea

→ Larnaka

New Harbour

▲ Aleppo

Hittin Square

Al Maghreb
Al Arabi St.

Governmental Centre

Martaqula Square

Azar

Omar Ibn al-Khattab Mosque

A. al Hamadani St.

Jamal Abdul Naser Avenue

M **Lattakia Museum**

Al-Ajan Mosque

14 Ramadan Avenue

Tourist Information

Avenue

Al Qouds St.

al Khattab Avenue

A. Bin Hariha St.

Saif al Daoula Street

al Ab. al Ghafiqi St.

Maysaloun Street

Bagdad

Al Yarmuk

Umar   bin   Street

Archaeological Site Cemetery

Abdel Qader al Jazair St.

Avenue

Al Mograby Mosque

Suria Ave.

Al Jazair Avenue

Borsaid

Ibn Sina Street

Street

Triumphal Arch

Al Yaman Place

Abdel Qader al Houssini Ave.

Bagdad

Avenue

al Khattab Avenue

Al Urouba Avenue

Homs, Damascus

Hosain Mosque

Umar   bin   al Khattab   Avenue

Al Urouba   Avenue

N

South Korniche

0   600 m

Beirut

Mediterranean Sea

Paris Avenue (Corniche)

Paris Avenue

American University of Beirut

Post Hall (AUB Archaeological Museum)

AIN MRE

RAS BEIRUT

JAMAA

John Kennedy St

Bliss St

Bliss St

Clemenceau St

Sidani St

Maamari St

Negib Ardati St

Makdissi St

Omar ben Abd Aziz St

Sourati St

Roma St

TALE JOUNB

Kuwait St

Hamra St

Bahrain St

Sadat St

Jeanne d'Arc St

HAMRA

Lebanese National Library

MANARA

Baalbek St

Bank Lebar St

Qalaa St

Emile Edde

René Mouaw Garden

Salah ed Dine el Ayoubi

El Hussein St

KRAYTEM

SNOUBRA

Dunant St

Roma St

Mary Edde St

Chatila St

Madame Curie St

Khaled bin el Walid

Druze Cemetery

B. Maarouf

SANAYEH

Raoucheh Bay

Lebanese American University (LAU)

Rachid Karame St

Algeri Independ

Pigeon Rocks

RAOUCHEH

Australia St

Dermachkieh St

National Unity St

Knio St

Ibn Rochd St

DAR EL FATWA

Berlin St

Ain el Tineh St

Vienna St

Bechir St

El-Rachidine St

Qassaar St

Hachem St

Imam Hanife St

Khalil St

Abdallah es Sabbah St

Schubert St

Verdun St

Mazraa St

Amine Takey ed Dine St

Moaourijah

N

Blvd Saeb Salam

Unesco St

Blvd Saeb Sa

Chebli el Mallat St

Beirut Public Beach

Rafic el Hariri Ave

Farid Trad St

UNESCO

Unesco St

Moaourijah St

MSAY

Habib Chahla

Sunset Towers

Unesco Palace

Peter Medawar St

Sidon, Tyre

Beirut Rafic Hariri International Airport

0   800 m

BIEL Center

Georges Hotel

Public park

Marina Towers

Mir Majid Arsalan

Port of Beirut

Platinum Tower

Ahmad Chaouqi St

Souks

Charles Helou

MARFA

Venus Towers

Medieval wall

Al-Omari Mosque

Jounieh, Byblos, Tripoli

Omar ed Daouk St

Weygand

Archaeological Site

Charles Helou Ave

BAB IDRISS

Ottoman Military Hospital

Roman Baths

Nejmeh Square

Emir Assaf Mosque

Charles Helou

El Arz St

El Murr Tower

France St

Grand Serail

Parliament

Maronite Catholic Church

Martyrs Square

Pasteur St

Robert Mouawad Private Museum

Emir Bechir

Al-Amin Mosque

St Georges Greek Orthodox Cathedral

GEMMAYZE

Gouraud St

Maurice Barres

Armenian Church

SAIFI

Sursock St

Sursock Museum

MAR NICOLAS

Charles Malek Ave

PATRIARCAT

BACHOURA

General Fouad Chehab Ave

St Nicolas Park

St Nicolas Cathedral

FURN EL HAYEK

Osmane ben Affane St

Basta St

Hyane St

Damascus St

Museum of Prehistory

Furn el Hayek St

BORJ ABI HAIDAR

Ahmad Beyhum St

Ahmad Tabbara St

Bechara el Khoury St

Saint Joseph University

YESSOUIYEH

Abd el Wahab el Inglizi St

fiyeh St

Independence Ave

Achra

Elias Sarkis Ave

SSAITBE

Lebanese University

Selim Salam St

Mamoun St

Basta St

BASTA EL-FAWQA

Mohammed el Hout St

ACHRAFIEH

Abd el Ghani Arayssi St

Omar el Khatib St

Bechara el Khoury St

Damascus St

Christian and Jewish Cemeteries

NASRA

Christian Cemetery

Youssef es Saouda St

Haidar

Toufic Salem St

Habib Bacha es Saad

Mazraa St

Ouzaii St

EL AAMLIYE

RAS EN NABAA

Chayla Stadium

Hotel Dieu St

MAZRAA

Blvd Saeb Salam

Abdallah el Yafi Ave

Pine Residence

Hippodrome

National Museum

Ramot

Sderot Golda Meir

Yam Suf

Forest

Tombs of Sanhe

Museum of Jewish Art

Divrei Hayim

Ezr at Torah

Ohalei Yosef

LIFTA (MEI NEFTO 'AH)

Sderot Menachem Begin

Ze'anim Me'irot

Zichron Ya'akov

ROMEMA ILLIT

Shamgar Hamacabi

Binyamin Ya'akoson

Eli

Pnina Grossberg

Lod, Tel Aviv

Nefio'akh

Harav Sorotzkin

Biblical Zoo

BUCH QUAF

Sderot Weizmann

Hamag

Petah Tikva

Harav Bar Ilan

Rehovot Izi

Nehemya

Giv'at Sha'ul

O holiav

Yirmiyahu

Malchei Yisra'el

Zefanya

Rabbi Yisra'el Najara

Amram Gaon

Ba'al Hashel'iltot

ROMEMA

Kikar Rokach

Hahashmona'im

Peri Hadash

Mat'akhi

Kanfei Nesharim

Tzion

Ben Dor

Hatevi

Central Bus Station

Sarei Yisra'el

Haturim

Yechezkel

Rashi

David Yellin

Ha'nevi'im

Mesha Yahu

KIRYAT MOSHE

Sd. Hame'iri

Moshe

Sderot Herzl

ETZ HAYIM

Sd. Zalman

BINYANEI HA'UMA

Shazar

Jaffa Road

Agrippas

MAHANE YEHUDA

Yosef Ben-Mattinyahu

Jaffa Road

Farbstein

Hakron Hirsch

Convention Hall

Sderot Yitshak Rabin

Bank Yisra'el

Sd. HaNassi Hashish

Sd. HaNassi Hashiv

Ben Zvi

Bezalel

Ben Sappir

Mordechai Eliash

Agrippas

Strauss

MESH

Yad Vashem

David Wolffsohn

Sderot Herzl

Rabbi Binyamin

Joel Zusman

Eliezer Kaplan

Ben Zvi

Lod

Ussishkin

Tavor

Narkiss

King George V

Independ

Kadish Sliman Shahar

Kar'mon

Wohl Rose Park

Rothschild

KIRYAT BEN GURION

Nahalat Tzadok

Hakaryemet Leyiste'el

Jewish Agency

BEIT HAKEREM

Planetarium

Ruppin

KNESSET

Diskin

Abarbanel

Ramban

Terra Sancta Coll.

Habana'i

Brodesky

University Stadium

Hebrew University

Bible Lands Museum

Shrine of the Book

Sderot Hayim Harazz

Rashba

Sd. Ben Maimon

REHAVIA

SHECHUNAT HAPOL'ALIM

Yehuda Burla

Avraham Granot

Israel Museum

Ruppin

Benyamin Mijudela

Derech Aza

Molcho

Monastery of the Cross

NEVEH GRANOT

KIRYAT SHMU'EL

Van Leer Foundation

Jerusalem Theatre

Jah

Shmuel Beyth

Bezalel Bazak

GIV'AT MORDECHAI

Zalman Shneur

Botanical Gardens

Yehoshua Yabin

Harav Herzog

Tchernichowsky

Hatayasim

Harav Berlin

Hapalmach

Eli Cohen

Hagdud Ha'ivli

Islamic Art Museum

Chopin St.

Teth Benovember

EMEK RAFA'IM

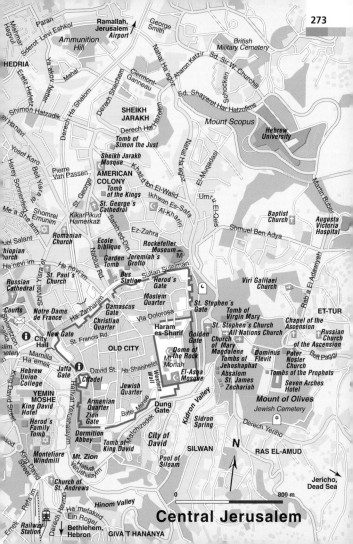

Central Jerusalem

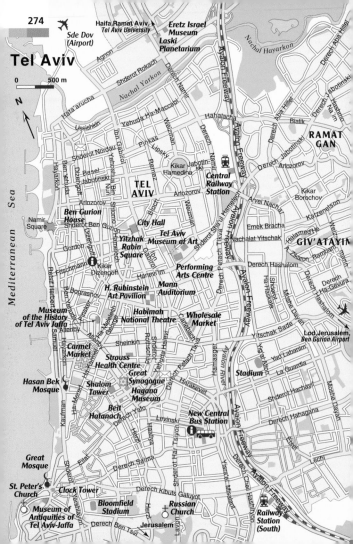

Mediterranean Sea

Montazah Palace, Aboukir, Royal Jewellery Museum

Chatby Necropolis

Port Said

el-Iskandar el-Akbar

A. Rahman Rochdy

Cairo Airport

el-Geish

Shallalat Gardens

Midan el-Miya

el-Huriyа

A. Rahman Rochdy

el-Malaab

Nabil el-Quaggad

el-Mamoum

Nemasha

Fine Arts Museum

el-Huriya

1 km

500 m

N

Fort of el-Silsila

Bibliotheca Alexandrina

Sultan Abd el-Aziz

Sofer

Riyad Pacha

Salah Mustafa

Alexandria National Museum

Dr Ibrahim Abd el-Said

Sofer

Iskandar el-Akbar

CHATBY

Champollion

Khartoum Column

Greco-Roman Museum

el-Malaab

Stadium

Masr Train Station

el-Corniche (el-Corniche)

El-Qaid Mosque

26 Yulyu

Saad Zaghloul

Amin Fikry

el-Sultan Husein

Amin Fikry

Zaghloul

Cavafy Museum

Roman Theatre Kom el-Dikka

Lumu

el-Huriya

el-Malaab

Muharram

el-Gumhuriya

Land submerged by water

Midan Saad Zaghloul

Midan Ramleh

Nabia

el-Ghorfa el-Togariya

el-Ahd

Saliyah

Elijahu Ha-Navi Synagogue

St Mark's Cathedral

Nabi Daniel

Nabi Daniel Mosque

French Cultural Centre

Villa of Birds

Cairo

el-Attarine

Eastern Harbour

Midan Saad

Nabia Daniel

Amr

Salah Harb

Talaat Harb

Ahmed Orabi

el-Mitwalli

Salah el-Din

el-Mitwalli

Salah Salem

Tawfiq

St Catherine

Gohar el-Qaid

Abou el-Dardaa

Pompey's Pillar, Kom el-Shuqafa

Midan Ahmed 26 Yulyu

Said Orabi

EL-MANCHIYA

Midan Orabi

Midan Tahrir

el-Gazair

Ibrahim el-Awal

el-Bab el-Akhdar

el-Gazair

el-Corniche

Terbana Mosque

el-Shorbagi Mosque

Zinga el-Sitta

Souk

Midan el-Nasr

Salah Salem

Ahmed Orabi

Nokraski

el-Nasr

el-Bahariya

Fort Qaitbey

Aquarium

26 Yulyu

Mohammed Kourahin

Faransa

el-Tabbukh

Nokraski

Said el-Tabbukh

Saiyyd

Abu Abbas el-Mursi Mosque

Ras el-Tin

Ismail Sabri

Safar Pacha

el-Bahariya

GUMRUK

Fish Market

Fort of el-Atta

ANFUSHI

Anfushi Bay

Qasr Ras el-Tin

RAS EL-TIN

Shipping Terminal

Western Harbour

Alexandria

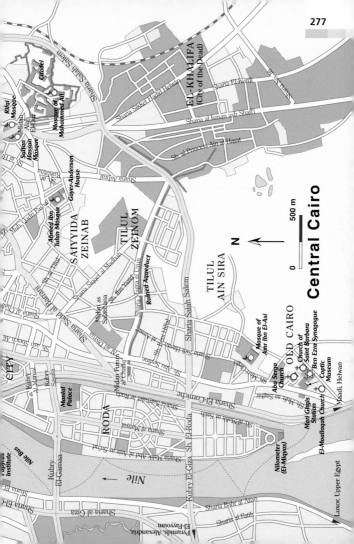

Central Cairo

0 ⎯⎯ 500 m

N

EL-KHALIFA
(City of the Dead)

Citadel

Rifai Mosque

Sultan Hassan Mosque

Mosque of Mohammed Ali

Midan Salah ad-Din

Gayer-Anderson House

Ahmed Ibn Tulun Mosque

SAYYIDA ZEINAB

TILUL ZEINOM

Manial Palace

RODA

Nilometer (El-Miqyos)

Mari Girgis Station

Abu Serga Church

El-Moallaqah Church

Coptic Museum

Church of Saint Barbara

Ben Ezra Synagogue

Mosque of Amr Ibn El-Asi

OLD CAIRO

TILUL AIN SIRA

Sharia Salah Salem

Shari'a al-Azhar

Ruined Aqueduct

Maidan as Salahana

Shari'a Saqet al Madbah

Nile

Papyrus Institute

Nile bus

Kubri El-Gamaa

Kubri El-Giza

Sharia Bahr al Azan

Sharia El-Fatih

Pyramids, Alexandria, El-Fayoum

Luxor, Upper Egypt

Maadi, Helwan

Sharia El-Corniche

Valletta

1 Greek-Catholic Church
2 Auberge d'Aragon
3 Archbishop's Palace
4 Carmelite Church
5 Manoel Theatre
6 Grand Master's Palace and Armoury
7 Old Valletta Market
8 National Museum of Archaeology
9 St. Andrew
10 St. Barbara
11 St. Paul's Anglican Cathedral
12 St. Catherine of Italy
13 Our Lady of Victories
14 Auberge de Castille et Léon

0   200 m

N

St. Elmo Point
Abercrombie's Bastion
Ball's Bastion
St. Gregory's Bastion
Fort St. Elmo
St. Lazarus Bastion

National War Museum
St. Elmo Place
St. Elmo Granaries
St. Lazarus Curtain

St. Elmo Bay
Jews Sally Port
French Curtain
Fountain Street
Spur St.
St. Joseph Street
Old Hospital St.
North St.
Toni Bajada Lane
Mediterranean Conference Centre (Sacra Infermeria)
Old Wells St.
Irish St.

English Curtain
St. Sebastian
Curtain
St. Sebastian St.
Republic Street
St. Nicholas St.
Lower Barracca Gardens

St. Sebastian Bastion
St. Michael St.
St. Charles St.
Bull St.
St. Anne St.
St. Dominic Street
Casa Rocca Piccola
St. Christopher St.
St. Frederick St.
St. Christopher St.
St. Paul St.
Jesuit Church
St. Roque's Church
Fish Market

German Curtain
Marsamxett St.
Bishop Lane
West St.
Bounty St.
Old Bakery St.
Archbishop St.
Mint St.
Archbishop St.
Felix Street
St. Ursula's Church
Inq. U. Mediterr.

Water Polo Pitch
St. Salvatore Bastion
Old Theatre St.
Palace Square
Grand Master's Palace
Old Theatre St.
Barriera Wharf

Old Theatre St.
Republic Square
Wartime Experience
St. John's Co-Cathedral
National Library
St. Paul Shipwrecked Church
St. Barbara Bastion

Mattia Preti Sq.
West St.
St. Patrick St.
Gt. Siege Sq.
St. Lucia St.
St. John St.
St. John Sq.
St. Paul St.
St. Ursula St.
East St.
Victoria Gate

St. Andrew's Bastion
St. Andrew St.
St. Mark St.
Old Bakery St.
St. John Street
Merchants Street

Melita Street
Museum of Fine Arts
Vassalli St.
Strait St.
Old Theatre St.
Zachary St.
Melita Street
St. Paul Street
Parisio Palace
Upper Barracca Gardens
Saluting Battery

St. Michael's Bastion
Sappers St.
South Street
Windmill St.
Ordnance St.
Castle Place
Old Customs House

Hastings Gardens
St. John's Cavalier
Ditch
Pope Pius V St.
St. James's Cavalier
St. James's Bastion
Lascaris War Rooms
Lascaris Wharf

Tritons Fountain
City Gate
Girolamu Caassar Ave.
Nelson Rd.

Great Siege Road
FLORIANA

Marsamxett Harbour
Grand Harbour

General Editor
Barbara Ender-Jones

Introduction and History
Jack Altman

Concept
Karin Palazzolo

Layout
Luc Malherbe
Sylvain Botter

Cartography
JPM Publications
Mathieu Germay
Jonathan Reymond

Copyright © 2012
JPM Publications S.A.
12, avenue William-Fraisse,
1006 Lausanne, Switzerland
information@jpmguides.com
http://www.jpmguides.com/

Printed in Germany
13754.00.11093
Edition 2012